Transformation

Far and wide, God's people are tuning in to His mandate to disciple nations. A passion is rapidly arising for pursuing aggressive, intentional social transformation. Ed Silvoso is one who has been clearly hearing what the Spirit is saying to the churches, and his brilliant new book, strong on theory and intense on practice, is just what we all need to begin to take giant steps toward God's ultimate destiny for the world.

C. Peter Wagner
Presiding Apostle, International Coalition of Apostles

The genius of this extraordinary book is that, like a wonderful meal, it can be enjoyed by everyone. Ed Silvoso sparks the mind with the "meat" of challenging paradigms yet satisfies the intuition with the "potatoes" of solid examples. He challenges our Scriptural prejudices and adds the Tabasco of godly wisdom, then finishes with a personal "dessert" that brought tears to my eyes and satisfaction to my heart. This banquet will quickly leave a hunger to minister in the marketplace and leave a godly legacy.

Dr. Francis S. Oda
CEO, Group 70 International
Senior Pastor, New Life Church Honolulu
Chair, ITN Global Council

Ed Silvoso is a twenty-first-century Abraham—having received an (impossible) word, he has the courage to believe it can be done. Ed's insight into Scripture causes the familiar passages to blaze with color and fills the reader with expectancy of a world where the marketplace flourishes with believers that dare minister. *Transformation* is not a book; it is a manual for the brave, a masterpiece for the theologian, and a road map for the entrepreneur.

Dr. Phil Nordin
Pastor, Jubilee Christian Centre, Calgary, Alberta
Author, *Power Thoughts* series

When God was looking for someone to herald the message of transformation to the nations of the world, Ed Silvoso stood up and said, "Here I am, Lord, send me," and God took him up on it. Ed's latest book is not only theoretical and biblical but also practical and real. Reading this book will deposit real faith to believe that Jesus Christ uses real people in real life situations to really change the world. Ed's insightful definition of faith as "the revelation of what is yet to happen" will challenge you to reach for nothing short of the transforming lifestyle God has purposed for all His children to experience.

John Isaacs
Senior Pastor, KingsWay Community Church, San Jose, CA
Founder and President, Pray the Bay

Without question, Ed Silvoso is the most insightful biblical tour guide I know. This book takes the reader on a journey of God's thoughts that only the Holy Spirit can reveal. It is a must-read!

Clifford E. Daugherty, Ed.D.
President and Superintendent
Valley Christian Schools, San Jose, CA

While many have talked and prayed for transformation, there has been a void of practical solutions for how to actually reach cities and nations for God. Ed Silvoso has done us all a favor with this groundbreaking book! If you read *Anointed for Business*, you need to carefully study this book. It is a how-to manual for transformation.

Cindy Jacobs
President and Cofounder, Generals International
Dallas, TX

Ed Silvoso has once again made the complex understandable by masterfully articulating a framework and guide for deep and lasting transformation in the marketplace. You will be inspired to see that indeed the whole world can experience the fullness of life that Jesus Christ died to give in this first heaven on Earth. You will be convinced that the elimination of systemic poverty is perhaps the most important and overlooked task for ushering in God's kingdom on Earth. And whether you're a pastor or politician, farmer or food processor, entrepreneur or lawyer, doctor or social worker, you will be compelled to live differently! Thank you, Ed, for this great gift!

Doug Seebeck
Executive Director, Partners Worldwide

When you read *Transformation*, you will see that Ed is definitely leaps ahead in his understanding of discipling nations. He is an anointed, biblical teacher who has his ear tuned to the voice and heart of God. Buckle up and prepare for take-off . . . this book is sure to shift you into new paradigms of transformation!

Chuck Ripka
President, Rivers International and Ripka Enterprises
Author, *God Out of the Box*

The faith at work movement has entered a new phase. We're now seeing first-hand what can happen when men and women across the world apply their faith at work. Ed Silvoso's book *Transformation* is *the* new handbook on workplace, city and nation transformation. Every practitioner should read this book.

Os Hillman
President, MarketplaceLeaders and International Coalition of Workplace Ministries
Author, *The 9 to 5 Window*

Ed Silvoso has presented the heart of God and the mind of Christ for the twenty-first-century Church. The truths Ed shares from the Bible, along with personal life experiences, will challenge saints to demonstrate the kingdom of God and transform their areas of influence. This book could be the catalyst that begins the fulfillment of Christ's determined purpose for the kingdoms of this world to become the kingdom of our God and His saints.

Dr. Bill Hamon
Bishop, Christian International Ministries Network (CIMN)
Author, *Day of the Saints*

Although embraced by Christians centuries ago, the truth Ed Silvoso describes—God's plan for blessing the nations—needs to be reaffirmed as a primary objective by Christ followers. In this book, Ed brings to light insights, both for those in the marketplace and those in the pulpit, of how to see the kingdom of God affect their city, their region, and their nation. Applying these insights will help Christians fulfill their calling the "other 6.5 days a week" and result in wonderful benefits for the struggling world around us.

Dave Seeba
CPA and President of Seeba & Associates
Silicon Valley CPA firm

Once again Ed takes us deeper into the Word and expands our vision so that we can and must respond to the Word of God. The Five Pivotal Paradigms are the marching orders of every Christian. Understand and apply these paradigms in the marketplace and you will see cities and nations won for Christ. A must-read!

Jack Serra
Founder, The M&M Consulting Group
Author, *Marketplace, Marriage and Revival: The Spiritual Connection*

The Lord has given Ed Silvoso five new paradigms—new ways of thinking—that stretch us as believers farther than we have ever been stretched before. We are going beyond revival to the transformation of society; beyond the salvation of people to the salvation of nations. Perhaps the most amazing paradigm shift of all is that Christians will eliminate systemic poverty. Ed Silvoso's new book, *Transformation*, will help you to see what you have never seen and do what you have never done.

Rick Heeren
Author, *Thank God It's Monday* and *The Threshing Floor*
Editor, *The Elk River Story*
Minneapolis, MN

This book is a three-legged stool you can set your life on. It is theologically sound, biblically grounded, and imminently practical. It's a great book!

Dave Beelen
Senior Pastor, Madison Square Church
Grand Rapids, MI

transformation

CHANGE THE
MARKETPLACE
AND YOU CHANGE
THE WORLD

ED SILVOSO

Regal

From Gospel Light
Ventura, California, U.S.A.

Published by Regal Books
From Gospel Light
Ventura, California, U.S.A.
Printed in the U.S.A.

Library of Congress Cataloging-in-Publication Data
Silvoso, Ed.
  Transformation : change the marketplace and you change the world / Ed Silvoso.
    p. cm.
  ISBN 978-0-8307-4475-6 (hard cover) — ISBN 978-0-8307-4514-2 (international trade paper)
  1. Employees—Religious life. 2. Religion in the workplace. I. Title.
  BV4593.S55 2007
  248.8'8—dc22
                                                                                        2007021802

1 2 3 4 5 6 7 8 9 10 / 10 09 08 07

Rights for publishing this book in other languages are contracted by Gospel Light Worldwide, the international nonprofit ministry of Gospel Light. For additional information, visit www.gospellightworldwide.org.

To our dear friends Graham and Lauren Power,
marketplace ministers who model the transformational principles
that are the essence of this book

Contents

CHAPTER 1

Real People, Real Change—In Real Time

A couple married for over 20 years is out for a Sunday afternoon drive. All of a sudden, a red convertible, the top down and rock music at full blast, overtakes them and stops right in front of them at the red light. The driver's seat seems to be occupied by one body with two heads, male and female, passionately bestowing expressions of love on each other. Exuberant life, resonant laughter and overflowing joy suddenly fill the intersection.

Becoming aware of the space that separates her—on the passenger side—from her husband at the wheel, the wife forlornly asks, "What ever happened to us? Look at them, so close, and look at the gap between us." The husband, hands on the steering wheel, looks at her and says, "I never moved."

Some people have allowed a similar gap to develop between them and their dreams, *but the dreams are still there.* They haven't moved. Better yet, God, the inspirer of those dreams, hasn't moved either. This is what this book is about, a renewal of your heart and mind so that you will recapture your dreams and fulfill your destiny.

Something extraordinary is going on all over the world. Ordinary people are doing extraordinary things that are radically transforming schools, companies, prisons, cities, and even nations. Today millions of men and women are walking out their call to full-time ministry in the marketplace. These people work as stockbrokers, lawyers, entrepreneurs, farmers, chief operating officers, news reporters, teachers, police officers, plumbers, receptionists, cooks, and much more.

Many already know that they are called to play a vital part in the establishment of God's kingdom on Earth. They believe they are ministers, and they have turned their jobs into ministerial vehicles.

A pineapple grower in Africa chooses to buy a parcel of land for his workers before buying himself a home, giving his employees not only economic freedom but also an unbeatable leadership model. Subsequently he becomes the largest pineapple grower in the country and at present cares for 665 children in several orphanages and educates 1,531 students affected by the HIV/AIDS scourge, in a school that his business funds.

An American lawyer, representing an airline filing for bankruptcy, and another attorney, working on behalf of the creditors, agree to pray together to discern the best resolution to a most difficult case involving millions of dollars on one hand and thousands of jobs on the other. They pray for a win-win resolution—and "out of the blue" (God's blue!), a solution is found that allows the airline to come out of bankruptcy court in record time, properly fitted to succeed in the marketplace. The miraculous is hard to ignore, and the outcome causes other lawyers to reevaluate the value of prayer in their profession.

The CEO of an oil company in Minnesota presides over a meeting in which his management team discusses how to add 2,500 churches to the 500 churches *already* planted overseas as part of *their business plan.* Under his direction, the group also regularly *and joyfully* allocates tens of thousands of dollars to help eradicate systemic poverty, provide training for aspiring entrepreneurs, and launch Kingdom companies in the nations served by these churches.

After being sworn in, the Commissioner for Tax Revenue in a Third World nation erects an altar to God in her office and invites God-fearing associates to join her in conducting spiritual warfare against the corruption that has kept fiscal revenues from being collected, turning tax evasion into a national sport. Later, at the end of the first year, receipts increase to a record level. More remarkably yet, leading merchants begin to come to the Commissioner to repent for tax evasion and agree to pay long-overdue taxes!

A businessman facing a major loss in his company has a supernatural experience and, as a result, dedicates his firm to God. In the next eight years, he sees his profits increase beyond anything imaginable, with a 65 percent increase in growth the first year and 385 percent the last two years. This enables him and his wife to help feed 5 percent of the population of their county.

A city in the American Midwest, once plagued by the highest national per capita teenage suicide rate, its schools in ruin, and a clandestine drug lab flooding the market with methamphetamine, becomes a beacon of peace and prosperity. The reason? The mayor, along with pulpit and marketplace leaders, invites God to set up residence in town, and every Tuesday they spend half a day in the equivalent of a spiritual staff meeting with the Lord, bringing before Him different needs for His guidance and/or intervention. The city's spiritual atmosphere improves so much that prayer for miracles is routinely offered in banks, car dealerships, motorcycle showrooms, doctors' offices, restaurants and law offices.

A student in his senior year at a violent, drug-prevalent high school has an encounter with God that launches a movement that first transforms his campus and then impacts 76 other schools in the state, reducing crime and disciplinary referrals, improving attendance and grade point averages, and infusing the students, teachers and administrators with newfound hope.

Real Transformation

Everywhere I go, from Argentina to Uganda to the USA, I meet ordinary people and hear these extraordinary stories of dramatic change. This is real transformation taking place in real time as the result of a singular discovery: that God passionately cares—not just for people, but also for the marketplace and for cities and nations.

This transformation movement is different because it is spiritual without being religious. Even though faith in God is its central tenet, there is no religious flavor to it. In fact, more than in houses of worship, it is primarily taking place in the marketplace. It is revolutionary without being rebellious. It is contagious without being infectious. It is empowering without being overpowering. It is personal while at the same time touching cities and nations. It is both death defying and life-giving, because it is being facilitated by people who are overcoming systemic evil by the blood shed on the cross by the Holy One, people who have exchanged their lives for *His* life (see Rev. 12:11).

Essential to this movement are *five pivotal paradigms for transformation*—keys that constitute the backbone of this book. These paradigms, when embraced, will open our eyes to the most inspiring spiritual panorama and reveal a source of power so magnificent and vast that we will be immediately compelled to tap into it to bring transformation to our lives, our families, our jobs, our cities, and eventually our world.

Transformation is what this book is all about. These five pivotal paradigms, examined in the chapters that follow, have the potential to turn you into a world changer, just as it was with our predecessors, about whom it was said over 2,000 years ago, "These that have turned the world upside down" (Acts 17:6, *ASV*).

But before we discuss these paradigms, you will need to wrestle to the ground four questions that will define your destiny.

CHAPTER 2

The Four Questions That Will Shape Your Destiny

On September 23, 1779, during the American Revolutionary War, one of the fiercest engagements in naval history took place off the coast of Scotland. Privateer John Paul Jones, the 32-year-old Scotland-born captain of the flagship *Bonhomme Richard*, battled against the superior 44-gun British Royal Navy frigate *Serapis*. After relentless pounding by the enemy's mightier guns, Jones's ship was ablaze and precariously holding itself above water, with many of his men dead or sprawled wounded across the bloodied decks, the few still standing by his side beyond exhaustion. Captain Pearson of the *Serapis* hailed Jones and inquired politely, "Sir, are you ready to strike your colors and surrender?" To which Jones replied, "Surrender, sir? I have not yet begun to fight!" And he proceeded to lead his decimated forces in a furious counterattack. The enemy was overpowered, the *Serapis* surrendered, and Jones took command of the mighty British frigate.

The choice Captain Jones made in a split second came from something embedded in the very fiber of his soul. If it caught him by surprise, it most assuredly caught his adversary off guard; and the result was a decisive victory in the path to birthing a new nation with a glorious destiny.

Living vs. Existing

This book is about transformation and the paradigms and principles that undergird it. Transformation does not happen in a vacuum. It is brought about by people who have tapped into a well of resolve and a sense of purpose deep and powerful enough to enable them to overcome the ominous and menacing challenges that stand at its gates like intimidating guardians. This book tells true stories of how and why these people are changing the course of history in neighborhoods, marketplaces and nations around the world.

When the weight of destiny hangs in the balance, as happened to Captain John Paul Jones, there are four basic questions that lead us to that source of resolve and purpose—questions that every human being wrestles with at some point in his or her life. How we answer them will shape our decisions and determine our lifestyle. They mark the difference between merely *existing* and really *living*; between stagnating like a swamp and flowing like a majestic mountain river with unimpeded force during a Spring thaw; between being changed by the world or being a world changer. They shape our future and even the future of those around us.

Let's examine these four crucial questions.

Question #1: *Is There a God?*

The first question lays the foundation for all the others: *Is there a God?*

Do you remember when that question first came up in your mind? I recall it very vividly. I was about four years old, growing up in Argentina, where every night I saw my mother, a devout Catholic, kneel by her bed to hold a monologue with someone I knew was not in the room. Puzzled, I asked her, "Mom, who are you talking to?"

Very matter of factly, she said, "I am talking to God."

I inquired further, "Who is God?"

To this she responded, "God is the one who made the world."

Religion was not a popular subject around our dinner table as my father was a vocal atheist, and its exclusion was some sort of a truce between his unbelief and my mother's beliefs.

My infantile but nonetheless logical four-year-old mind pondered my mother's comment to an irrefutable conclusion: Somebody made the toys I played with; they did not make themselves. Therefore, somebody must have made the world, and He must be God.

Perhaps you came to believe there is a God in a similar way that I did, or maybe in an entirely different way; but the vast majority of people answer this question affirmatively because it takes a lot *more* "faith" to reject all notion of a higher power than to embrace it. For example, imagine that you parachute into the Amazon jungles in South America where, upon landing, you find to your utter surprise a table exquisitely set in the middle of the forest with steaming food on it, background music gently playing, and an elegantly inscribed note stating, "Welcome. Enjoy it!" After the initial shock, I'm sure the first question in your mind would be, *Who put this here?*

The odds of someone tossing the parts of a wristwatch into the air and having it land on their wrist, assembled, fastened properly and telling the right time, are greater than the chances that the vast universes that we are discovering today came together by some uncontrolled explosion. Since, as a child, I knew that someone made my toys, it was absolutely logical for me to conclude that Someone bigger than me made the world.

Question #2: *Does God Care?*

Determining that there actually is a God leads to the second question: *Does He care?* There are hundreds of thousands of gods worshiped in the world today, most of them passively enshrined in cold temples, their presence confined to the material they are made of. In and of themselves, these "gods" are but inanimate objects, utterly oblivious to human concerns. So, does God *really* care?

When we examine the universe and see how marvelously designed it is and how precisely it is run, when we observe how one season follows the other in perfect harmony, each one unique and at the same time complementary to the others, when we see how the earth compensates for the damage humans relentlessly inflict on her, and how "miracle cures" are found for lethal conditions that emerge as a result of our irresponsible behavior (particularly when, in light of our tremendous potential for evil, how *much more evil* could have happened on any given day that actually *did not* happen), we are driven to the conclusion that God indeed cares for the world He created.

Granted, tragedies occur. The river of history flows bloody and polluted by lethal debris as a result of man's capacity for evil. But in the midst of all this human suffering, the God who cares is there. It is the influence of His power and constant presence that, in spite of tragedies, makes the world a better place today than it was a hundred years ago. This points to the existence of a greater power actively restraining catastrophic terrorist acts, worldwide plagues, monumental political disasters, and unabated human stupidity with lethal global consequences. Otherwise, the end would have come a long time ago. There must be a God watching over the earth.

Question #3: *Does God Care for Me?*

This conclusion leads to the third question: If there is a God who cares for the world, *does He care for me?* This is a most important question because there is no personal benefit in believing that there is a God who cares unless we realize that He cares for us *personally.*

The day I proposed to Ruth, my wife, we had gone for a stroll in the beautiful hills of Cordoba, Argentina. Hand in hand we walked on the sunny bank of a lovely creek, enjoying the idyllic view and listening to the murmur of the water as it cascaded from one rock to the next, while butterflies engaged in a multicolor game of flower-hopping in the lush vegetation flanking our path. A turn in the brook provided us with some welcome privacy, so we tiptoed on rocks barely above water level to reach a promontory in the middle of the creek where Ruth sat on a large rock while I sat at her feet on a smaller one.

There is no personal benefit in believing that there is a God who cares unless we realize that He cares for us *personally.*

After getting lost one more time in her beautiful green eyes, I asked, "Ruth, do you love me?" ardently hoping for an affirmative answer while struggling to keep my doubts under control.

She could have replied, "I love the flowers and the hills" or "I love my aunt Marjorie and my cousin Willy" or more inclusively yet, "I love the whole world." However, none of those answers would have meant much to me at that moment because my question was very personal: "Do you love *me?*" Only when she said yes, did everything else become relevant.

This is also true when it comes to the question, "Does the God who cares for the world care for you *personally?*" This is where the God of the Bible comes through with undeniable "competitive advantage." Yes! God cares for us. From the very beginning He created the very best, including humankind. When man fell into sin, it was He who came to the rescue to make restoration possible, to the point of sending His very best, Jesus, who in spite of having done nothing but good, was crucified like a criminal by the very people He came to save. In the midst of that cruel death, He forgave us and then descended to the deepest part of Hades to dethrone the powers of darkness that held us captive; He then returned victoriously to earth, full of divine power and in splendid majesty to say to us, *I love you and there is nothing you can do about it.*

The message is compelling beyond measure: His love is unlimited and unconditional. In fact, He assured us that when we believe in Him as our Lord and Savior, He will have our names inscribed by angels in the Book of Life and no one will be able to take us away from Him. The reason God allowed us to inflict the most undeserved punishment on Him was to provide us with incontrovertible and unassailable proof that His love is absolutely unconditional and therefore can and will conquer *everything.*

So, we know that there is a God who cares and that He cares for us personally.

Question #4: *Does God Care About What We Do?*
In order to find not just success but also specifically significance in life, a fourth question must be answered: If there is a God who cares for me, *does He care about what I do?* Does He care about my job, about my career, with the same intensity that He cares for me? Is He interested in exercising His power to help me solve the problems I face at work as much as He is interested in my personal holiness?

Unfortunately we don't always answer this question affirmatively. Or if we do, somehow, deep down, we harbor the misbelief that even though God may watch out for us in the workplace, His heart is not fully in it, because His interest is in the welfare of our soul and in our spending eternity with Him.

This faulty perception of the scope of divine intention is most unfortunate, because unless we understand that God cares about what we do *as much as He cares about our eternal soul,* our life on Earth, and particularly our role in the workplace, then we will never rise past the level of being mere survivors in a spiritual prisoner-of-war camp. With this perspective, we won't get to heaven without first going through some sort of hell on Earth. That would be a monumental misperception, because His design is for us to take over the POW camp and turn it into a training ground from which to orchestrate the liberation of other camps until the whole earth has come under His lordship.

This type of shortsighted and incomplete thinking would be like the story I heard about a British lad who spent all his savings to buy a ticket on a transatlantic luxury cruiser and skipped the meals, carefully rationing the stale crackers he brought on board as food *because he didn't realize that every meal was included in the price of his ticket!*

What we embrace about the scope of God's caring for us not only affects our lives during the 167 hours of the week that we are not in a church service, but it also affects the world around us. God is not with us only when we are sitting in a church pew. Where is He on Monday? Or, for that matter, Tuesday through Saturday? Where is He when life's challenges lay siege to us in an environment that at times turns overtly hostile? We spend the bulk of our waking hours some-where in the marketplace. It is there that we face the circumstances day in and day out that continually test, and sometimes crush, our self-esteem and sense of personal worth, both of which are vital to succeeding in life. What is the use of believing in God if He cannot be *with us* and *for us* in such a crucial place as our career or work envi-ronment? The answer is simple: God is omnipresent—He's *everywhere, and as I intend to show in this book, He cares for what you do in the market-place as much as He cares for you!*

The Divine Role Model

We derive, at least at an embryonic level, our notion of God as a father from the influence, or lack of influence, of our natural fathers. As a child I had an experience that illustrates how key it is that the one who embod-ies the strongest role model in our life also demonstrates that he cares about what we do (or, in my case, what I was supposed to do but found myself unable to do).

When I was growing up, there was a chore that the children took turns doing. Twice a day we would go to an ice shed behind the house and bring the drinks to accompany our meals. These beverages were kept in a cooler in this storage room at the end of a long path flanked by tall, thick trees.

I always tried to draw the lunch assignment for this chore because I was afraid of doing it at night, but I didn't always succeed. One dread-ful evening, I stood frozen with fear at the head of the path that led to the shed, while in the dining room the family was waiting for me to bring the drinks. Out in the menacing darkness, the sound of the wind rust-ling the leaves and stirring the branches caused me to imagine monsters lurking behind every tree.

My father, noticing that I was taking too long for a relatively simple task, came out to check on me. Seeing me immobile at the head of the path, he discerned what was going on. Looking me in the eye, with a calming voice he asked, "Son, you are afraid, aren't you?"

"Yes," I answered timidly.

"Are you frightened of the darkness?" he inquired further.

Again I assented.

"Do the tree branches look as if they're trying to grab you?"

One more time I nodded with embarrassment. I felt I had failed my assignment—not for lack of trying, but from being overwhelmed by what I perceived to be a hostile environment. I felt helpless and especially humiliated for being seen in such a state by my father.

At that moment he took my hand in his and said in a firm voice, "Let's go, son. We'll do it together." The instant his hand enveloped mine, all fear evaporated, and at that moment *I knew* that I was going to succeed, even though nothing on the outside had changed. The darkness was still there. The menacing trees did not go away. The wind continued to rustle the leaves. The distance to the ice shed did not diminish. *But I was no longer afraid.* Instead, I felt empowered, and I was able to bring the drinks to the dinner table under the reassuring gaze of my father, who had now become my partner.

I always knew that my father cared for me, but that night I *experienced* that he also cared about *what I was expected to do*—my job—and that he was willing and (to my surprise) eager to come alongside me to ensure that I would succeed. So many people go through life feeling alone and helpless, when right from the start God is next to them, ready to take their hand in His because *He* cares *about what they do!*

Jesus, who came to reveal God's loving nature and compassionate character, exemplified this through His miracles. In John 2, Jesus was a guest at a wedding and was made aware that the caterer had run out of wine. He immediately solved the problem by turning water into wine of such high quality that the caterer, who moments before faced public scorn, was enthusiastically congratulated.

Peter and John, along with their brothers, owned fishing boats that on a particular day, as told in John 21, were returning to port empty. Despite having been out all night, they had caught nothing. For professional fishermen, this was a major problem. It was the equivalent of a broker losing his largest account, or a lucrative house sale falling through when the agent needs the commission for a make-it-or-break-it payment on his own mortgage. No fish meant there would be no sales. No sales meant there would be no income, which in turn resulted in no food on the table.

What did Jesus do? Did He tell them to pray harder? Did He question their spirituality? On the contrary, He told them precisely where to cast the net to get a most extraordinary catch. This type of "marketplace miracle" was a common occurrence with Jesus.

Matthew 17 tells about how Peter came to Jesus in obvious distress because his taxes were overdue. This is a situation many people can identify with today. The mere fact that Peter would bring it up to Jesus shows that He was considered a sympathetic source. How did Jesus respond? He did not spiritualize the problem. Knowing that Peter was a professional fisherman, he told him to go fishing, and a coin would be found in the mouth of the first fish he caught. Being a practical man, Jesus told Peter that while he was at it he should use whatever change was left over to pay His taxes as well!

God *Is* in Our Work

God cares about our job because of the cause-and-effect relationship that exists between our identity and our work. What we do in life is an external expression of who we are inside. Because of this connection, these two dimensions should not be dichotomized. It is often said, *Don't let what you do determine who you are.* While there is some seminal truth in this statement, a deeper aspect also needs to be understood: *Who we are determines what we do.* Doctors, lawyers, politicians, educators, people working in the service industry, have chosen that specific occupation because it best reflects who they are. This is because God planted seeds in the inner recesses of our soul at the moment of conception that, as we mature, ultimately sprout into a trade, a vocation or a profession. Because God planted the seeds, His involvement is required for them to develop properly. This is why it is a monumental tragedy not to understand that God cares about what we do *just as much as He cares about who we are.*

If all God cared about was our soul, then ministers would hold us under the baptismal waters longer than three minutes so that they could facilitate a speedy transition to eternity! Fortunately, this is not the way it is done. In fact, as people emerge from the waters, they are told to *walk in newness of life*. In marketplace terminology this is the equivalent of saying, "develop a partnership with God in the workplace," because doing so will shape our soul in His image as we learn from Him how to resolve everyday challenges while holding His hand, drawing power from Him, and benefiting from His guidance to experience new and better ways of doing things. The scope of the newness of life we hear so much about in church goes beyond the external perimeter of our soul. Using our soul as a staging ground, we are to take God's renewing power to the outer confines of our sphere of influence until it has been transformed.

■ ■ ■

God cares about what we do just as much as He cares about who we are.

■ ■ ■

God and a Fortune 500 Company

This is not a fantasy; it is something that is happening more and more. For example, I know a career woman named Marissa (not her real name), who holds a high position in a Fortune 500 company, who came to realize that, in addition to caring about her job, God also has designs and a purpose for the company she works for. This conviction led her to declare, "I am not just an executive but also the pastor of this corporation." And she began to see her job as a spiritual exercise. As a result, every morning she set aside time to pray for the company, for her boss, for her employees and associates, and for the deals and transactions that are part of her normal workload.

One day as she was praying, the Holy Spirit alerted her to the fact that a recent corporate acquisition was flawed. In fact, He provided her with specific information about how the CEO of the recently acquired company had fooled the auditors during the due diligence phase leading up to the transaction. Later that day, as part of her interaction with the Chief Financial Officer, she disclosed to him this explosive information. The CFO was surprised at first, but since she was providing very specific details, he asked how trustworthy her source was.

"Absolutely," she replied. What else could she say, since God was the "informant"? But the CFO demanded to know who the source was. When she demurred, he pressed and pulled rank on her. Reluctantly, she blurted out, "God told me about it."

At that moment the CFO's state of mind went from surprise to shock. "God?" he said. "And what does God have to do with our company?"

By way of explanation, she gave him the three-minute version of my book *Anointed for Business*, putting in plain words that God cares about what people do in the workplace and how important corporations are to Him—theirs included.

Her boss said, "I don't know about that, but I am left with no choice but to investigate this further." He proceeded to dispatch a team of auditors to check the records, this time with the blueprint of how the alleged fraud had been perpetrated.

A few days later the CFO announced that everything she had reported turned out to be correct, and that the specifics she provided were key to the success of the auditing team. After a brief pause, he went on to ask, albeit with a sense of trepidation, "What else did God tell you? Did He say anything about me?"

Your Turn

As strange as Marissa's story sounds, it is not without biblical precedent. Joseph and Daniel lived and worked in secular contexts that benefited immensely from the divine revelations entrusted to them—revelations that resulted in great prosperity for those they worked for. In fact, the rulers of two world empires were so impacted by the extraordinary insights Joseph and Daniel provided, concerning complex marketplace issues that resulted in significant improvements in the quality of life in their kingdoms, that eventually they came to believe in, and revere, their God.

What about you?

What are you going to do with the rest of your life? Are you going to stand immobilized at the head of the trail leading to your destiny, caving in to the prospect of failure while being buffeted by fear and feelings of inadequacy? Remember, your destiny awaits you at the end of a path blocked by menacing giants. To achieve it, you need to overcome those giants, and there is only one right way to do that: with God at your side.

If you have not done it yet, now is the time to place your hand in the hand of your Maker to access the power that will enable you to become everything He has meant you to be. Yes, there is a God who cares for the world. In fact, He made it. He also cares personally for you. He is *your* Maker, but He cares about what you do too; and to that end He has a magnificent plan for your life.

Like Captain John Paul Jones's warship over two centuries ago, today your ship may look ready to go down, damaged by the pounding of incessant adversity, with surrender sounding like an appealing option. However, if you realize that God cares about *what you do as much as He cares about you,* you will transcend your present circumstances and find the strength to say, *"Surrender? I have not even begun to fight!"*

I encourage and even implore you right now to let His hand envelop yours. Agree with Him about how much He cares about you *and for* you. Pray this prayer now: "Lord Jesus, I invite You to come into my heart, to forgive my sins and to fill me with your presence. Also take my hand in Yours. I know You will never let it go. Amen." And now with Him at your side, begin the journey to claim your destiny and transform your world!

CHAPTER 3

The Five Pivotal Paradigms
for Transformation

It finally dawned on me that I was in deep medical trouble when my eye surgeon told me, "Well, you were first in line for brains . . . but last for eyes." Several top-notched eye specialists had examined me previously, and one by one they had referred me to "someone more experienced on this matter." Now I was at the end of the line and about to start a surgical journey down the road to six eye surgeries, hence the reason for my doctor's dry humor.

By the time I was onto my fifth surgery, Ruth and I had come to know everybody at the hospital—doctors, nurses, receptionists, volunteers, even the janitors. But on that particular day, I noticed the nurse was prepping my *left* eye and I knew that the scheduled surgery was for the *right* one! She had already placed an adhesive plastic arrow on the left side of my forehead pointing to the eye to be operated on. I asked her to check, and sure enough my suspicions were confirmed; it was the wrong eye.

I insisted on now having two adhesive arrows placed, one indicating "this eye" and the other "NOT this eye." I then proceeded to bring up the issue with the nurse, the anesthesiologist and the nurses aide taking me to surgery. When I was about to broach the subject with the operating surgeon, he said, "I know, I know. It is the right eye. Everybody within 10 miles of this hospital has heard about it. Relax!"

Because the subject was of vital importance to me, I insisted on making sure everybody got it right. They not only got it, but they also joyfully complied. Unfortunately, God doesn't always get the same cooperation from us on issues that He considers of great importance. All through the Bible He has placed fluorescent red markers pointing us to the things He wants us to fix on in this world—the cities and nations in desperate need of "surgery"—but somehow we keep focusing on something else.

From God's point of view, the ultimate destiny of Christians is not to become the foremost experts in foxhole design and maintenance, countermarches, defensive maneuvers or siege management.

The army led by Jesus is designed and commissioned to advance decisively, to bring down the gates of Hades and to overcome the evil that is entrenched in the world until God's glory has been poured on peoples and nations. No matter how clearly this is spelled out in the Scriptures, we seem to "prep the wrong eye." To make this change, we need to embrace new paradigms and gain new vision.

We associate lenses with the eyes, but there are also intellectual "lenses" that, once placed over our mind, can impact our understanding—for better or for worse. Likewise, the Church today is beset by myriad "optical" difficulties when it comes to seeing the fullness of our purpose and potential as change agents in the societies in which we live. Some folks are functionally nearsighted, others are farsighted, some have tunnel vision, some can't focus, and some have cataracts. If, for example, an optometrist mistakenly prescribes reading glasses for someone who needs glasses for distance, the user would not be able to focus on objects far away. Being unable to see the long view, the patient would eventually give up and miss the big picture entirely.

The issue is that while we have been *looking*, we have not been *seeing* all there is to see. Because we have looked through religious lenses, we have not seen the marketplace, much less its great importance to God's kingdom. By exclusively discipling individuals, we have missed the higher prize of bringing transformation to nations. It's time that we put on kingdom-of-God glasses that will enable us to see the Church operating 24/7 in the marketplace, to see the real objectives and the real enemies, and to see the integration of all that gives us the power to disciple nations.

The brief stories you have read here so far, and many others you will read in the pages ahead, came about because the principals involved operate out of a different mindset. In essence, they embraced new paradigms that afforded them a clearer and more comprehensive view.

The Five Paradigms

There are five pivotal paradigms essential for sustainable transformation to take place, each of which we will examine in detail in the chapters ahead. These paradigms are:

1. The Great Commission is about discipling nations, not just people.

2. The marketplace (the heart of the nation) has already been redeemed by Jesus and now needs to be reclaimed by His followers.

3. Labor is the premier expression of worship on Earth, and every believer is a minister.

4. Our primary call is not to build the Church but to take the kingdom of God where the kingdom of darkness is still entrenched in order for Jesus to build His Church.

5. The premier social indicator that transformation has taken place is the elimination of *systemic* poverty.

These paradigms might seem radical, and are not necessarily what we hear from the pulpit every week, but they are thoroughly biblical and clearly reflect God's perspective. However, to be able to see them, we need to wear the right lenses, because it is our tendency to be short-sighted when processing divine instructions; that is, we tend to focus on what is closer in the present at the expense of capturing the full scope of all that God has in store for us and wants to accomplish through us.

By exclusively discipling individuals, we have missed the higher prize of bringing transformation to nations.

A clear example of this is found in Acts 1:4-8 where Jesus is dispensing last-minute instructions to His followers as He awaits the white cloud that will take Him back to heaven. He is telling the disciples to tarry in Jerusalem until they have been baptized with the Holy Spirit. By this He meant that they should stay in Jerusalem in order to receive the power required to disciple nations all over the world. Undoubtedly Jesus is looking through the distance portion of the lenses.

How did the disciples process this information? I dare say *nearsightedly*, as revealed by their inquiry: "Are you going to restore the Kingdom to Israel at this time?" Basically they were asking, "When the Holy Spirit comes, are we going to be vindicated before our nation and, as a result, will Jerusalem become the center of the world with the nations coming to us?"

Since Jesus, in the gospels, had promised them a kingdom, it is not unlikely that they saw the promised infilling by the Holy Spirit as the threshold to access such a kingdom. But Jesus had a different focus. He told them not to wait for nations to come to them, but to *go to the nations*. He specifically instructed them to begin by discipling a city (Jerusalem), and from there to move up to a region (Judea), and once they had acquired some experience in the subject of regional discipleship, to go on and tackle the first nation (Samaria), and after that *not to stop until they had reached the ends of the earth*—all nations (see Acts 1:8). What a contrast! In essence, Jesus was saying that it is not about you, *it's about God* and God is about nations!

Clearly, God intends to restore the Kingdom to Israel. He does pour out His Spirit upon people to endow them with supernatural power to overcome personal challenges. The problem is that the disciples focused on the immediate dimension at the expense of the bigger picture. For the Bible to make sense, for its principles to become relevant, and for the promised results to materialize, a series of paradigm shifts are necessary to allow us to become *disciplers of nations,* empowered by the redemptive work of Christ to fully *reclaim the marketplace* and *worship God with our jobs* so that we can *take the kingdom of God where evil is still entrenched* so that nations will have honor and glory restored.

Church on Weekdays

For many, the shifting of paradigms began with a very practical question, *Where is God on Monday?* Or, for that matter, every other day of the week besides Sunday? The truth is, as a growing number of people are discovering, God is passionately interested *and invested* in human affairs *all the time*. Consequently, He is willing to bring His presence and His power to bear, first in our immediate sphere of influence, and eventually in our cities and even our nation.

Let's take a look at some examples of how this can occur.

Lieutenant Governor Welcomes Jesus into Paradise

Hawaii, one of the most alluring and hospitable American states, has scored a number of negative "firsts." The first abortion clinic opened in Honolulu in the '70s. The first homosexual marriage initiative was introduced there. A strong liberal lobby in Hawaii is relentlessly pushing for the islands to be at least the second state to approve assisted suicide legislation (Oregon has the discredit of being the first). When people think of the most liberal state in the Union, they usually name Massachusetts; but socially speaking, Hawaii is far more liberal. Aided by strong unions, it has had continuous left-of-center administrations since it became a state in the 1950s—a string unbroken until a 2002 upset election.

Things began to change on December 8, 2004, when Lieutenant Governor James "Duke" Aiona led 6,000 believers in a corporate invocation, inviting Jesus, publicly and officially to come into the state to make it God's Hawaii. This solemn act was the climax of a canopy of prayer raised over the islands that day and the prayer walk of 77 school campuses across the state.

What took place is no different than what we read in 2 Chronicles 7:14: "If my people, upon whom my Name is invoked, humble themselves and pray and seek my face, and turn from their wicked ways, I will hear their prayer, I will forgive their sins and I will heal the land."

In Hawaii, that prayer exercise reflected the new understanding about the need to disciple nations and the right to reclaim the marketplace (in this case education) for the kingdom of God.

Anybody familiar with the acidic American constitutional debate on the separation of church and state knows that participating in (and, in the case of Hawaii's Lieutenant Governor, leading) such an overt public religious exercise is tantamount to political suicide. However, this was not about the institutional *church* and state; it was all about *God* and the problems of the state. Hence, the dramatic and extraordinary changes that began to take place shortly after the statewide prayer made believers of many unbelievers, to the point that even the secular media began to report good news.

Following the raising of the canopy of prayer, crime and disciplinary referrals in school campuses decreased dramatically. In some schools, grade point averages and graduation rates reached record highs. In another school, teenage pregnancy dropped significantly. Best of all, in many schools, campus drug dealers, who used to operate with impunity due to the complicity of students, were exposed and arrested. All of this constituted clear validation that the kingdom of God was taking over areas where evil had been systemically entrenched. Churches "adopted" schools and took offerings to purchase much-needed equipment or to pay for repairs. Believers volunteered as athletic coaches, spiritual advisors and campus counselors, and prayer became common at track meets, sporting matches and even at faculty meetings.

Once prayer became a "normal" activity on campus, students regularly made it a practice to hold hands in small circles to publicly pray for the principal, the teachers and fellow students. Soon afterwards, reports of miraculous answers to those prayers fueled greater interest in God's presence on school grounds, and many students *and administrators* experienced life changing encounters with Jesus.

In the context of the prayer exercise, in January 2005, 134 Kingdom-minded persons from across the Islands came to hear and share reports, hopes and dreams for the future. This led to a spontaneous gathering of 900 transformation-hungry Christians in February 2005, which in turn resulted in an Anointed for Business seminar the following May for 2,500 believers. During the closing session of this seminar, 200 pastors commissioned 2,300 church members as marketplace ministers in an inspiring ceremony that set the stage for the newly commissioned to turn their jobs into their ministry. The following week, scores of transformation groups were launched (most of them around lunch breaks) in hospitals, ranches, the waterfront, stores, banks, car dealerships, attorney's offices, schools and hotels. Prayers began to be offered all over the marketplace for Hawaii to become God's Hawaii, just as the Lieutenant Governor had prayed the previous December.

Democrats and Republicans Praying Together in Chambers

The results became evident right away, proving that the gates of Hades cannot prevail against Jesus' people. The ancient bitter animosity between Republicans and Democrats took a direct hit when the Republican Lieutenant Governor and a leading Democratic state senator publicly asked for forgiveness on behalf of their respective parties. Subsequently, spirituality in politics became prevalent among legislators and government workers. At least 50 people have joined a newly established prayer meeting in the state building. The political climate improved so much that *both parties* rated the 2006 legislative session as "the best ever," and closed it by singing "Amazing Grace" *in chambers*!

At the city level, shortly after a fiercely fought election, the mayor of Honolulu (a Mormon and a Democrat) opened his term in office with prayer convocation to seek God's favor for the city, and afterward prayed regularly with pastors in his office seeking God's guidance and favor. A year later, at what was billed as the mayor's *"annual* prayer service," he gave eloquent testimony that intercession and God's favor were the reason for the remarkable municipal breakthroughs of the previous 12 months. At this prayer service, government and community leaders representing the most diverse social and political streams held hands asking for God's blessing on the city and the state.

Breakthroughs also started to show up in the business community. The management of the leading car dealership introduced prayer for their employees and customers. This became so *normal* that people would call to ask, "I don't need a car but I need prayer. Can I come in?" A new bank that opened decided from the very beginning that they would give a percentage of their profits to charity. Crime decreased and the murder rate was cut in half.

The booming economy is now the best in the history of the state; and Hawaii now has the lowest unemployment rate in the nation. Median income rose from $53,554 to $58,112 in one year, while the poverty rate descended from 10.6 percent to 9.8 percent. And on April 20, 2007, local newspapers covered a friendly dialogue between Democrat and Republican legislators to refund to the taxpayers the fiscal surplus of the previous two years as the state constitution mandated.

Across Hawaii, Christian youth are leading peers to the Lord in unprecedented numbers, voluntary worship services are being held in school campuses, and pastors are being asked to serve as spiritual advisors. Furthermore, in the tough docks of Honolulu it has become "typical" to see sturdy stevedores lifting heavily tattooed arms in prayer; while in a growing number of boardrooms, divine guidance is sought by CEOs and senior management as part of the regular corporate agenda.

In the town of Nanakuli, historically one of the poorest and most hopeless places in the state, believers adopted every square inch of the city and prayer-walked the entire community, inviting Jesus to set up residence in it, and especially on its school campuses. Shortly afterward, the National Football League donated one million dollars to build youth centers in the area, most of which will operate in conjunction with the same schools where Jesus was invited in. At about the same time, a nearby prison began to experience radical transformation when the newly appointed warden invited Jesus to make it "Jesus' prison." In less than six months, half of the inmates became believers, were baptized, transformed, and are now actively involved in building a Christian ward that is setting the bar for the rest of the prison.

■ ■ ■

To see what we have never seen, we must do what we have never done, or else we will continue to see what we always see.

■ ■ ■

On the island of Maui, businessman Myles Kawakami gave God control over his company. The business began to prosper and Myles has been faithfully writing checks from God's 51 percent portion of the profits to bless poor people and social undertakings, while watching his income increase. Myles and his wife, Joyce, feed thousands of needy people, in addition to funding a significant number of projects. Myles says, "It would be foolish not to give away 51 percent every month, because the 49 percent I get to keep is greater than the 100 percent I used to keep, due to God's extraordinary prosperity."

Tahiti: President Gets Baptized

Breakthroughs have also gone beyond Hawaii. Francis Oda, chairman and CEO of Group 70, arguably the leading architectural firm in the state, was in Tahiti to participate in an architectural contest for the renewal of the capital's city, Papeete, and its waterfront. Francis holds dual ministry citizenship as an architect and as senior pastor of a congregation in Honolulu. Because of that combination, he knows that his pastoral duties are not confined to Sundays. This is why he saw himself as a channel for God's kingdom to become manifested in Tahiti, even though the stated reason for his trip was an architectural assignment. Francis understood that he was called to disciple nations and to reclaim the marketplace, and that his job was a vehicle to take God's kingdom where evil was still entrenched.

During an official meeting, the president of Tahiti asked for Francis's opinion on what to build on the location of a project he had just stopped. Francis asked specific questions to get the best possible grasp on the subject, and after pondering the information, he suggested building a museum. The president stated that it might be better to consider an alternative placement and proceeded to give him the reasons for it. Acknowledging the president's reasoning, Francis said, "If you put it there, the project may turn out to be good, but if you place it on the waterfront, it will become world famous." As soon as his words were uttered, a sepulchral silence fell on the meeting. The president abruptly changed the subject and Francis became aware of a cultural tenet that Tahitians never violate: One does not contradict the president's opinion, especially in public.

However, soon afterward the president returned with a wink and a twinkle in his eyes and told him, "I like your idea, but can I say that it was my idea? And can you make a presentation in two days' time?" Francis, vividly relieved, agreed to the presentation, while wondering how he would find the time to do it on such a tight schedule.

The next morning, while he was "prayer swimming"—interceding for his host nation—the Lord began to download to him a magnificent new design for the building depicting a history of French Polynesia. This proved to be a challenge, because Francis was in his swimming trunks and had no writing material handy. But, like the prophets of old, he began to make notes in the sand, while his assistant (unlike the biblical scribes), who had also been swimming, ran to the hotel to fetch a digital camera to photograph God's revelation before it was erased by the tide!

For the next two days, Francis and his associate found themselves feverishly drawing to have the document ready on time. To compound matters further, just a few hours before the dinner where Francis was expected to present his work before the president and invited VIPs, he received a phone call from an assistant to the president requesting Francis's opinion on how to solve an engineering challenge affecting the docks, the beaches, and the highways in the downtown area. "The president would appreciate if you can have a solution on this subject also," intoned the assistant in the most natural manner.

Both requests represented challenges beyond anything humanly possible. But Francis, as a marketplace minister deputized by God, had a direct line to the Creator, and he put it to good use. After he prayed, God gave him a most inspired insight on how to resolve the challenge *and gave him the time and the energy to make all necessary drafts!*

What emerged for both projects was so extraordinary and riveting that the president was elated and inquired again how Francis had come up with such a brilliant concept in such a short time. Very straightforwardly, Francis stated, "It was God." As surprising as that sounds, it did make sense, even though at first it startled the president, because 13 French engineers had been working on the second project for six months and had not been able to come up with anything remotely close to what Francis had designed.

One thing led to another, and eventually the president, his wife, Francis's collaborating Tahitian architect Teiva Raffin, Teiva's partners and Teiva's Iranian wife received the Lord. Francis baptized them and, after laying hands on them, they were filled with the Holy Spirit. Not long afterward, the president asked Teiva Raffin, now fellow believer, to offer a prayer for Tahiti during an official gathering—a definite first!

Biblical Results for Modern Times

Stories like this eloquently testify that these pivotal paradigms, when embraced with childlike faith and Spirit-led persistency and dependency, produce the same results that we read in the Scriptures.

Yes, the Bible is a reliable record of God's intervention in human affairs, and these stories are proof that God is very involved in the transformation of nations. Its narratives are not meant to be mere memorials to ancient times, but are meant to serve as launching pads for contemporary emulations. It is about time to stop seeing the Bible as an echo of the past and to let it be what it is meant to be: *the* guiding voice for the future. To see what we have never seen, we must do what we have never done, or else we will continue to see what we always see. Embracing these five paradigms is the first step of a long and glorious journey.

CHAPTER 4

Altitude and Attitude

*Paradigm #1: The Great Commission is about
discipling entire nations, not just people.*

Three brick masons labored diligently side by side in the heat of the
day, covered with the dust of bricks and mortar, their backs aching and
their clothes sopping with perspiration. With callused hands, they
arduously laid brick upon brick on what appeared to be a huge project.
Out of curiosity, a passer-by asked the first mason what he was doing.
With more than a tinge of resentment, he replied, "I'm sticking bricks
together. Can't you see?" Even more curious, the questioner proceeded
to the second mason with the same query, which elicited a slightly less
mundane response. "I'm building a wall," he said. Not yet satisfied, the
man approached the third bricklayer with the same question. The man
paused, wiped his brow and, looking up to take in the sight of something
that did not yet exist, replied with a twinkle in his eye, "I am building
a *cathedral*!"

Even though all three were doing the same grueling task, only one
was actually enjoying it, because he had his eyes on the ultimate design
instead of just the immediate task. It is very easy to guess which one of
the three woke up every morning motivated to go to work: definitely the
one who saw each brick with the eyes of his imagination as part of the
cathedral he could not see in the natural—*yet*. In reality, possessing a
greater vision allowed him to look beyond the ordinary and incomplete
and see the grandeur of the finished product, changing his attitude
about an otherwise tedious job. His attitude determined his altitude!

Attitude will always determine our altitude. But in order to aim high,
we need to know deep down in our heart how much has been entrusted
to us by God. Such knowledge will permit us to see beyond the workaday
tasks that clamor each day for our attention. Then, like the third mason,
every brick in our hands will be more than a plain brick; it will be an
essential piece of a great cathedral.

Not Only People, but Also Nations

Right after the resurrection, Jesus called His disciples to a mountain in Galilee to give them final instructions in the context of His imminent return to heaven. On this momentous occasion, He chose not to talk about heaven but about Earth, and specifically nations—and not just one nation, but *all the nations.* The heart of His farewell address is known as the Great Commission (see Matt. 28:18-20), and this is what He said:

> All authority has been given to Me in heaven and on earth. Go therefore and make disciples all the nations, baptizing them in the name of the Father and the Son and the Holy Spirit, teaching them to observe all that I have commanded you; and lo, I am with you always, even to the end of the age.

The *ultimate* goal of the Great Commission, contrary to contemporary religious lore, is not simply making disciples of people, but also discipling, teaching and baptizing *nations.* What distinguishes a nation is the uniqueness of its people, its culture, and its government, in some cases its language, and definitely its natural boundaries. Jesus explained to His audience that since all power had been granted to Him on Earth, *His deputies are expected to use it to disciple the nations that populate the planet.*

As if this assignment were not challenging enough, Jesus entrusted it initially to followers who had never lived outside Israel. This group was so exclusively Jewish in their worldview that they had no appreciation, much less love, for other nations, making them the least likely to succeed as international ambassadors of good news. In addition, none of them was a religious leader. Some were businessmen, others were government employees, and John was just a teenager at the time. There were also women with a humble standing in the community.

Very much like the first two bricklayers, these folks did not see much to brag about when it came to the routine that consumed most of their energies. Nevertheless, Jesus confidently appointed them to their task by giving them a blueprint that provided meaning to their daily chores: *You will disciple nations!*

It cannot go unnoticed that even though some of these disciples had walked with Jesus on Earth and seen mighty miracles, they still had serious doubts about their capabilities (see Matt. 18:17), which Jesus ministered to directly in the context of the Great Commission when He reassured them with these words: "All authority has been given to Me . . . and lo, I am with you always, even to the end of the age." He was telling them that through Him, the "cathedral" is buildable. And to prove that *it can be done*, it's as if the Lord deliberately chose those who seemed least likely to succeed.

A Process in Four Steps

Moments before returning to heaven, Jesus broke down the Great Commission into sequential steps (see Acts 1:8), instructing His disciples to move from the simpler to the more complex ones. He told them to begin "small," with *just* a city (Jerusalem), and once they had succeeded, to tackle a region (Judea), and from there they were to disciple their first nation (Samaria). After having done that, they were to keep going, nation after nation, until they had reached the ends of the earth. That is a very impressive set of marching orders for a bunch of novices.

How did they fare? Our first indicator is found in Acts 5:28, where we read that the opposition objected (which in itself is generally a sign that progress is being made!) and decried them, saying, "You have filled Jerusalem with your teaching." That statement suggests that in just a few weeks they had reached the first milestone. Jerusalem, as a city, was so impacted by Jesus' disciples that its streets became corridors for the power of God to flow unimpeded. People on cots and palettes were lined up on the streets to receive ministry, and multitudes gathered at Solomon's Portico to be touched by the power of Jesus in the disciples. So prevalent was the presence of God that merely Peter's shadow was enough for miracles to take place. Furthermore, neighboring cities brought their sick, who, once healed, returned home with the good news that a city can indeed be entirely filled by the transforming power of God.

As a result, in the following chapters of the book of Acts we see an ever-expanding wave develop that takes the gospel to cities and regions until, in Acts 19:10, we learn that *all* who lived in Asia had heard the word of the Lord. It is estimated that no less than one million people, encompassing more than 10 nations, resided in the Roman province of Asia. The divine record certifies that *all* of them heard the word of the

Lord—a major milestone as far as discipling nations is concerned. And just to make sure that we do not miss the magnitude and completeness of this milestone, the text states that *both Jews and Gentiles* heard the word of God, a clear sign that the movement impacted more than just synagogues.

Obviously, hearing the word of the Lord did not refer to simply exposing people to a cursory presentation of the gospel, such as passing out evangelistic tracts or airing a five-minute gospel message or a weekly 40-minute sermon, but to people seeing and experiencing a live, working, ongoing 24/7 demonstration of what Jesus taught His disciples.

Nation-Discipling Impact

Just so we do not assume that what is reported in Acts 19 was a one-time occurrence, in Romans 15:19 Paul states that he had fully preached the gospel "from Jerusalem and round about, as far as Illyricum." This means that he had fully saturated these areas across the Adriatic Sea from Italy with the preaching of the gospel. In fact, he went on to say, "with no further place for me [to disciple] in these regions" (v. 23), and so he had set his sight on the *nation* of Spain. The prevailing, imperfect understanding of world geography at the time could suggest that Paul may have perceived Spain to be at the limits of the known world—the end of the earth!

The Early Church was not driven by church planting but by a mission to disciple nations.

Luke's reporting in the book of Acts on the spread of the gospel and Paul's region- and nation-focused terminology in this particular passage highlight a secondary but most important point: The Early Church was not driven by church planting but by a mission to disciple nations. In fact, there is not a single command in the New Testament directing us to plant churches, much less instructions on how to do it. This does not mean that the disciples did not plant churches; they did, intentionally and proactively. But church planting in the New Testament was the *by-product* of discipling and impacting cities, regions and nations, and not the other way around. Today we plant good churches that do not have "discipling nations" as their primary objective.

You may be thinking that it's easier for excitable Argentines like me to believe the seemingly impossible notion that nations can be discipled, taught and baptized. But all I am doing is reading through long-distance lenses the same passages we have been looking at for too long through reading glasses. Nations were promised to Abraham, father of the faith. Nations were the ultimate objective of Jesus' redemptive work. In fact, He spoke of nations being admitted into His kingdom (see Rev. 15:4). The nations were present at ground zero when the Church was born on the Day of Pentecost, and saved nations from all over the earth will pass through the pearly gates when the New Jerusalem descends from heaven. Nations—many nations, saved nations—epitomize God's redemptive passion.

Incontrovertible proof of this is found in Revelation 21:24-27. In this passage, the biblical equivalent of the two-minute warning in an American football match (that brief segment of time before the end of the game), we read that *nations will bring their honor and glory to God,* and that the rulers of those nations will lead them in a majestic procession that seems to be an unending one, since the gates through which they march will never close. And so as to leave no room for the slightest doubt that these are saved nations, the passage states that only those whose *names have been written in the Lamb's book of life* will be part of this awesome parade.

This represents clear, compelling and inspiring evidence that nations can and will be *discipled*—and by "discipled" I mean that they will be taught and will practice *everything that Jesus taught.* Also, the statement that they are bringing their *honor and glory to God* shows that these are not nations in tatters after being yanked in the nick of time from the jaws of the Antichrist. These are nations that have glory and possess honor in sufficient abundance to bring them as offerings to God. These are *saved* nations, led by their rulers in a public thanksgiving parade. Basically, these are nations whose God is the Lord!

The assignment first given to the apostles has not been voided. It has been issued to you and me also. *The discipling of nations is our primary task on Earth.* This notion is so overwhelming that we end up downgrading it to the simpler task of making *individual* disciples, since we don't know how to disciple a nation, much less all the nations. Rather than reject or diminish the assignment, let us step into it slowly but securely by going from the known to the unknown.

To disciple someone means to turn that person into a follower of the teachings you espouse. In the case of a nation, it means to impact its life so that it will conform to a set of specific values and develop a corresponding behavior. Nations have been, and are being, discipled all the time. The Romans "discipled" nations by conquering and imposing on them the *Pax Romana.* Lenin and his followers "discipled" Russia and the Soviet Union by molding in a regimented and all-encompassing way the lives of millions with Communist philosophy. Mao did the same in China, the largest nation on Earth. Militant Muslims actively take over nations and disciple them *a la* Ayatollah Khomeini; and even though they do not use the term "disciple," they are making entire populations into followers—disciples—of Mohammad.

The issue is *not* whether a nation can be discipled, because it happens all the time and it will continue to happen. The question is, Can a nation be impacted in such a way that it will become *a disciple of Jesus*? Can His teachings impregnate its people *and its institutions* so that the nation will reflect the character of Christ? And at this point, the critical factor is not Jesus Himself, but what His followers are willing to do to see nations become His followers. Would they take His teachings to a nation until those teachings are embraced *at a national level*? They should, because Christians have a competitive advantage. When Lenin took over Russia, or the Muslims Iran, their teachers Marx and Mohammad had been dead for a long time. The deciding factor was the boldness, resolve and commitment of their disciples.

This is why I say that we Christians must play the critical role because we have *a triple advantage*, which sadly we have not pressed—*yet*. First, unlike Mao and Mohammad, Jesus is alive. Second, His teachings provide healthy win-win solutions to the problems that afflict the entire world, instead of favoring one group over another or making the demise of one the solution to the problems of the other. And third, the world is now clamoring for His message in light of the fact that hatred and class and religious struggles have already had their turn *and are not helping*!

Play to Win

The Church needs to cease being a spectator and play as if it is convinced that it can and will win. The first step is to realize that we are called *and empowered* to disciple nations and will succeed *if we try*. At first, trying could mean scoring small victories that may be followed by major setbacks; but as long as we are heading in the right direction—to disciple nations—we are bound to win in the end.

The following examples show that things will definitely move *in the right direction* once we exchange the bleachers for the playing field:

Bermuda: Premier Calls on God

Joan Simmons, a marketplace Christian from Bermuda, caught the vision for nation transformation at our conference in Argentina. Once she became convinced that the ultimate objective was the discipling of Bermuda, she discerned that the key to this was the highest-ranking official in the land. Upon her return home, she made an appointment with the premier, the Hon. William A. Scott. She was fully persuaded that it was God's will that she seek such a meeting, since discipling a nation was God's idea to begin with! Sure enough, she was granted the interview. She explained to the premier the need *and the advantage* to call on God for Bermuda's unsolved problems to be fixed. She got no argument from Mr. Scott, who was keenly aware of the many challenges that had defied every political solution thrown at them. He agreed to put before Parliament a resolution for a National Day of Prayer. (I love the practicality of marketplace leaders. Like light switches, they have only two positions, ON and OFF, and when they are ON, they go for it!)

As the premier got up, indicating that the meeting had come to an end, Joan asked if he would bear a second question. The premier assented and retook his seat. Joan proceeded to explain that calling for a Day of Prayer was important, but more important yet was for him as the premier to invite Jesus into his heart, since doing so would give him direct access to God to intercede on behalf of Bermuda on account of the office he held. The premier agreed and inquired, "How do I do that?" Joan reached for his hand and said, "Please repeat this prayer after me." He did it and right there, in his own office, he walked into the kingdom of God.

The resolution was approved by Parliament with support from both parties, and on September 13, 2005, Ruth and I arrived in Bermuda to be the keynote speakers at the event scheduled for the next day. Mr. Scott sent one of his cabinet ministers to welcome us at the airport, and the next morning he received Joan and us in his office. He was very happy about the upcoming prayer convocation at the National Sports Centre, but more so with Joan, to whom he referred as "Joan the Baptist"! We prayed together in his office, and that night he came to the rally to read the proclamation calling on God to bless Bermuda.

The next day he hosted an official lunch for Ruth and me at Camden House, the premier's official residence, which was attended by parliamentarians from both parties, captains of industry and leading clergymen. Mr. Scott again recognized "Joan the Baptist" as the one who made him aware of the need to call on God for national problems, and proceeded to make the most candid statement: "I believe the time has come for government and prayer to be reconnected. I have asked our guest of honor, Mr. Silvoso, to tell us how."

What a great set up—especially for Ruth and me, who are totally, irretrievably committed to national transformation! I stood up, thanked our host, acknowledged the distinguished guests around the table and proceeded to give the 20-minute version of *Anointed for Business*, as well as the principles presented in this book. I closed by inviting everybody to hold hands and repeat after me an invocation asking God's forgiveness for personal and national sins and for God to bless Bermuda. When we were done, everybody was elated. God was in the house and they felt it!

Bermuda is still a long way from being transformed, but Joan was absolutely wise to choose the premier as the point of inception for nation transformation, because as the highest-ranking official he feels the greatest pressure from problems that defy political solutions, making him open to her message. But her choice was the direct result of grappling with the notion that *nations must be discipled*. I doubt she would have gone for it if she had continued to operate in the old paradigm of only discipling people.

An incipient transformation movement has been launched in Bermuda, and even though Mr. Scott is no longer the premier, his response and actions clearly show how *eager* the world is—political leaders in particular—to hear that God cares for the nations they lead.

The Philippines: Pastors Repent and President Believes

This deeply set interest—I dare say *thirst*—for God's involvement in nations was clearly put on display in the Philippines in 2000 when I had the privilege of leading 3,000 pastors in a public act of repentance for ungodly hostility toward President Estrada. One of the main sources for this widespread anger, even raging fury in some cases, was the widespread disappointment among Christian leaders that the current head of state defeated their born-again champion in the last presidential election. This was further compounded by persistent reports of open debauchery and all-night drinking parties at the presidential palace and residence. President Estrada, a former movie star with several marriages to his discredit and a reputation as a ladies' man, made no secret, in public or in private, that he was not a religious person. Consequently, the hostility on the part of Christian leaders against him was painfully palpable.

What prompted the repentance exercise was a warning I received in prayer. The morning prior to the meeting with the pastors, the Lord alerted me to the fact that because of their anger toward the president, they did not have clean hands (that is, hands without anger and dissention, as required in Timothy 2:1-10). Worse yet, they had failed to obey God's command to pray for those in authority over the nation in order to make possible that the nation will lead a tranquil and quiet life in all godliness and dignity, as promised by God in the same passage. At the time Paul wrote those words, Caesar and his heathen, ungodly appointees, made a most unrighteous collection of rulers that made the president of the Philippines look mild in comparison (since he had not used his power to persecute, much less execute, Christians as the Romans had done).

God's warning led me to change my message, and I instead preached on the Timothy 2 passage. God moved mightily. When I made a call to repentance, all 3,000 pastors fell to their knees. Anticipating that outcome, I'd had the organizers prepare 3,000 sheets of paper and pencils, which were quickly passed around so that each pastor could write a letter of apology to the president, along with a promise to pray for him regularly. To my total astonishment, all the pastors did so, and then came forward to deposit them in a great pile by the platform. It was an awesome moment!

However, on account of the rift between the pastors and the government, no one seemed to have a way to communicate with the president.

But it was obvious that the audience was open, if not eager, to do something about that. After the initial uncertainty, both a politician and a retired general offered to let the president know what had taken place in the meeting.

The next day when I walked into the stadium, I was introduced to a member of the cabinet, who had been sent by the president to collect the letters and thank the audience. Everybody was in awe! Apparently not many people expected the president to appreciate what had transpired the day before. We invited the official to address the crowd, and after expressing thanks, she asked permission to convey "a prayer request to the pastors" on behalf of the president. At that moment, one could feel the tension in the air created on one hand by the excitement of what was being said and on the other by the belief that nothing good could come out of a president who was "such a sinner."

I could see the pastors sitting on the edge of their seats, ready to devour every word about to be spoken. And the official shocked everybody again by saying, "The president would like for you to pray for protection against the forces of evil that are buffeting the nation, because he is powerless against them without your help." Such a request, coming from someone that until just the day before had been seen as Spiritual Public Enemy #1, and was now asking to play on the same team, was beyond anything imaginable. But it was also undeniable since it was happening right before our eyes.

We called a representative group of pastors to come to the platform to pray for the president in the person of his emissary. It was a most special moment. When we were done, I felt led to say to her, "Please, tell the president that Jesus is standing at the door of his heart and of the palace, waiting to be invited in. And when He is invited in, Jesus will come in and will change things for the better." The anointing was so palpable that this lady fell on the platform, obviously under the power of God. As she was going down, she cried out, "I am not worthy to deliver such a message. I am a sinner!" I kindly exhorted her to do it anyway, and though reluctant at first, she agreed. Later on I learned that she had been a Catholic nun who grew disenchanted with organized religion, renounced her vows, and became a leftist politician. But on this day, sensing again the power and the presence of God in her life, she was overwhelmed by the fact that He would entrust her with such a mission after she had turned her back on Him.

What happened—in just 24 hours after the Church recognized its dereliction of duty toward the full scope of the Great Commission and took simple steps of obedience that proactively moved it in the direction of discipling the nation—was utterly amazing. But more—much more—was to come in very short order. The next morning, a lady visited me who was so close to the president as to be considered his sister. She came to thank me for what took place at the stadium and brought with her the president's daughter and granddaughter so that I could pray for them. I did more than that. I led them to the Lord, showed them how to become intercessors for the president, and gave them precise instructions to set up an intercessory altar at home.

■ ■ ■

When the Church lifts up its aim to focus on the nation, it will always find powerful grace from heaven and a receptive audience on Earth.

■ ■ ■

A few days later, when I was about to board the plane to return home, the politician who made the contact with the palace came running, visibly out of breath, to let me know that the president had received my message and would like Ruth and me to have dinner with him when we returned to the Philippines. Then it got even better. About a month later I received a letter from the president informing me that he had invited Jesus into his heart and into the government as instructed. When Ruth and I went back to the Philippines, we were invited to a private dinner with him and his family as well as some of his close friends. He was unable to make it because of a sudden military crisis in the south of the country, so his wife hosted the dinner. His children proudly showed us the prayer altar they had set up as per my instructions and pointed to the Bible passage the president had read that morning.

That night was like a revival meeting as we led everybody present to the Lord. When the president's son called him to report what a great time they were having, the president requested that we pray for him. To make it somehow more tangible, his son brought a large portrait of the president and we prayed laying hands on it as his wife gave him a play-by-play account on the phone.

I wish I could say that what we saw that night grew exponentially until it transformed the nation, but some time later President Estrada was forced to resign and was succeeded by his vice president, Mrs. Gloria Macapagal Arroyo, in a context of severe political upheaval. Nevertheless, shortly after her ascension, Mrs. Arroyo was led to Christ by some of the same pastors. During a subsequent visit to Manila, I was invited to pray with her at the palace. She wanted to be filled with the Holy Spirit and was desperate for stability to come to the nation. Sometime earlier, a group of senior army officers had rebelled against her and she had thrown them in jail. However, the same group of leaders that had prayed for Mrs. Arroyo also led those officers to Christ and began to disciple them.

The jury is still out as far as what the *immediate* outcome will be in the Philippines, a beautiful nation inhabited by the some of the nicest people in the world, but ridden with systemic corruption. However, what has become crystal clear is that when the Church lifts up its aim to focus on the *nation*, even if temporarily, it will always find powerful grace from heaven and a corresponding receptive audience on Earth, as in the case of the Philippines and Bermuda. Unfortunately in both countries, the final objective has not been completely reached, largely because, like everywhere else in the world, the Church is still unsure if it should be discipling nations, and therefore it regresses easily into the old paradigm of saving only souls, faithfully and courageously rescuing shipwreck victims while giving up on what they have come to see erroneously as a sinking ship.

Nations *Can* Transform

A second factor is that the Church also needs to learn to preach the gospel of the Kingdom and not just the Law and the prophets. In Luke 16:16, we read, "The Law and the Prophets were proclaimed until John; since that time the gospel of the kingdom of God has been preached, and everyone is forcing his way into it." Why would *everybody force* his or her way into God's kingdom? Well, why not? The kingdom of God consists of righteousness, peace, joy and power (see Rom. 14:17; 1 Cor. 4:20), which is what every person and every nation on Earth is clamoring for. We have been quick to offer these blessings to individuals but not to nations, much less in the person of their leaders—especially if they are not Christians.

We seem to be far more comfortable confronting sinners with the dos and don'ts of the law than with demonstrating the liberating and restoring power of God to nations that are eagerly awaiting the manifestation of the children of God (see Rom. 8:19).

The next testimony bears witness to the fact that nations can experience transformation (at least at an embryonic level), by showing how much one person can accomplish by preaching the gospel of the Kingdom after having embraced the call to disciple more than people.

Ukraine: God's Oil for Souls Program

In 1999, Ken Beaudry was a devout follower of Jesus but was still operating in the old paradigms. Then he and his wife, Carrie, went to Argentina to our international conference on nation transformation, where they were infused with the principles stating that he is a minister as much as his pastor is and that his job in the marketplace is his ministry vehicle to disciple cities and nations. They returned home determined to operate in the new paradigms. Since then, using their company (Beaudry Oil) as a ministry vehicle, they have planted over 500 churches in Ukraine and four neighboring nations.

Recently Ken wrote to me, "I was first invited to go to Ukraine in 1999 to teach on Christian work ethics. I was newly downloaded with all kinds of marketplace dynamics from my visit to Argentina. With this new perspective on the marketplace and the church, I went to teach business people."

His involvement coincided with a sovereign move of God in a nation that until not long ago was run by ruthless atheism. Ken and his team saw excellent results as Christians took the power and the presence of God to the workplace. In his words, "We set up prayer booths in connection with public prayer fairs for people to receive ministry. In addition, believers began to prayer-walk their neighborhoods and do evangelistic outreaches in nearby parks. As a result, we were planting one church per month."

What happened next can be best described as a spiritual explosion: A church-planting fire broke out all over the country. Even newly saved grandmothers went into villages to evangelize and teach people how to prayer-walk neighborhoods. In four years, 500 churches were planted, and local leaders started to go into Kyrgyzstan, Armenia, Afghanistan and Iran.

But this was only the beginning. In 2001 the Holy Spirit spoke these words to Ken: "You can do more." At that time, there was a desperate need to feed prisoners in Ukraine, and an average of 50 inmates a week were dying of tuberculosis. Ken had seen the graves. He and his partners made a corporate decision to provide food and to send teams to the prisons.

Within a year, a church with 300 members was planted inside the first prison. The authorities were impressed because transformation was impacting the toughest inmates. Word got out, and soon other prisons opened up. Today there are full-fledged churches in 11 prisons, some of which have Bible schools that train inmates to become pastors when they are released.

The Lord has led Beaudry Oil to make the discipling of Ukraine and the surrounding nations part of their "business plan." This is why it was not surprising when on January 5, 2007, during his prayer time, the Holy Spirit indicated to Ken to go to the next level: "You must plant churches in Israel." As a result, Beaudry Oil has an overall goal to plant churches in Israel among the approximately one million Russian-speaking Jews currently living there.

Ken and his associates connect traditional church planting with the new paradigms, such as focusing on the marketplace, equipping business people to view their businesses as ministry, reaching out to government officials, prayer-walking neighborhoods, attacking systemic poverty, and planting a vision for discipling nations. Ken explains it like this: "To us the church is like an Air Force fighter plane. Without the smart bombs, heat-seeking missiles and other state-of-the-art weaponry, it's just a jet, but when fully armed, it becomes amazingly effective. That is why we equip the churches we are planting to have vision for the marketplace, the government and other areas of influence, in order to see nations discipled."

It is so confirming to see Ken embrace the five pivotal paradigms. First he realized that God had redeemed the marketplace and was able to see labor as worship, and he began to teach that. Then, as his disciples applied the principles, they found themselves taking the kingdom of God to where evil was entrenched in society. As those gates came down, multitudes believed in Jesus and hundreds of churches were planted. A beachhead was established inside a prison where systemic poverty was removed. As a result of all this, faith for discipling nations became embedded in Ken's heart.

A Higher Level

My friend, this train is leaving the station. The question is, Will you be on it? Dare to believe God for your nation as a starting point, since that is where He sovereignly planted you. When the day described in Revelation 21:24-27 arrives, wouldn't you want to see *your* nation with its flag waving in the wind of the Spirit, ably led by virtuous leaders bowing before God, with millions more singing, *Honor and Glory forever and ever and ever?*

Faith comes by hearing and hearing by the word of God. You are hearing (by reading) the word of God *right now*. Let the Holy Spirit impart faith to you, a faith for nations. It is the same faith that allows you to do whatever you are already doing transformationally—*but at a higher level*. It is amazing how much clearer the vision becomes when we apply the right set of lenses! Like the story of the three masons, even though all three did the same work, one had his eyes beyond the immediate task. He was looking not at the coarse cement on the shovel or at the irritating dust on his fingers, but by faith he was seeing a cathedral develop, one brick at a time.

Let the Holy Spirit speak to you *now*. Let Him show you the nations of the earth and your call to disciple them. Aim high, as He always does.

What on Earth Did Jesus Come to Do?

*Paradigm #2: The marketplace (the heart of the nation)
has already been redeemed by Jesus and now needs to
be reclaimed by the Church.*

Several years ago, Ruth and I took with us a very precious young lady on an international trip. She was such a cheerful person and helped us a lot with our children. We had planned carefully and had saved adequately to stay in relatively nice hotels and eat in pleasant restaurants. But Ruth and I noticed that she only ate bread at the restaurant, and on the first day when we were checking out of the hotel, she was late coming down. When I went to find out the reason for her delay, to my surprise she was making the beds and cleaning the bathroom. When I inquired about her behavior, she very matter-of-factly replied, "I don't want you to have to pay extra. This is why I did not consume the food and now I am cleaning the room."

It took us a while to convince her that the price had already been paid, that she was not a burden to us in any way, and that provision had been made for her to enter into the fullness of every aspect of the journey.

So it is with God and His Church. We are too often guilty of holding back or getting involved in the menial chores rather than going for the bigger objectives because we didn't know or weren't convinced that the price for the latter had already been paid. Open your heart and your mind now to that provision. Your life is about to change.

We have asked the question, Can a nation or a city be discipled? Taking the Great Commission at face value as we have, the resounding and challenging answer is Yes! From this point forward, there are only two questions left: *How* will they be discipled, and will *we* embrace the call? My intent with the rest of this book is to answer the first question in such a way that you will find yourself so empowered and with such vision that you will *go for it, knowing that He has fully paid for everything you are asked to possess!*

e discovering the "how" is such a challenging proposition, let's
ch it by focusing on something that is familiar to us: salvation.
o we get saved? Basically, the power of God touches our heart—
the very center of our existence—and His transforming presence takes
up residence there. The same is true for cities or nations: Their "heart"
needs to be transformed; and the heart of cities and nations is the *marketplace*.[1] In the same fashion that a person cannot live without a heart,
cities and nations cannot exist without the marketplace. Therefore, this
is where salvation needs to be introduced in order for them to be saved.

One of the more riveting examples of a city impacted through the
marketplace is what took place during Jesus' visit to Jericho as recorded in Luke 19. Zacchaeus, the region's chief tax collector, was the crook
that everybody loved to hate. He had a well-deserved bad reputation.
His occupation was largely dishonorable and much of his wealth ill
gotten. His neighbors saw him as a traitor because, with the backing of
the Roman army, he extracted taxes from his fellow citizens to fill the
coffers of the hated oppressors. In the eyes of his contemporaries,
Zacchaeus was most likely incapable of any decent deed; and as a result,
his social standing was despicable.

Nevertheless, how is it that he was able to perform a deed worthy of
Mother Teresa that earned him public praise from none other than
Jesus Himself? More perplexing yet, how could Zacchaeus, only
moments after coming in touch with salvation, have done what contemporary, well-taught believers would not even consider doing in their
wildest dreams: give half of their wealth to the poor and offer to pay a
400-percent penalty to settle claims in lieu of punitive damages!

The answer is found in Jesus' words in Luke 19:10: "For the Son of
Man has come to seek and to save *that* which was lost" (emphasis added).
When asked what this verse means, most people reply that Jesus came to
seek and to save the lost. Although biblically speaking that is true, it is
not all that this particular verse teaches. There is much more.

Three Losses

Jesus stated specifically that He came to save *that* which was lost. In this
sentence, the word "that" points to something beyond people or souls.
To find out what it is, we need to review what was lost in the Garden
when sin first entered the world (see Gen. 3). I see three distinct losses.

First, *our direct and intimate relationship with God was lost,* since Adam and Eve (and subsequently their descendants) were barred from dwelling in His presence as a result of the original sin. No earthshaking revelation here.

Second, *the harmonious relationship between men and women was ruined,* specifically in the context of marriage, since after the Fall, Adam and Eve were no longer able to walk or work as full partners because Eve's desire (her *will*) was made subject to Adam. In other words, Adam was given control over Eve—which was not God's initial intention in putting them together. And even though Adam was an accomplice to the crime, since Eve's actions aided Satan's scheme, God bestowed on her a stiffer penalty.

God was obviously upset about the devil's defiling work, and His strict sentence on Adam and Eve was not out-shadowed by His stern four-part judgment on the deceiver. First, he demoted Satan: "You will be cursed more than all the animals." Second, he removed his driver's license, so to speak: "You will no longer walk but from now on you will crawl"—the modern equivalent of having to ride the bus instead of driving your own car. Third, God ruined his diet: "You will eat dust all the days of your life." But the most severe dimension of the punishment was the last one: "I will make the woman your enemy by putting enmity between you and her and between her seed and your seed." Next, God went on to announce a rematch, predicting the woman's victory by stating, "Satan will lay prostrated under her seed with a bruised head" (see Gen. 3:14-15). Because the devil knows that God's words are true, he is aware that a rematch, in which he will be the loser, is bound to happen. (This is why in my book *Women—God's Secret Weapon,* I go into great detail to show that Jesus came to restore harmony between genders as a ramp-up to that rematch.)

The third loss, the one that is central to this book, was *the marketplace.* Watch how the Fall affected business, government and education: The business sector was impaled when the ground ceased to yield bountiful fruit, forcing man to trade the sweat of his brow for the fruit of the land. The government dimension was negatively impacted because rebellion impregnated the creation, making man's rule over it an ongoing challenge. And divinely inspired education was interrupted when God stopped coming down in the cool of the afternoon to instruct and to fellowship with His creatures.

Jesus Redeemed Everything

Jesus did not come only to save *souls* (as important and as precious as that is), but also to seek, find and recover *everything* that was lost. This introduces a key insight that is needed to capture the full scope of the atonement and that is corroborated by Colossians 1:20: "For it was the Father's *good pleasure* [meaning that God did not do it reluctantly but intentionally and joyfully] to reconcile *all things* to Himself, whether things *on earth* or things *in heaven*" (emphasis added). This last sentence underscores the totality of the reconciliation effected by the Lord. Heaven and Earth encompass the entire universe.

This is confirmed by Ephesians 1:7-10, where we find a similar statement: "In whom we have our *redemption* through His *blood* . . . according to the riches of His *grace* . . . to sum up all things in Christ, the things in the heavens and the things upon the earth" (*ASV*, emphasis added). Three key words in this passage underscore that this overarching reconciliation is absolutely central to Jesus' redemptive mission: "redemption," "blood" and "grace." If someone says "coffee, bacon and eggs," one word immediately pops up: "breakfast." Right? And when we hear "redemption, blood and grace"? *The Cross!* The redemption that Jesus wrought is all encompassing and had as its objective the recovery of *everything* that had been lost.

It is paradoxical that when a destitute blind beggar named Bartimaeus had a transforming encounter with Jesus, *everybody* praised God. But when the Donald Trump of Jericho—Zacchaeus, a powerful marketplace leader—had a similar experience, *everybody* got upset, even after Zacchaeus had given 50 percent of his money to the poor, had placed the balance of his wealth in an escrow account to settle claims, and had offered to pay fourfold punitive damages. The Jerichoans' strong feelings against Zacchaeus blinded them to the astonishing dimension of what had actually happened. Jesus made the statement in Luke 19:10 to enlighten them as to the extraordinary scope of the salvation experienced by Zacchaeus, since it impacted not just him, *but his household as well.*

Why was Zacchaeus able to do, after a very brief time with Jesus, what well-trained, properly discipled, mature believers never do—that is, to give 50 percent of their wealth to the poor? The answer is found in Jesus' words in verse 9: "Today salvation has come *to this house*" (emphasis added). He specifically stated that salvation had impacted not just Zacchaeus but also *his house*.

In the Bible, "house" or "household" encompasses not just the individual and his or her extended family, but also the marketplace, because the vast majority of the population worked from their homes. The tax collector processed collections at home. The fishermen lived by the sea. The farmer worked the land where he resided. The physician took care of patients in his house. The garment maker worked at home. Additionally, parents, children and even grandchildren shared the same occupation, making family and business part of the same equation.

Therefore, according to Jesus, Zacchaeus's spontaneous decision to use his wealth for godly purposes (see v. 8) made it evident that salvation *had come to his business*. And to make sure that such an important point is not lost, Jesus' next words state that He came to seek and save *that* which was lost. Jesus was explaining that because He found and recovered Zacchaeus *and his business*, both of them experienced salvation, and as a result, folks at both ends of the social spectrum were being impacted: the poor, whom he chose to help, and his fellow merchants, to whom he offered restitution.

God's Kingdom in the Marketplace

It is equally enlightening that Jesus prefaced His words in Luke 19:10 with the statement that Zacchaeus was *also a son of Abraham* (see v. 9). Abraham became the father of the faith because he believed God when He told him that Abraham was going to be the father of *nations* (see Gen. 12:2). God is after nations, and that was Jesus' objective in Jericho. The kingdom of God came first to Zacchaeus *and* his business, and this touched the people in the city by making them the direct beneficiaries of this all-encompassing spiritual experience.

Jesus, who was able to read people perfectly, discerned that the crowd was not tracking with what He was teaching. We see in verse 11 that the audience did not get His point, because they were not expecting the kingdom of God to come to their city (Jericho) or to other cities, but to just one place—Jerusalem (see Luke 19:11). In order to help the people understand His point about the progressive manifestation of the kingdom of God and that it will come to *every* place (not just to Jerusalem), and particularly the key role that marketplace people like

Zacchaeus would play in that process, Jesus proceeded to teach the parable of the minas.

A mina was a monetary unit, the equivalent of approximately 100 days' wages for a day laborer. In this parable, a nobleman goes away to secure title to his kingdom, and in the interim he entrusts one mina as investment capital to each one of his 10 servants. His instructions to them are very specific: *do business*—which, obviously, occurs in the marketplace. While the nobleman was away, his enemies took control of the kingdom (which includes the marketplace), but his servants continued to do business, in spite of (or perhaps because of) the new hostile environment. Upon his return, he asked for an accounting from everyone. One servant reported a gain of 10 minas, another 5, and a third no profit whatsoever. To the first two servants, he gave *authority over cities* in direct proportion to the rate of return on the investment. Once his servants were placed in authority over cities, the sovereign took *complete* control of the kingdom by disposing of his enemies (see Luke 19:11-27).

In such context, it is important to underline that the fullness of the kingdom of God on Earth—embodied in the New Jerusalem descending from heaven—marks the culminating moment when our Lord will take *complete* control of the earth, with nations as the welcoming audience (see Rev. 21:24-27). What is described in Revelation is the crowning moment when God's kingdom will have eliminated every remnant of the devil's empire on Earth—in essence: *the climax of a process dotted with city after city submitting to His authority* and care because of the activity of Kingdom-minded servants reclaiming *the marketplace of those cities.*

It is vital not to miss the connection in this parable between *business, authority* and *cities.* There is nothing ethereal here. Everything is absolutely down to earth: The nobleman instructed his servants to do business (in the marketplace) with the clear expectation to succeed (make a profit) so that they will be granted authority (government, influence) over cities for the kingdom of God to come to *those cities through them.*

This parable also explains why people such as Zacchaeus—believers operating in the marketplace—are key to the progressive establishment of God's kingdom, not just in one city (Jerusalem), but also everywhere on Earth. The fact that the servants had to do business in a hostile environment similar to what awaited Zacchaeus once Jesus left town, illustrates that Jesus expects His followers to bring transformation to what the enemy has usurped and defiled. God's point of entry for His kingdom is obviously the individual, but as soon as that person experiences salvation, he or she is expected to expand his or her focus to his or her sphere of influence in order to use it as a launching pad to reclaim *everything* that was lost, including cities and eventually nations. This is crucial for the picture presented in Revelation 21:24-27 of nations and leaders bringing their honor and glory to God to take place. This passage reveals the end *as God intends it to be!*

Redeeming and Reclaiming

Today, most believers, if asked when they expect to see the kingdom of God come to Earth, would reply, "When the new Jerusalem descends to Earth like a bride ready for her groom." If asked to elaborate on what will happen to cities such as London, New York, San Francisco and Beijing, they respond very matter of factly, "They are all going up in smoke. They are destined to burn." When pressed for the reason behind this bold assertion, they retort with a tinge of something that comes across as smugness: "Oh! We are expecting *the* city, whose builder and architect is God!"

These answers reveal two serious theological misconceptions. First, that we, the Church in general, have no theology for *the salvation of cities*. Apart from *people getting saved*, we have no hope for cities, much less for nations.

Second, we overlook Jesus' teaching that the end will come only *after* the gospel of the Kingdom has been proclaimed *in every place*. According to Matthew 24:14, "This gospel of the kingdom shall be preached [first] in the whole world for a testimony unto all the nations; and then shall the end come." Preaching the gospel *of the Kingdom* requires *much more* than just elementary forms of proclamation, such as placing a gospel tract under every door or buying radio time to cover the planet with evangelistic programs 24/7.

Preaching (declaring, or making known) the gospel of the Kingdom means stating and also enforcing the will of the King. In biblical times, when a sovereign sent heralds to proclaim a decree, the moment the proclamation was made, the will of the monarch became law in that area. It is the modern equivalent of a Supreme Court decision. The moment it is announced, it becomes the law of the land, preempting and taking precedence over anything contrary to it. That is why *proclaiming the gospel of the Kingdom in every nation* must be understood as nothing short of the will of God being enforced, similar to the parable of the minas, where the king's servants were given governmental authority.

In my estimation, the main reason we have such difficulty understanding that proclaiming *the gospel of the Kingdom* will bring cities and nations to God is because we have embraced the misconception that such proclamation is to be done by clerics in religious settings to reluctant heathens—whereas, in the examples in the Scriptures, good news is presented to people in the marketplace, who readily embrace it because it meets deeply felt needs. If the heart of the city—the marketplace—is touched, the city is impacted.

Olmos Prison: When Heaven Took on Hell

In very few places is this type of transformation as tangible as prisons in the province of Buenos Aires, Argentina. In the 1980s at Olmos Prison, inmates enlisted in murderous gangs, and the church of Satan held regular services—including animal sacrifices—turning the prison into a cesspool seeping with evil and corruption. The diabolical system at Olmos made it intentionally impossible for Christians to find a job there or for pastors to minister inside its walls. Since there were no believers among the inmates, it became a solidly un-Christian and anti-Christian stronghold. Just as in Luke 19, the kingdom was taken over by evil people, but God was about to send someone by the name of Juan *to do business with Kingdom principles* there.

When Juan Zuccarelli, a pastor in a nearby town, requested permission to hold evangelistic meetings, he was unceremoniously rebuffed. But God told him to "infiltrate" the satanic perimeter by applying for a job as a guard. When he did, he was turned down. Nevertheless, he persisted until the authorities reluctantly decided to go through the motions of processing his application while threatening him with physical harm if he persevered, and with death if against all odds he landed the job.

It was not easy. In fact, it was very dangerous for Juan to persist, since he was systematically singled out for abuse and threats in front of the other candidates. But he came across a divinely ordained break when the officer who had harassed him the most went into asthmatic arrest and began to suffocate. While everybody stood immobilized, Juan rebuked the demons tormenting the officer and laid hands on him to impart divine healing. God honored Juan's prayers by providing deliverance on the spot. As a result, the officer turned from adversary to advocate and eventually mentor.

Juan got the job and soon afterward held the first evangelistic service in the history of the prison, at which hundreds of inmates received the Lord, launching a process that within a few years led to 60 percent of the inmates becoming believers. In the intervening time, the gangs were dismantled and the church of Satan was put out of commission by a combination of dramatic conversions in their ranks or by death as a result of internal fights. What used to be permeated by systemic evil was replaced by righteousness.

This was possible because Juan saw his job as his ministry, and his position in the prison as a channel for the power of God to be directed against the works of the devil. Like the servants in the parable of the minas, Juan *did business*—in his case, working as a guard at first. Then, as God enabled him to come up with inspired solutions to longstanding prison problems, his success invested him with authority and he subsequently became a trouble-shooter and counselor to the director of the Prison Bureau.

The dramatic changes at Olmos Prison motivated the authorities to ask for similar programs in other prisons in the province of Buenos Aires. This is how transformed inmates filled with evangelistic zeal began to be systematically transferred to other jails to launch transformation processes. Before long, similar breakthroughs were in evidence all over; so much so that in 2002 the authorities asked Juan to start and run the first Christian prison in the nation. This is how Unit 25, officially named "Christ the Only Hope Prison," was born and became a place where guards and inmates pray together. Prisoners learn the Word of God throughout the week and teach it to their families on visitation days. Attractive curtains have replaced cell bars to provide greater freedom of movement, and income-generating workshops allow inmates to support their families. In addition, the prisoners fast two days a week. And from the food they save and the contents of the care packages they receive, they tithe to feed children in a nearby slum. Best of all, the rate of recidivism has gone down from 50 percent to less than 5 percent.[2]

This level of *extraordinary* success is impacting prisons in several other countries, proving that when salvation comes to a person's household, his sphere of influence will also experience it—and beyond.

Institutions, cities and nations being changed through the marketplace is not a foreign concept to politicians. They work shrewdly from this principle all the time to impact the marketplace, improve the economy, change legislation, revamp education, and so forth, so that when election time comes, they look good enough to be re-elected. The marketplace is the key.

This is also possible in the evangelistic realm, because in Argentina there are cities where it is very difficult for sinners to go to hell. For example, in the Buenos Aires suburb of Adrogué, my good friend Pastor Eduardo Lorenzo has been pioneering the vision for transformation for years. Today, if a sinner insists on going to hell, he or she can eventually make it, *but not without first having a heaven of a time getting there*. The reason is that the churches operate 24/7 *all over the marketplace*. Each block has a shepherd assigned to pray for and minister to every resident. Every business and school campus has been adopted in prayer. Key government officials have someone interceding for them. The church has taken control of the marketplace and, by extension, of the city itself.

Guatemala: Mobilizing Believers to Reclaim the Marketplace

Failing to grasp this principle will unnecessarily and tragically concede our cities and nations to the devil—*even if the majority of the population ends up going to heaven!* A clear example of this is found in Guatemala. Of all the nations in Latin America with a sizable born-again population, Guatemala is at the very top. It is estimated that between 47 percent and 52 percent of the people are evangelicals—and when born-again Catholics are added to the numbers, the percentage can easily reach 75 percent. This means that three out of four Guatemalans are saved. In addition, the country has had two born-again presidents who preached the gospel enthusiastically to the nation. Evangelistically speaking, Guatemala is a dream come true.

However, when it comes to measuring its overall confidence rating among nations in Latin America, Guatemala consistently ranks near the bottom, barely ahead of Haiti. How can a nation where the vast majority of the population is born again register so low, barely edging out Haiti, a country immersed in and dominated by witchcraft? The answer points to evidence that even though the Church in Guatemala excels at making disciples of *people,* it is not discipling the *nation*. This paradigm has not shifted in Guatemala yet, even though leading figures are making significant progress in that direction.

Harold Caballeros, a lawyer and the founder of one of the most influential churches in Guatemala, has been equipping and mobilizing believers to reclaim the marketplace. Recently he founded a university to repossess education, and he is seriously considering running for president. Harold would not be doing any of this unless he had seen the pivotal role of the marketplace in the transformation process. His willingness and courage to sail on totally uncharted waters is admirable.

Access to the Same Weapons

Understanding the full scope of redemption is key because it equips the people "in the pew" to go to work on Mondays convinced that they have the same anointing and divine assurance of victory with which their pastors come to the pulpit on Sundays. It is not easy to be a pastor, especially in light of the relentless attacks of the evil one on them and on their congregations. But they are fully persuaded that the gates of Hades can never prevail against the Church. And that is why, when the Church is under attack, pastors confidently stand their ground and pray, preach, teach, exhort and counsel *until the evil one flees.* A pastor never surrenders his congregation to the enemy, because he knows that victory is guaranteed by the power and the scope of the Atonement itself.[3]

On the other hand, Christians in the marketplace with an incomplete understanding of what Jesus accomplished through His death and resurrection often too easily resign themselves to defeat. They see the devil messing with their jobs and, after praying and seeing no immediate change, dejectedly declare, *"Let the will of God be done."* Why? Because they are not persuaded that they have access to the same spiritual arsenal their pastors do. They believe that there is a God who cares for them *but not for their work!*

Zacchaeus's business was never the same after salvation came *to his household.* What used to be a lair of evil turned into a beacon of righteousness, and everybody in Jericho was impacted, both rich and poor. Salvation is like light: once introduced it expands until it touches everything.

God's Bank and the *New York Times*

Chuck Ripka is a marketplace minister who until recently was the senior vice president of the Riverview Community Bank in Elk River, Minnesota.[4] The night before opening its doors in 2003, Chuck and the

CEO prayer-walked its facilities, laid hands on desks and computers, and opened the door of the Bank for Jesus to come in.

It wasn't long before all the employees had received Christ as their Savior. Chuck then proceeded to explain to them that they were ministers of God and that the bank was their ministry and the customers their flock. From that moment on, clients were regularly offered prayer as a "free banking service." In over two years, more than 60 miracles were recorded during business hours, and more than 100 people came to the Lord on the premises. Prayer came to be perceived by the general population as so germane to the bank that one day (as shown in the DVD *Transformation in the Marketplace with Ed Silvoso*) a lady showed up, as she put it, "because my marriage is finished, I fear, and I came to the bank for prayer."[5]

The *New York Times* sent a reporter to do a story on the bank. At first, true to his profession, the reporter was skeptical, even cynical. But as he moved in and out of the resident presence of God in the bank, hearing veritable stories of lives, families and businesses transformed, he began to ask spiritual questions. Eventually, he received the Lord and went on to write a superb piece titled "God's Bank," which became the cover story for the *New York Times Magazine* on October 30, 2004.

As a result of the worldwide impact of that journalistic piece, film crews from as far away as France and Japan descended on the bank and produced riveting television stories of institutions, lives, and even a city touched by God. People from out of state, as well as from other countries, have called the bank, asking, "Is this God's bank? If so, I want to move my money there." These actions made it possible for the bank to grow at a rate of almost a million dollars a week during the first two years, making it one of the fastest growing community banks in the state of Minnesota and in the nation.

It would have taken Chuck the rest of his life to make an impression half that size if he had used traditional means. But because salvation *came to the bank*, the bank experienced the benefits of Jesus' life and power, just as Zacchaeus's business did 2,000 years ago. It is amazing how much can be accomplished when we let salvation touch not just one soul, but a household also!

To fully grasp the scope of the Great Commission, we need to understand that Jesus did not pay solely for souls but for *all* that was lost, including the marketplace, and as a result, those who work in it are empowered *and expected* to reclaim it for His kingdom!

CHAPTER 6

Bridging the Pulpit and the Marketplace

When we talk about *ministry,* we usually think about preachers, evangelists, missionaries, youth pastors and Christian education directors—the people who commit their lives to serving us and others in churches and so-called "parachurch" organizations. I have been making a strong point in this book about the calling and anointing also given by God to marketplace people for ministry in their spheres of influence. However, it has become very evident that there is a gap between the pulpit and the marketplace that needs to be bridged.

We have a good understanding of ministry in the church and of those called to serve behind a pulpit, but it is harder for us to comprehend how a person not called "pastor," "reverend," or "missionary" can also be a full-fledged minister and what form that *ministry* will take. We must not only bridge this gap, but also learn to use that bridge intelligently to come in touch with the power and the grace that God has deposited in both camps if we are to see transformation happen.

There is definitely a call from God to pastors to lead congregations, a calling I generalize under the term "pulpit ministry." Where would we be today without those dedicated men and women who devote their lives to ministering to us, day and night. The call to the pulpit is a sacred one, but it is not the only call to ministry. The Scriptures state that every believer is a priest (see Eph. 4:12; Rev. 1:6; 5:10; 20:6). Since priests are ministers, it follows that there has to be a call to ministry in the marketplace, as that is where the bulk of church members operate day in and day out. This becomes an even more critical component when we understand that *labor is the premier expression of worship,* voiding the misconception that quitting a job is a requisite for "entering the ministry."

Vertical Ministry and Horizontal Ministry

Today the greatest implementational challenge we face is the integration of the vertical and horizontal aspects of ministry. The first step to overcoming this challenge is the coining of more adequate terminology.

In the past we have called pastors "clergy" and church members "laity." In the new paradigm, I refer to them as "pulpit ministers" and "marketplace ministers." Both are ministers with identical callings, but with spheres of influence and expertise that are very distinct and at the same time strategically complementary.

Pulpit Ministers

Pulpit ministers naturally focus on the vertical dimension of life. They have invested time and energy to acquire the scriptural knowledge necessary to explain in theological terms the character of God, the essence and the consequences of sin, the fundamental nature of the atonement, and so forth. On the other hand, marketplace ministers, by virtue of their occupation, are primarily immersed in life's horizontal side. They are constantly aware of how one action affects the next to produce and sustain the processes that constitute life in the marketplace. Their bottom line has to do with clientele, supporters and pupils, all of which are built around interaction and relationships.

Most pulpit ministers have limited experience when it comes to the horizontal aspect, except what they are able to acquire by running or being part of a church staff and fellowshipping with the members of their congregation. In the course of carrying out their ministry, they do interact with the marketplace, but primarily out of an "us" and "them" mindset, and never as an integral part of it. This shortage of parameters restricts their effectiveness outside of the church building, especially when it comes to conceiving and conveying specific ways for members to apply their teaching in everyday situations. This is why marketplace ministers so often find themselves puzzled as to how to implement on Mondays what they heard their ministers teach so eloquently the day before.

Marketplace Ministers

The vast majority of marketplace ministers have been called to influence others through relationships and channels in the workplace. The object of my book *Anointed for Business* was to help these people understand joyfully and embrace unashamedly that calling.

Marketplace ministers are so very much in touch with (and battered by) the world, its people and its systems that they often lose touch with the vertical life-giving dimension that is meant to invigorate and infuse them with divine power for everyday living. The result is that they show up on Sundays in a survival mode so thirsty for water that they hold their cup up to a fire hydrant. The "pulpit" does its best to make sure the pressure is turned up as high as possible, but the gap is rarely closed.

Four Misbeliefs that Derail the Church

These two dimensions must be integrated. The revelational understanding that comes from the pulpit's vertical flow of anointing must connect with the marketplace's corresponding horizontal flow, which is the application of transformation in the day-to-day life of Christians throughout the city and nation. Unless this happens, we will continue to feed *four major misbeliefs* that have derailed the Church from achieving the purposes of her Builder:[1]

The first one is that *there is a God-ordained division between clergy and laity*, the implication being that one is subservient to the other. This division is not scriptural for the simple reason that neither word ("clergy" nor "laity") shows up in the Bible (the closest we find is the word *laos*, which basically means "people").

This, in turn, leads to the second misconception, that *the church is designed to operate primarily inside a building, often referred to as the sanctuary, and mostly on Sundays*. This identification with a building not only lacks validation in the examples of church activity found in the New Testament, but it is also a contradiction of what the term itself means. "Church" comes from the Greek word *ecclesia*, which signifies a gathering or assembly; and as such, it describes people, not a building. Confining church to a building once a week preempts any possibility for marketplace ministers to exercise their calling.

The third misbelief is that *marketplace ministers are not as spiritual as pulpit ministers, mostly because they hold a job in the marketplace*. The underlying assumption (which is monastic in origin) is that those involved in secular affairs lack the purity required to understand spiritual matters. Time and again I have watched church members curse themselves, so to speak, by saying, "Ed, I am not a minister. I am just a layman." As if demoting themselves to laymen were not enough, they add further downward thrust by inserting the qualifier "*just.*" When I ask what they mean by "layman," they answer with a visible degree of shame, as if confessing to some perverse sin, "Well, I work for a living."

All through the Bible, working in the marketplace was a plus, never a minus, for people to attain spirituality or to receive divine revelation.

Abraham did not become the father of the faith by quitting his job and buying a mountain in order to turn it into a prayer retreat where he could spend the rest of his life ruminating on how to acquire such status. On the contrary, he received the call *in the marketplace* and he exercised it for the rest of his life *in the marketplace*, developing and tempering his faith by its constant application to everyday situations. The heroes of the faith listed in Hebrews 11 are what we would call today *marketplace ministers*. There is no biblical basis to assume that holding a job is a disqualifier for spirituality; quite the contrary.

--- ■ ■ ■ ---

It is fundamental to grasp the spiritual dimension of our job so as to leave no doubt that we need access to spiritual resources in order to succeed.

--- ■ ■ ■ ---

Furthermore, when the time came for God to introduce the Early Church to the most revolutionary theological truth that Gentiles do not need to become Jewish proselytes as a precondition to be saved, He did it by supernaturally orchestrating a meeting of marketplace leaders: Cornelius (a high ranking military man) and Peter (a partner in a fishing company who was the guest of Simon, a merchant in leather goods). Such was the context in which this earth-shaking revelation was brought forth.

The fourth misconception is that *the primary role of Christians in the marketplace is to make money to fund the vision of those in the pulpit.* Taken to an extreme this can become a form of spiritual indenture, where people arbitrarily considered to be of lesser spiritual standing are expected to work for the benefit of somebody who belongs to a privileged class. Time and again church members get the impression that somehow they got the shorter end of the stick by not receiving a call to the pulpit, and that the only option left to them is to pinch their noses and venture into the unsavory world of the marketplace to access resources with which to support someone else's vision. The double jeopardy is that the ministry they are supporting will likely have little impact on the work environment where they are earning the money. There is something definitely missing in this picture.

Importance of the Call to the Marketplace

The first two misconceptions (that there is a God-ordained classification between clergy and laity, and that the Church must operate primarily inside a building, usually on Sundays) severely discriminate against marketplace ministers. As bad as this is, much worse is the message the third and fourth misbeliefs convey (that they are incapable of spiritual depth, and consequently must be relegated to the role of financial supporters), because these misbeliefs illegitimatize them as far as ministry is concerned. By convincing them that spirituality is off limits, it robs them of the confidence needed to access the divine power that is necessary for transformation to take place in the marketplace.

These misconceptions constitute lethal weapons that turn the balance of power in the devil's favor, since the horizontal and the vertical dimensions of the priesthood of all believers must be integrated for the Church to do the job for which it has been empowered by the Holy Spirit. A major key for this is to understand that spirituality is not only possible in the marketplace, but it is also *required*!

Spiritual Solutions

This is no small matter, because spiritual problems require spiritual solutions. If our job and placement in the marketplace are intrinsically spiritual, secular training alone would not be enough to solve problems that have spiritual dimensions and spiritual roots. Everything has a spiritual dimension; therefore, the old paradigm that dichotomizes "secular" and "sacred" is not valid.

For example, in the Bible, whenever God met with a human being, the subject was always a problem on Earth that was out of alignment with God's will in heaven, and the meeting was usually called by God to convey an assignment for humans to fix it.

It is fundamental to grasp the spiritual dimension of our job so as to leave no doubt that we need access to spiritual resources in order to succeed. Our work is God's work. There is only one way to do God's work in the marketplace effectively, and that is *by* and *through* the Spirit of God. To do it any other way is bound to have negative and often tragic consequences.

This was the case in the Old Testament when God commissioned two edifices for His presence to dwell in. The first assignment went to

Moses, who was asked to construct the Tent of the Covenant. The second went to Solomon, who was assigned to build the Temple. Both men successfully completed their tasks, but with diametrically opposite results: Moses drew closer to God, but Solomon backslid spiritually.

How can men carrying on such sacred projects meet fates that were so different? What made Moses grow stronger and Solomon weaker as they implemented on Earth designs drafted by God in heaven? The answer is found in whom these men relied upon to carry out the tasks entrusted to them. Moses depended on Bezalel, an artisan and the first biblical character reported to be filled with the Spirit of God (see Exod. 31). Bezalel was a capable craftsman, but after being filled with the Spirit he was able to do his job in the fullness and power of God, rather than solely in his natural strength and abilities. Whatever Bezalel learned in trade school (most likely from his father, as was the custom in biblical times) was elevated to supernatural heights by the Spirit of God dwelling in him.

On the other hand, Solomon hired pagan temple builders (mainly from his heathen friend Hiram, the king of Lebanon) to build God's house. This was a most unfortunate and lethal spiritual error, since God is three times holy and Solomon hired ungodly people to erect His earthly sanctuary. I suspect that what motivated Solomon to do this was that Hiram's men were the best contemporary temple builders, but they were not filled with the Spirit of God. As such, they depended exclusively on their own abilities rather than on God's. Worse yet, being unbelievers, they channeled evil into Solomon's kingdom and eventually into his personal life as well.

In the preceding chapters we read how God revealed His will to ordinary people who followed His leading until the initial vision took shape and became tangible. This was, in essence, how *natural people learned to live supernaturally*. Like Bezalel, the Old Testament artisan, the players in these stories already had a natural level of training and expertise, *but they did not limit themselves to it*. Instead, time and again, when facing obstacles that exceeded those abilities, they reached up to God to access revelational wisdom *so that His will would be done on Earth as it is already done in heaven*.

Contemporary Examples

In Elk River, Minnesota, third-term mayor Stephanie Klinzing has dedicated the city to the Lord and invited Him to set up residence in town. Mayor Klinzing was elected by the people to public office, and with that came a certain level of power. The mayor, along with a group of marketplace and pulpit ministers, prays every Tuesday for divine power to handle city affairs, and as a result they see miracles by adding God's power to their natural abilities and resources.[2]

The evidence is that the economy of the city is in an upward spiral and the spiritual atmosphere is so appealing that two major national companies have located their key data-processing divisions there, making it one of the leading boomtowns in Minnesota. Even though there is a human factor, the underlying reason is simple: God is in town. The city elders and leaders now go regularly to Him for guidance, and people take the power and the presence of God to work every day because they believe that they are called to disciple their city and to reclaim the marketplace so that God's will shall be done in Elk River.

This town once had the highest per capita rate of teenage suicides in the USA. Today, they have none. Its school system, once in ruins and pitifully inadequate, is now a model of excellence. A large methamphetamine lab that used to operate with impunity, always one step ahead of the authorities, was put out of business after the chief of police attended a Tuesday prayer meeting to be prayed for by the mayor and her associates *for supernatural revelation* to locate the elusive lab. And God answered prayers offered by both pulpit and marketplace ministers who work in unity and harmony to pastor the city!

The same principle was activated in the transformation story about Hawaii. These folks came to understand that in order to see what they had never seen, they needed to do what they had not done before, because if they kept doing what they always did, they would continue to see what they always saw. In this case it involved genuine repentance on the part of both pulpit and marketplace ministers and a public commissioning of the latter to pastor the state 24/7.

By bridging the gap, they brought excellence to their pastoral sphere of influence in the marketplace, and in so doing they were able to attain higher levels of influence.

Four Levels of Involvement in the Marketplace

As discussed in *Anointed for Business,* I have noted that there are four levels at which Christians find themselves in the marketplace.

At the very lowest level are *those who are struggling (and failing) in the workplace.* These folks constantly suffer setbacks that cause them to lose ground. Even though some well-meaning spiritual counselors may try to justify this state of failure by pointing out that it builds Christian character, this does not constitute abundant life. As General Patton is portrayed saying in the movie by the same name, "The secret to win the war is not to die for your country but to make the enemy die for his."

The second level consists of *Christians who apply biblical principles in the marketplace*. This is where the vast majority of believers are today (I would say as many as 90 percent are at this level), but the problem is that they apply principles not so much to change the marketplace but to *keep the marketplace from changing them*. In other words, they have settled for a draw. No team can win a championship by ending every game in a draw. We need to apply biblical principles to win!

This takes us to the third level: *Christians who apply biblical principles in the marketplace to do business in the power and the fullness of the Holy Spirit*. This means that when they go to work, they *expect* to be led by the Holy Spirit. They *count* on God empowering and providing them with *supernatural* insights. These folks never surrender, but press forward, in prayer, intercession, supplication and spiritual perseverance until the gates of Hades, blocking their path, becomes a pile of debris after being confronted with supernatural weapons that are mighty in God for the destruction of such strongholds.

But the highest level consists of those who operate in the power and the fullness of the Holy Spirit *to bring transformation to the marketplace*. Their objective is not simply to have a good day at work but also to see first their job and eventually their industry, city and nation transformed. This is why they consistently take the presence and the power of God where evil is entrenched until it crumbles and becomes nothing more than a pile of rubble. In other words, they are marketplace ministers who do not dichotomize work and pulpit, because they have blended them into one.

No one exemplifies this better than the apostle Paul. He was trained as a rabbi but he also had an income-producing trade as a tent maker that naturally allowed him to be part of the marketplace in the cities where he ministered. He was a most successful church planter before, but he brought transformation to entire regions when he integrated the horizontal and the vertical dimensions of ministry. By synergizing these two dimensions, Paul discovered the key to city, region and nation transformation.

CHAPTER 7

The Marketplace:
The Forum for Transformation

Very late at night, a person was searching for something under a street-light. When the policeman on duty asked him what he was doing, he replied, "I am looking for my keys which I dropped half a block away." Perplexed the officer inquired, "Why are you searching here then?" The reply was even more mystifying, "Because there is no light over there."

The lesson is simple: It is not enough to know what to look for but we must also look for it in the right place, *even if it is dark!*

When Paul got saved, God told him that he had been chosen to take the gospel to the Gentiles and to kings and to the children of Israel, in that order (see Acts 9:15; 26:17-18). However, when Paul (and Barnabas) was sent out to do missionary work, he began preaching in the synagogues of the Jews—the wrong place to be looking for Gentiles and kings (see Acts 13:1-5). Nevertheless, for the next few years, Paul—believing that his mission would be accomplished by working from an enlightened religious structure—led a band of evangelists that did a great work establishing churches. He did faithfully and efficiently what most pastors do today. He preached (usually once a week) to God-fearing people in religious settings (the synagogue), leading many of them to the Lord and planting exemplary churches. He was so success-ful that 2,000 years later, when we study evangelism and church plant-ing, Paul is *the* model we aspire to emulate. His example is the best when it comes to church planting.

While Paul saw the transformation of many individual lives dur-ing this time, he was not effectively reaching the Gentiles, and as a result, he did not see what God had planned—sustainable transforma-tion impacting a city, region or nation—until many years later when he ministered in Ephesus, where it was recorded that "All who lived in Asia heard the word of the Lord, both Jews and Gentiles." The "Asia" referred to was the Roman province of Asia, of which Ephesus was the leading city. It is estimated that as many as 14 nations existed in that province, numbering in excess of a million people. That everybody in such a diverse cultural and ethnic mosaic had heard the word of God was a definite first as far as the expansion of the Church in the New Testament. In fact, the text clearly states that it was accomplished through uncommon means: "God was performing extraordinary miracles by the hands of Paul" (see v. 11).

How did this happen? Upon arriving in Ephesus, Paul tried his usual approach one more time by going to the synagogue (a segregated religious place) to preach; but, as in Corinth before, he did not meet with success. After three futile months in the synagogue, in utter frustration he relocated his base of operations to the marketplace, to a school known as "the school of Tyrannus." It is from here that the transformation process of cities and regions began suddenly and expanded rapidly.

It is very important that we not lose sight of the trail that this revelational process took. First, the power of God manifested itself in the marketplace (not in the synagogue), from where it became known to everyone in the city (Ephesus), and by two years later the entire region (Asia) had been impacted. The progression went from the *marketplace* to the *city* (Ephesus) to the *region* (see Acts 19:1-12).

Corinth: The Detonator

However, what eventually ignited in Ephesus had already detonated in Corinth, as reported in Acts 18. Paul had just completed a not-so-successful evangelistic thrust in Athens, where he had preached eloquently to the Empire's intellectual elite, with dismal results. Only a woman and a few men believed, while the rest told him they would listen to him some other time—which amounted to a polite "get lost!"

Upon landing in Corinth, Paul, a pulpit minister, met Aquila and Priscilla, a married couple who were artisans and marketplace ministers and who shared the same trade with him. Paul established a business with them and moved into the marketplace, and Aquila and Priscilla integrated their trade with the pulpit. Paul never left the pulpit; he simply moved it to the marketplace. Nor did his business associates abandon the marketplace; they merely applied the spiritual authority and revelation that had come to them, to enlighten others spiritually.

For the next three months, Paul worked as a tentmaker and preached on the Sabbath. After a most frustrating attempt at establishing his evangelistic base in the synagogue, Paul and his new friends left it and moved into a house (marketplace) not far away. Since the term "house" in the Bible encompasses both the home and the workplace, it is safe to assume that Paul and Aquila and Priscilla operated their business out of that particular house.

Given Paul's all-consuming objective to present Christ and His claims to as many people as possible—with his stated intention upon leaving the synagogue, "to preach to the Gentiles"—it is safe to assume that Paul and his associates ministered daily to pagan people in a spiritually dark, non-religious setting (the marketplace), as opposed to what they did before—preaching once a week to devout people (Jews) in a religious venue. In other words, Paul and his team turned their jobs into a ministry vehicle; and the results were initially impressive and eventually astounding.

■ ■ ■

Paul and his team turned their jobs into a ministry vehicle; and the results were initially impressive and eventually astounding.

■ ■ ■

Shortly after the relocation to the marketplace, Crispus, the principal of the synagogue, and his entire household believed in the Lord. Soon afterward, many people in Corinth "were believing and being baptized." The tense in the verbs (*were believing* and *were being baptized*) indicates that this activity was an ongoing process, as opposed to a one-time occurrence. The well was deep, and the conversion of Crispus was the priming of the pump.

Need for Divine Reassurance

In fact, so many Gentiles came to believe in Jesus that Paul was apparently caught off guard by the voluminous response and most likely became unsure if he was doing the right thing. His perplexity was so great that it precipitated an unsolicited divine house-call one night from Jesus, who reassured Paul and instructed him not to stop, telling him that He was with him in the marketplace, that no harm would come to him since he was doing exactly what the Lord wanted him to do, and that He had "many people in the city" (Acts 18:10). This last sentence reflected God's seal of approval on Paul's new base of operation and activities in the marketplace as the key to seeing the ungodly population reached with the gospel. In fact, Paul was finally looking in the right place for what God sent him to find (Gentiles), even if it was a dark one.

The obvious implication of "I have many in the city" was that these people were not in the synagogue, and they were very likely not in the Kingdom. Nonetheless, God had His eye on them, and Paul, by head-quartering his ministry in the marketplace, was in a position to get in touch with the people God had in mind. What we see here is a breakthrough that was totally unexpected. And the text leaves no doubt that what triggered this mass movement was the conversion of Crispus and his entire household.

Who was Crispus and why did his decision impact so many so powerfully and so quickly? We know that Crispus was a principal in the synagogue, which implies that he was a leader in the city as well, because the synagogues did not have professional clergy. He was there-fore a godly man and obviously had high social visibility, because the report of his conversion immediately became news all over town. By impacting Crispus *and his household*, the city was impacted. This is what I call an evangelist's dream: to be used to lead to Christ a person so prominent that his conversion results in massive salvations across an entire metropolis.

Building on his success in Corinth, Paul was able to put into place a more developed model in Ephesus, and in about the same time it took him to saturate the city of Corinth, he was now able to impact an entire region. The key for both breakthroughs was Paul's partnership with marketplace ministers in an association he turned into a spiritual beachhead in the heart of Corinth and Ephesus.

For the first 16 years of his ministry, Paul did what most pulpit min-isters do today: He preached to God-fearing people in religious settings with notable results. But he did not see a city or a region transformed until he partnered with the marketplace. The vertical intersected the horizontal, and the results rippled across the pages of history and the corridors of time, to this very day, leaving us a model to emulate.

How feasible is this today? I believe it is very much so, because if people of high social profile like Bill and Melissa Gates, for example, were to experience an extraordinary manifestation of the power of God in their lives and as a result were to bring the gospel of the Kingdom to Microsoft Enterprises (which is their marketplace "household"), then millions of people would be impacted. All Bill Gates would need to do is to send an email or a text message to his entire database of tens of millions of electronic addresses, and the whole Western world would be touched.

What Paul experienced in Corinth was an exceptional and mighty move of God in an ungodly setting (the marketplace) where a large number of conversions were sparked by the impact of the gospel on the first-century equivalent of Bill Gates.

Hollywood Used by God?

Something very close to what I am talking about took place in late February 2004 when Mel Gibson premiered his movie *The Passion of the Christ*. During the weeks leading up to the debut, most of the world's media became the global purveyors of the gospel through interviews and special programs. When the movie was released, thousands of movie theaters were turned into forums for the kingdom of God, where the power of the visual word made a life-changing impact on millions. The image of theaters packed with teary-eyed unbelievers is too vivid to forget. Regardless of Mr. Gibson's difficulties before and after the movie, it was an event that illustrated a moment in time when God had his eye on someone "in the city" and used him. The Church would have done well to have captured it for the Kingdom by putting the presence and power of God on display by praying for people and their needs *right there in the theaters.*

Paul's choice of the marketplace as a forum for the gospel resulted in an exceptional move of God in an unusual and ungodly setting— turning it into a godly one. That was unusual, considering that previously they had tried to run him out of town. But it gets more impressive when we consider exactly who it was who had tried to do this: people in the marketplace—so much so that Paul taught the word of God for a year and a half to multitudes of new believers *in the marketplace.* And how did Paul teach the Word to folks who, unlike synagogue members, had no biblical background? Years later, Paul alluded to his methodology when he revealed that he did not do it with words of human wisdom, nor (perhaps recalling the stinging setback in Athens) did he teach the way we do today—with the audience taking notes while the presenter talks. Rather, Paul told the Corinthians, that he taught with "demonstration of the Spirit and of power" (1 Cor. 2:4).

Miracles Are the Best Teachers

I believe that the most effective way to teach the word of God in the marketplace is in a context of miracles. Again in reference to the story of Juan Zuccarelli, Juan was able to change a very hostile environment at Olmos Prison when God used him to heal the officer abusing him. Later on, when the most violent and depraved inmates were radically changed, the authorities gave Juan permission to minister at will to the entire prison population. When prisoners with AIDS were healed in answer to bold prayer, many more became believers. A miracle, especially in the context of a power encounter, is the most powerful key to opening up an institution, a city and even a nation.

The most effective way to teach the word of God in the marketplace is in a context of miracles.

The process at Olmos Prison went beyond basic evangelism. New converts went through spiritual deliverance, were filled with the Holy Spirit and baptized right away, and immediately began to exhibit an unusual level of spirituality. Folks who had been believers for only a few days embraced a lifestyle of holiness that usually takes believers outside of a prison years to attain. The reason is that one miracle seems to provide the equivalent of 1,000 hours of instruction, not in content but in depth of perception and readiness to apply what the new believer learns. Paul taught the word of God for a year and a half in *demonstration* of the Spirit and of power.

In downtown Buenos Aires, for example, there is a restaurant where the vast majority of the waiters have become believers. When we visit that restaurant, the moment we walk through the door we are greeted with hugs, handshakes and exclamations of, "Praise the Lord." Having a meal there is like being in a revival camp. Even though they haven't joined a church yet because they work 6 days a week, 12 to 14 hours a day, and need to spend time with their families when they get off of work, their level of spirituality is outstanding.

How could these new converts have attained and maintained such a high level of faith and spiritual impetus? Because the breakthrough that resulted in so many of them trusting Christ came as the direct result of a *miracle*. In the late '90s we had gone to that restaurant, and when the meal was served, instead of just praying for the food we offered to pray for the owner. He told us that he had been diagnosed with an aggressive form of pancreatic cancer, leaving him a short time to live. We prayed for him that night, and a short time later he reported that the cancer was gone. That miracle is responsible for what we see in the restaurant today. The waiters believe God for miracles because they were saved in a context of miracles. I like to say that this is a restaurant where you can order your food with the blessing on it or on the side!

The reception that Paul received from the pagans in Corinth challenges the long-held belief that as far as the world is concerned nothing but hostility is to be expected. Nothing can be farther from the truth. Tribulations are to be expected but not wholesale rejection, because in Romans 8:19 we read that the entire creation is eagerly awaiting the manifestation of the sons (children) of God. This is an encouraging declaration since it states that the world is expecting us with a high degree of eagerness.

Peacemakers Cannot Be Hostile

Why is it then that we are not welcomed by the world? I believe it is because we violate the principle spelled out in Matthew 5:9: "Blessed are the peacemakers, for they shall be called sons [children] of God." We usually do not approach the world as peacemakers. Quite the contrary, we tend to preach a gospel of condemnation. However, every time we bring an end to a hostile situation in the world by accessing the power of God, whether that situation be sickness, problems in marriage, oppression, systemic poverty, or financial challenges in the workplace, we are recognized as peacemakers, because that is what peacemakers do—they put an end to hostilities.

That is what happened after we prayed for a healing miracle at the restaurant in Buenos Aires, where the owner was dying and the employees were at imminent risk of losing their jobs, a most hostile situation, spiritually speaking.

Corinth, a city that was dominated by systemic demonic pagan worship was able to experience the liberating power of God because Paul moved his base of operation to the marketplace by turning his tent-making corporation into a ministry base.

When President Ronald Reagan passed away, according to custom and protocol, he was granted a state funeral. Twenty-five heads of state, 11 former leaders, the 4 living former U.S. presidents, and more than 180 ambassadors and foreign ministers participated in what was supposed to have been a secular ceremony—except that the gospel was presented at every turn. Scripture reading and hymns and testimonials of the former president's faith permeated every aspect of the weeklong event, which moved from California to Washington, D.C. and back to California again. Round the clock worldwide media coverage—through television, radio, newspapers, magazines and the Internet—made this solemn and inspiring occasion an international event.

However, the climax came in the final moments at the Reagan Library in California before the internment. As the sun was majestically setting over the Pacific Ocean, the most distinguished gathering of world leaders, including Prince Charles, Margaret Thatcher, Mikhail Gorbachev, Brian Mulroney, and hundreds of others, listened attentively while President Reagan's son Michael gave the most clear witness of the gospel those leaders may have ever heard. Furthermore, it was broadcast to every nation on Earth, and millions more heard and felt the impact of the love of Christ.

It would have taken *billions* of dollars for professional evangelists to reach that kind of an audience. Nevertheless it happened gracefully and naturally. Best of all, it reached the most unchurched audience imaginable, because it was produced and took place *in the marketplace*! And that is where the lost are, and consequently the place where we need to go looking for them, *even if it is dark*!

CHAPTER 8

Doing Church 24/7 in the Right Place

An oxymoron is a contradictory statement that cancels itself by eliminating any possible credibility. Can you imagine, for instance, a honeymoon manual developed by eunuchs? The word itself is contradictory. *Oxy* means "sharp"; *moros* means "dull." Nevertheless, many oxymora have found their way into our common vocabulary, like "with all deliberate speed" or "jumbo shrimp" or "pretty ugly." And truth be known, when the term "marketplace minister" was uttered, it used to create a perplexing "deafening silence." However, it is encouraging to see how ministry in the marketplace is gaining credibility in church circles. More Christians than ever see themselves as viable ministers in the arenas of business, education and government. More pastors are beginning to see marketplace ministry as a natural Monday through Friday expression of the Church. It is wonderfully non-contradictory.

As this phenomenon spreads, so does the desire and the need to know how to launch marketplace ministries. As a result, a growing number of organizations now dedicate their time and resources to offer this service. We can be pleased about all of this attention and energy. However, I wish to submit a crucial caution that a local church-*based* marketplace ministry *is* an oxymoron as contradictory and dysfunctional as a parking garage for orbiting satellites. Transformation will not happen by making marketplace ministries part of the program of the *local* church. Marketplace ministry is not marketplace ministry unless it happens *in* the marketplace. For this to take place, we need to understand that church is not a building; it is people actively invested all over the city, 24/7.

Two Setbacks and Two Victories

In Paul's 16-year transition from teaching pastor in Antioch to spiritual architect of transformation in the Roman province of Asia, he experienced two major setbacks and two decisive victories, which prove with incontrovertible clarity the strategic value of moving the Church base of operations to the marketplace, as well as the perils of not doing so. If I were a lawyer building a case before a judge and jury, what follows would constitute my leading argument for this premise.

Setback #1: Pisidian Antioch

The first setback took place in Pisidian Antioch. It was painfully disappointing because it stalled a most promising revival that in barely two weeks had impacted not only the city but also the surrounding region. In Acts 13:44 and 49 we read that "nearly the whole city assembled to hear the word of the Lord . . . and the word of the Lord was being spread through the whole region."

The beginning could not have been better. Upon arriving in town, Paul and Barnabas began preaching in the synagogue on the Sabbath and made such an impact that apparently the Gentile proselytes, who were not confined by Jewish traditions to once-a-week gatherings, continued to receive teaching during the week (see Acts 13:43b). As a result, on the next Sabbath, nearly the whole city came together to hear the apostles. This was a major breakthrough because, in addition to the Jews and the God-fearing Gentiles that Paul and Barnabas had ministered to before, practically everybody in town was now hearing the gospel.

Unfortunately the Jewish leaders became jealous and withdrew their welcome to the apostles, who by now had moved their base of operations out of the synagogue to concentrate on the receptive Gentiles. In spite of the opposition, success greeted them immediately because, "when the Gentiles heard this, they began rejoicing and glorifying the word of the Lord; and as many as had been appointed to eternal life believed" (Acts 13:48). The message was also welcomed beyond the city because "the word of the Lord was being spread through the whole region" (Acts 13:49).

For a Jew of Jews, as Paul describes himself, exchanging the religious setting of the synagogue for the pagan environment of the Gentiles was a most radical move. Nevertheless it was one that Paul justified by citing what God had said to him, "I have placed you as a light for the Gentiles, that you may bring salvation to the end of the earth" (Acts 13:47). Even though Paul never actually met Jesus face to face during His earthly life, evidently he was well acquainted with the Great Commission and the "ends of the earth" as its final objective.

It is hard not to envisage Paul's and Barnabas's satisfaction as they found themselves in the vortex of an expanding revival that impacted Pisidian Antioch and the surrounding region, pointing them to the ends of the earth so soon after the beginning of their missionary thrust. Unfortunately, it did not last because "the Jews incited the devout women of prominence and the leading men of the city, and instigated a persecution against Paul and Barnabas, and drove them out of their district" (Acts 13:50). The Establishment rose up in opposition and succeeded in shutting down the emerging revival, forcing Paul and Barnabas to leave town. We can only imagine their disappointment as they left behind the smoldering embers of such a promising spiritual awakening.

Marketplace ministry is not marketplace ministry until it happens *in* the marketplace.

Setback #2: Thessalonica

The second setback occurred in Thessalonica, where "Some of them [i.e., pious Jews] were persuaded and joined Paul and Silas, along with a large number of the God-fearing Greeks and a number of the leading women" (Acts 17:4). Again we see the blossoming of a transformation thrust impacting a city and particularly its leading citizens. Yet, once more, the powers-that-be turned against Paul and shut him down: "But the Jews, becoming jealous and taking along some wicked men from the marketplace, formed a mob and set the city in an uproar" (Acts 17:5). This forced the apostles to flee, and "the brethren immediately sent Paul and Silas away by night" (Acts 17:10), leaving another revival to whither.

The establishment succeeded in not just running them out of town in Pisidian Antioch and Thessalonica, but it was also emboldened enough to dispatch religious posses to two other towns with similar results: Lystra, where "Jews *came from Antioch* and Iconium, and having won over the crowds, they stoned Paul and dragged him out of the city, supposing him to be dead" (Acts 14:19, emphasis added); and Berea,

where many Jewish leaders "believed, along with a number of prominent Greek women and men" (Acts 17:12). The high social standing of
those who believed initially suggests that a major breakthrough was in
the making there, "but when the Jews *of Thessalonica* found out that the
word of God had been proclaimed by Paul in Berea also, they came
there as well, agitating and stirring up the crowds" (Acts 17:13, emphasis added). This forced another apostolic flight, and "immediately the
brethren sent Paul out to go as far as the sea" (Acts 17:14).

What we see here is Paul being outflanked by the opposition and
forced to leave town because of the clever manipulation of city leaders
and the agitation of crowds by an influential group in spite of the favor-
able response by a large part of the population. The reason his adversaries
were able to do this constitutes an important lesson that should not be
ignored, which I will address after we examine Paul's two major victories.

Victory #1: Corinth

Paul's first transformational success took place in Corinth, where at
first he divided his time between a tent-making partnership with Aquila
and Priscilla and the proclamation of the gospel in the synagogue on
the Sabbath. Apparently the latter must have turned into a very
demanding task because two recently arrived associates joined the
business to free him to preach (see Acts 18:5). But even his full-time
dedication and passionate proclamation were not enough to convince
the religious establishment because, "when they resisted and blas-
phemed, he [Paul] shook out his garments and said to them . . .
'From now on I will go to the Gentiles'" (Acts 18:6). Paul left the synagogue and "went to the house of a man named Titius Justus, a wor-
shiper of God, whose house was next to the synagogue" (Acts 18:7).
As we have already seen, soon thereafter Crispus's conversion opened
a floodgate of other conversions.

However, the opposition, true to form, did not wait long to strike:
"The Jews with one accord rose up against Paul and brought him
before the judgment seat" (Acts 18:12). Once again Paul was forcibly
taken to court, but unlike his prior experiences in Pisidian Antioch and
Thessalonica, this time the presiding magistrate "drove them [Paul's
accusers] away from the judgment seat" (Acts 18:16). In the vernacular,
the judge threw the case out and sided with Paul, who felt emboldened
enough to stay in town a year and a half ministering unhindered and

launching a transformation movement that soon afterwards impacted the whole region.

Victory #2: Ephesus

The second breakthrough began in Ephesus and quickly expanded to the entire region: "All who lived in Asia heard the word of the Lord" (Acts 19:10). It was a movement characterized by unusual manifestations of divine power: "God was performing extraordinary miracles by the hands of Paul" (Acts 19:11). Paul's ministry went beyond setting victims free from witchcraft to disabling the evil system behind it: "Those who practiced magic brought their books together and began burning them in the sight of everyone" (Acts 19:19). So potent was the movement that no obstacle was able to stand in its way, and "the word of the Lord was growing mightily and prevailing" (Acts 19:20).

The opposition, once again, did not delay in materializing. Soon, "there arose no small stir" (Acts 19:23, *ASV*) and an angry mob filled the city with "confusion, and they rushed with one accord into the theater" (v. 29) with murderous intentions, dragging along two of Paul's associates. Since the riot was fueled by fear of an economic collapse in the leading local industry (witchcraft), members of the local "Chamber of Commerce," threatened in their pocketbooks, were eager to pulverize the emerging movement, as had happened in other cities before.

However, something was different this time: the Asiarchs (governors of Asia) had become Paul's friends (see Acts 19:31). After hearing reports of the situation, they urged him not to go to the theater, where two of Paul's associates were in danger of being lynched. Obviously, the Asiarchs knew how to work the system, because soon afterwards we read that the town clerk quieted the multitude, advised the crowd that they had no case, proceeded to let Paul's associates go free, and dismissed the assembly, urging them to disband or face contempt charges (see Acts 19:35-40). Conditions in the area became so safe afterwards that Paul felt free to leave the emerging church by itself while he traveled to Macedonia for ministry.

The Decisive Value of a Marketplace-Based Ministry

In these passages in the book of Acts, we have a very instructional narrative in which four cities were swept by revival: two rejected and stalled it, while the other two embraced and expanded it. Why the defeats and why the victories?

In comparing the two sets of cases, the contrast I see is that in Pisidian and Thessalonica Paul was seen by the population in general and the authorities in particular as an outsider with a religious message that came across as being divisive and unhelpful or inconsequential to the city in general. This is so because in both cities Paul made the synagogue the focus of his attention and his base of operations. His interaction with Gentiles was limited to the God-fearing ones who gravitated toward the synagogue, a status that would make them atypical Gentiles. Consequently, his influence on the leading non-Jewish citizens was minimal at best.

■ ■ ■

As long as our focus is exclusively religious, society will not welcome us or any form of growth or expansion of our ministry that produces no benefit to the community at large.

■ ■ ■

On the other hand, in Corinth and Ephesus, Paul's public image was closer to the heart of the city, for two reasons. First, his base of operations was in the marketplace, the epicenter of commerce. And second, Paul was "one of them" since the bulk of his time was spent in the community as a tent-maker (a member of the local Chamber of Commerce, so to speak) with an established and reputable business, which he turned into a channel to benefit the community.

Why would the Asiarchs sympathize with Paul and be willing to be known as Paul's friends? After all, these folks were pagans, pledged first and foremost to the Roman establishment, whose policy was not to promote one religion over another, much less tolerate religious unrest—something that made Christianity naturally unpalatable to them. Why would they defend Paul against a riot instigated by the most powerful union in the region? I believe they mobilized their political muscle on behalf of Paul because *he was valuable, not just to the Church, but also to the city and to the region they oversaw.*

We see evidence of this later on when Paul recounts how he used his position in the marketplace to equip the church: "I did not shrink from declaring to you anything that was profitable, and teaching you publicly and from house to house" (Acts 20:20). Notice his reference to the wide scope of his teaching: "*anything* that was profitable"; and to ministry taking place in the marketplace: "teaching you publicly and house to house." Ministry in the synagogue was not public, but restricted to Jews and proselytes. The word "house," as explained earlier, alludes to the marketplace as well.

Next, Paul goes on to explain that his business was profitable enough for him to enjoy a comfortable standard of living: "You yourselves know that these hands ministered to my own needs and to the men who were with me." It provided enough surplus to address social needs (see Acts 20:34-35).

I don't believe Paul is referring here to peripheral charity, such as occasional donations to the needy, but to something much deeper and far more systemic, because of his reference to no other than the Lord Jesus as the standard-setter: "Remember the words of the Lord Jesus, that He Himself said, 'It is more blessed to give than to receive'" (Acts 20:35). Paul used his business as a transformational prototype to meet social needs so that his many disciples would emulate him ("In everything I showed you") as part of a process designed to impact not just people but also the socio-economic systems, both of which helped to improve conditions in the city and beyond, producing favor with the governors of Asia, *who saw Paul as an asset to the region.*

Nowadays, pastors, who are an invaluable asset to their congregations, are not missed by the city when they move on, because usually the focus *and fruit* of their labor are centered mostly on their congregations. How many pastors do we know that are *personal* friends of the governor or the mayor or the chief of police to the point where those officials stand by them when their ministries come under attack by powerful local interest? I daresay a scarce minority. As long as our focus is exclusively religious, society will not welcome us or *any form of growth or expansion of our ministry that produces no benefit to the community at large.* This becomes evident when growing congregations find themselves in a dispute with City Hall over building or users' permits; or the fact that the secular media sees no value in reporting religious news, since they see no significance for such news *as far as the daily life of the city is concerned.*

The Value of Influential Friends in Government

However, when ministers take care of the needy in the city or in institutions such as the prisons in Argentina, the authorities resolutely defend them when they come under attack.

When Unit 25, Christ the Only Hope Prison, was established, it became an island of righteousness in a sea of corruption at high tide. How high the tide was in such a raging sea became evident the first day that state contractors came to the new prison to do the usual delivery of food. The butcher, the baker and the poultry vendors each asked how much of the provisions *paid by the government* should be rerouted to a shop in town *owned surreptitiously by the warden* (a hard-to-track kickback), something that was standard practice in the system. When the warden explained that Unit 25 was a Christian prison and that everything the inmates were entitled to should be delivered, the suppliers thought he was putting up a front to protect himself, so they approached the assistant warden, who gave them the same answer. Puzzled, they went to the comptroller, also a Christian, who demanded that they stop playing the corruption game and deliver the provisions as stipulated or run the risk of becoming a permanent resident of the prison instead of a provider!

The vendors repented of their ways and eventually became Christians, but the upshot of the story is that the inmates ended up with an abundance of food, which they put to good use. Because they fasted twice a week, with what they saved plus the tithes from care packages sent by their families, they began to provide food to children in a nearby slum. In fact, the soup kitchen that they supplied received special recognition as the best-run social enterprise in the city.

The challenging side was that Unit 25's honesty exposed the systemic corruption in other prisons whose perpetrators then summarily threatened the Christians in charge for setting an example of honesty that broke the code of silence that had made systemic corruption possible. When the Christians stood firm, false accusations and cleverly devised rumors were made to discredit them. However, when things came to a head, the authorities defended the Christians.

Like the Asiarchs, they came to appreciate what an asset they were to the system.

The Winning Strategy

Paul's strategy in Ephesus consisted of four parts: *work hard* (in his business in the marketplace) to generate resources *to help the needy* (poor), and in so doing, to *emulate Christ* in order to be perceived (by society) as a *giver instead of a taker*. In truth, what Paul finally discovered after a decade and a half of ministry is exactly what the Early Church found itself doing spontaneously on the first day of existence, as reported in Acts 2:45-47 (emphasis added):

> And all those who had believed were together and had all things in common; and they began selling their property and possessions and were sharing them with *all*, as *anyone* might have need. Day by day continuing with one mind in the temple, and breaking bread from house to house, they were taking their meals together with gladness and sincerity of heart, praising God and having favor with *all the people*. And the Lord was adding to their number day by day those who were being saved.

Let's look at that passage a little more closely. The Early Church pooled its resources and shared them with those in need. Traditionally we interpret this to be a private exercise done indoors for the benefit of church members exclusively. However, the text uses the words "all" and "anyone" to identify the beneficiaries. These two are expansive, not restrictive, terms; and because the next verse describes daily public meals and activities held outdoors, in the Temple and house to house (the marketplace), it strongly suggests that it was done to benefit more than just church members.

A statement that further confirms this is found in verse 47, where we read that the Church had favor with "all the people." Here the term "people" describes persons outside the congregation, because the next sentence explains that many of those were "added daily *to the Church*." Therefore, when we connect the word "all" in verse 45 with the phrase "all the people" in verse 47, it becomes even clearer that the Early Church took care of *anyone* in need, and not just its own members!

The statement that the Church *had favor* with *all the people* in the city parallels what Paul experienced with the Ephesians, and this favor was instrumental in many of them joining the Church. As an evangelist, I was very intrigued by this reference to *divinely orchestrated daily additions* of new believers, since what drives an evangelist is the passion to see multitudes added to the Church. The text specifies that the Lord added every day *those* (plural) who were to be saved. The lowest plural number is the number two. If God were to add the very minimum of two people a day to the Church every day for 365 days of the year, it stands to reason that every congregation would grow by 730 new members a year—a figure that is hardly the average today.

The Exponential Value of Doing Favors

Since *having favor* with the outsiders seems to be the key here, I asked the Lord what the secret was to obtaining such favor as mentioned in Acts 2:47. I must confess that I was looking for a very elaborate explanation. That is why I was surprised when the Lord showed me how simple it is: In order to have favor with the people, *we need to do favors for the people*. And if we do favors for *all the people*, we will gain favor (confidence, loyalty, appreciation, openness, etc.) with *all of them*. That is exactly what the Early Church did as part of its lifestyle, creating an environment that made conversions appealing and compelling.

In addition, the Lord pointed out to me that the text shows that the Early Church was open for business *every day*, because meals were public expressions of Church meetings. I imagine the Lord thinking (probably with a hint of disappointment) that many churches today are open for business only once a week just for a few hours, and it's a rare occasion when some of those minutes are effectively used to make a compelling presentation to give the few visitors who dare venture into its religious gatherings an opportunity to receive the Lord. No wonder so few are added every year—if any at all!

In this passage we also see that the Early Church operated not in one, but in two dimensions: "praising God" (the *vertical* dimension connecting them to God), and "having favor with all the people" (the *horizontal* dimension connecting them to the city). These dimensions working in tandem made possible the divinely orchestrated daily additions. In general, churches today do a good job in the field of praise, since it is a central part of the program, but they tend to fall short on the horizontal level (obtaining favor with people outside the church), simply because those folks are not the intentional object of their favors.

■ ■ ■

In order to have favor with the people, we need to do favors for the people.

■ ■ ■

Paul was able to launch and sustain transformational processes outside the synagogue because he turned his business into a vehicle to bridge the gap between pulpit and marketplace ministers. This allowed him to lead by example, bringing not only the message of the gospel *but the transforming lifestyle of the gospel* to the marketplace 24/7 by caring for the needy in such a way that ungodly people saw the practical value of godliness. He was contributing to the lifeblood of day-to-day existence. As a result, he gained favor in the city, and particularly with its leaders— something that proved most helpful when the opposition tried to drive him out of town.

The new attacks against this new and emerging movement were instigated not by religious leaders but by a system at work in the marketplace, and through its child, a union. Because the gospel had proliferated *in the marketplace,* as opposed to just inside a building, and had impacted the economy of the region, it debunked the systemic stronghold that the devil had established over it by merging economic and evil spiritual components into the fiber of the local economy. Paul and his associates were able to deal with this issue from the inside out by establishing his base of operation in the heart of the city, the marketplace.

How to Bridge the Gap

Even though I focus on Paul's record when I describe this shift to the marketplace, it is necessary to clarify that the responsibility for such a shift should not be confined to pulpit ministers. It will take both pulpit *and* marketplace ministers to succeed. Marketplace ministers need to be very proactive in turning their jobs into ministry beachheads.

This is why I constantly encourage traditional pastors to add to their pastoral routine visits to each one of their members *in the workplace*, to assist them with hands-on marketplace pastoral training.

To replicate this today, we need to resolve the tension between the pulpit and the marketplace. Paul would have never reached Asia through the pulpit (synagogue) *alone*. This is true today as well. We are blessed to have ministers in Asia, Latin America and Africa who pastor very large congregations. This extraordinary group of highly gifted leaders has led multitudes to faith in Christ, and many have hundreds of thousands in their congregations (one in particular is fast approaching two million members), *but none of them has transformed a city, much less a nation, yet.* The reason is very simple: It cannot be done from the pulpit *alone*.

A Strategic Partnership

Having said that, we now need to balance that statement by recognizing that Paul could not have reached Asia *without* the role played by the synagogues, namely as spiritual outposts of the oracles of God, where the Scriptures were read every week. Nowadays it has become dangerously fashionable, even enjoyable, to disqualify the relevance of the church by popularizing conclusions arising exclusively from social research that is tantamount to an obituary for the church. Some go as far as advocating the emergence of a "new" church disconnected from the "old" one. I am afraid that we will soon find out that we cannot reach the world without our modern-day *synagogues*. Rather than writing them off, we need to resolve the tension between the pulpit and the marketplace, not eliminate it by choosing one over the other.

To accomplish this, I suggest a four-step progression:

1. To change the city, or the nation, the marketplace needs to be transformed.

2. To transform the marketplace, marketplace ministers need to be recognized.

3. To recognize marketplace ministers, pulpit ministers (such as Paul in Acts 18 and 19) must reach out to them and partner with them.

4. To channel into the marketplace the spiritual wealth in the "synagogue" (the local church) through the strategic placement of marketplace ministers.

In Hawaii, the turning point in this partnership progression was the commissioning of approximately 2,300 marketplace ministers by close to 300 pastors at the end of the Anointed for Business seminar. That was the moment when pulpit ministers publicly and on the record validated as ministry peers their marketplace counterparts. I had the privilege of being part of that ceremony, and it was one of the most profound ministerial experiences I've ever participated in.

First, the pulpit pastors knelt before the audience to ask forgiveness for having perpetuated a non-biblical concept of the church by dividing it into laity and clergy. Next, the marketplace ministers asked forgiveness for hiding behind clichés to avoid taking on their God-given place in ministry. Tears flowed profusely on both sides. Finally, the pulpit ministers anointed and released the marketplace ministers to pastor their spheres of influence—hotels, restaurants, schools, hospitals, and so forth. Everybody felt the sacredness of the hour. It was as if a fine mist had descended on the assembly. Everything reached a majestic climax when pulpit and marketplace ministers embraced and made a public commitment to work side by side until the nation of Hawaii has been saved.

Since then, a myriad of small transformation groups have sprung up in the marketplace, and as a result, Hawaii is experiencing transformation on an increasing number of levels.

The Target Is the World, *Not* the Pew

The key is to intentionally *connect the pulpit with the marketplace* to take the kingdom of God "to the Gentiles"—the unchurched, those who do not have our religious values and whose conduct is unappealing to us. The key word here is *to take*, since it highlights that we are *to go* rather than wait for them to come to us.

This thrust into the world goes counter to what we have been trained to do, and it will take a deliberate effort to reverse it because, except for occasional evangelistic forays, our traditional focus is primarily on the pew, and not on the marketplace. This is due to the fact that seminary training is designed to equip ministers to pastor believers, not unbelievers—much less cities or nations.

I once saw a full page ad in a leading Christian magazine that was posted by a major seminary. The ad featured an action shot of an eloquent preacher. Under this preacher's photo was the caption: "Our passion is the people in the pew." I remember asking out loud, "What about those who are *not* in the pew, the multitudes that will never set foot inside our stained-glass-window-studded walls?" The inertia created and fed by such a limiting perspective and the resulting tradition is difficult, if not impossible, to reign in without a radical shift in paradigms such as the ones described in this book.

The Weight of Cultural Inertia

From Paul's own experience we can gain a helpful insight on the destructive hold that tradition can exercise. In his account to King Agrippa of his call to the ministry, Paul clearly stated that God sent him to the Gentiles: "I have appeared to you, to appoint you a minister and a witness . . . [to the] Gentiles, to whom I am sending you, to open their eyes so that they may turn from darkness to light and from the dominion of Satan to God, that they may receive forgiveness of sins and an inheritance among those who have been sanctified by faith in Me" (Acts 26:16-18). Paul's understanding that he was sent to the Gentiles is something that he reiterated when he explained to the Galatians that he was appointed as an apostle to the uncircumcision (Gentiles) in the same manner that Peter was to the circumcision (Jews) (see Gal. 2:7-9).

■ ■ ■

The key is to intentionally connect the pulpit with the marketplace to take the kingdom of God to the unchurched.

■ ■ ■

However, when Paul and Barnabas first went out from Antioch, we read that they began to preach *in the synagogues* (see Acts 13:5), which was the wrong place if he was called to the Gentiles. Could that be a big part of the reason he did not see transformation of a city or a region *until he left the synagogue and did what he was originally called to do*—to go to the Gentiles (see 1 Cor. 18:6)?

I believe Paul's 16-year detour from directly pursuing his ministry objectives was caused by cultural inertia. It took him that long to overcome it because his religious training overrode the new spiritual revelation and precise divine instructions. This is true of many leaders today. Most ministers answered the call to the pulpit because of passion, or at least intense love, for the lost. They entered the ministry prompted by a strong desire to see many people come to the Lord. But at some point in the journey, a detour occurred that resulted in them now spending 99 percent or more of their time with believers. No wonder so many are frustrated. However, the problem is solved when they stop looking at their congregations as sheep that need a shepherd and begin to equip and commission them to be shepherds to the sheep in the city (the "Gentiles") who dwell outside of our "synagogues."

To illustrate how God is turning this around, when our team was in a police station in Fort Worth, Texas, filming material for the *Transformation in the Marketplace* DVD series, Captain Kenneth Flynn and Sergeant Mark Thorne told the story of CAPA, the local Clergy and Police Association. Captain Flynn had seen the positive effects of ministers and policemen working together before; so when the two connected in his new post in the city, he sent Sgt. Thorne to recruit pastors to help pastor in the marketplace. "If I can get them to ride in a patrol car, I can get them outside the walls of their churches to see the city," Sgt. Thorne said.

What began with 12 pastors grew to involve 120 pastors in less than 5 years. The results are tangible. Today, according to some surveys, Fort Worth is among the top 10 safest cities in America, an accomplishment credited in great part to CAPA. CAPA members attend the Minister's Police Academy at the Fort Worth Police/Fire Training Center. Pastors are saying, "We never really saw the inside of our community before. Now we not only see it, but we are also able to do something for it."

When Hurricanes Katrina and Rita brought 90,000 evacuees from the Gulf Coast to Fort Worth in 2005, CAPA mobilized its members in just a few hours to provide critical relief. The city saw that the Church was able to do much more than have meetings for its members. Captain Flynn revealed, "I *entered* the ministry when I became a Captain with this police department."

During the video shoot, a woman called the police department in desperation. Sgt. Thorne took the call, and within minutes was praying with her over the phone. On another occasion, after leading in prayer at a community meeting, someone said to him, "Sergeant, I think you have missed your calling. You should have been a minister." He politely responded, "No, I have not missed my calling. I *am* a minister—a minister in the marketplace serving the Fort Worth Police department."[1]

In order to shift from *pastoring sheep* to *equipping ministers,* the key is to remind ourselves that pulpit ministers are called to equip *others* to do the work of the ministry, according to Ephesians 4:11. This shift will make them focus on the marketplace. This is a win-win combination, because pastors will see large numbers come to Christ through those they equip, thereby fulfilling their original vision. And marketplace ministers will bring transformation to where they spend the bulk of their working hours, thereby turning it into a place of *real* worship. Best of all, cities, regions, and eventually nations will experience much-needed transformation, just as it was with Paul in Asia.

CHAPTER 9

Worship in the Workplace

Paradigm #3: Labor is worship and every believer is a minister.

Ken Beaudry, the CEO of Beaudry Oil in Elk River, Minnesota, had received unwelcome news. One of his top salespersons had turned in his resignation to go work for a competitor. Though not what Ken wanted to hear, he nevertheless applied a transformational principle to the situation and announced to the management team, "Since labor is worship, we are going to lay hands on this person and release him to be able to worship *at our competitor's company.*"

Worship in the marketplace has to do with us both being in *His* presence and realizing that He is in *our* presence right in the midst of our daily marketplace activities.

Imagine God being present at the meeting of the Board, listening attentively, offering timely counsel and giving experienced advice. Imagine Him showing up for the swing shift at the factory as assistant shift foreman whose assignment is to make things run well and help you look good. Imagine Him as a venerable icon on campus, a tutor to students and faculty alike, a friend of all the people, and an unheralded counselor to the system. Or imagine Him sitting in the balcony of every session of the legislature, or walking the halls of Congress, dropping nuggets of profound political insight and wisdom to those who are carrying the weight of the state on their shoulders. Imagine, then, how different all of us would look at our daily tasks and responsibilities if we were to understand how fully engaged and present God can be in each and every one of them.

Sadly, many Christians do not picture God in such practical context because they have been programmed to think of God primarily, if not exclusively, in a heavenly setting, as if earthly tasks are not appealing to Him. While most believers would say that they can seek God's help in the marketplace through prayer, very few may really picture God this way on an ongoing basis.

However, the scenarios above should not be alien to our daily experience. In Eden every day, God came down in the cool of the afternoon to walk and talk with the managers He had put in charge. He visited Adam and Eve in the Garden and had meaningful, productive fellowship with them in the middle of their workplace. The fact that God did so during times when it would be the most comfortable weather-wise ("in the cool of the afternoon") suggests that this was meant to be a pleasant time. There is no complete record of what was discussed during those visits, but we know that at least marriage, children, horticulture, livestock, land management, animal nomenclature, and diet were among the subjects.

Those *daily* visits were primarily for the benefit of Adam and Eve and for the job they had been assigned to do. But it was also a two-way street because I imagine God also reaped great enjoyment from it, similar to the joy grandparents get from interacting with their grandkids. It's not so much because of what the little ones can do for them, but the fact that by doing something together, the grandparents get *ministered to*. Just as grandchildren are a glory to their elders as an extension of themselves, so too were Adam and Eve to God. God was ministered to by finally being able to interact with people created in His own image *in a work context*. Whatever labor Adam did, he related it to worship, because that is exactly how God saw it.

According to the biblical record, during those divine visits the subject was always terrestrial. Even after sin had defiled creation, God's instructions addressed the imminent adverse response of the soil to man's labor, how pain and the bearing of children would be intertwined, and a negative turn in the relationship between husbands and wives. Though the spiritual dynamic had been fundamentally altered by sin, neither heaven nor hell was on the agenda. Every subject concerned issues *on Earth*.

This was also the case in similar encounters in the Bible. Whether it was Abraham, Joseph, Moses, Joshua, Gideon, or Peter, Paul and the disciples, the reason for those meetings between God and humans was always a situation on Earth and the dispensing of divine instructions, power and anointing to deal with it. No human being was ever asked by God to do something in heaven or for heaven.

The same is true today. Thanks to what Jesus redeemed on the cross, God is able to connect with us again in the workplace in a very personal way, because labor has been reestablished as worship.

Labor as Ministry

God designed us to be His ministers. Today the word "minister" is associated exclusively with religious, liturgical matters. But a minister is simply someone who looks after, cares for, or tends to, something or someone. A waiter, a doctor, a lawyer or a taxi driver is a minister, because through the services they render, *they minister to* people's needs. By carrying out God-given assignments, humans minister to Him and to those who benefit from such tasks, including the earth itself.

Since our ultimate objective as God's creatures is to worship Him, labor needs to be rediscovered as the *premier* expression of worship, as Paul alluded to when he wrote, "Whatever you do, do your work heartily, as for the Lord rather than for men" (Col. 3:23). If we leave labor out of the equation, worship on Earth is reduced to a sporadic, ethereal activity with very little impact on the horizontal dimension of life.

In the opening chapters of Genesis, there is no explicit mention of worship, because worship took place through labor. This may seem strange at first in light of our belief that man was created to worship God. But this is possible only if we dichotomize labor and worship, because God told Adam and Eve to care for the Garden as a ministry to God (the Creator), to each other (as they nurtured themselves), and to others (animals and plants). Thus labor and worship became interchangeable

This is evident throughout the Old Testament, where God's people were instructed to bring the fruit of their labor (animals, produce, crops, etc.) to offer them on the altar as an expression of worship. This was an act dependent on the fruit of man's work. This being the context, it is impossible not to see how centrally connected labor and worship are. In fact, in the Hebrew language both words have the same root. The Hebrew word *avad* means "to work," "to serve" and "to worship." The verb's sense of "worshiping" God is an extension of the idea of serving God in and with one's work. Music and songs did not become a main component of worship (at least not corporate, public, organized worship) until hundreds of years later during David's reign, when Levites and musicians were appointed to play music and lead singing.

In the same manner that the term "church" has become confused as being a building we go to rather than a people of God that we are, religious music has come to be seen as worship *to the exclusion or the downgrading of other forms of worship.* As a result, the subconscious tendency is that most Christians who on Sundays worship God to the tune of inspiring music, fail to see that what they do during the week is also meant by God to be worship. The horrendous by-product is that soon they consider Monday-to-Friday activities devoid of spiritual substance or significance— worse yet, as something that conspires against spirituality.

Most Christians who on Sundays worship God to the tune of inspiring music fail to see that what they do during the week is also meant by God to be worship.

Considering music indispensable to worship in the marketplace is in most cases impractical, intrusive, disturbing, and in fact, counterproductive. How can we introduce a music-based expression of worship in a lawyer's conference room while a deposition is in progress? Or in the cockpit of a commercial airplane? Or in an air traffic control tower in a busy airport? For Christians in the workplace, not being able to use music in the course of their daily job will reduce their worship time to a few private moments a day, if at all.

Labor = Worship
We need to capture the difference between what worship is and what it isn't, and between what it does and what it does not do, so that we can see its transcendental importance. Worship in the New Testament was remarkably different from in the Old Testament. The key to understanding Old Testament worship is that the religious practices involved and evolved around the priests, the sacrifices of the old covenant, and the temple. In the person of Jesus Christ, these practices have come to fulfillment once for all time. The close and permanent relationship that the Old Testament believers could not have with God is now possible through Jesus Christ. He is the High Priest (see Heb. 3:1; 4:14), the ultimate and complete sacrificial lamb (see Heb. 9:14,26; John 1:29), and the true temple (see John 2:21; 1 Cor. 6:19). Through His atoning sacrificial death on the cross, the barrier (our sin) to coming face to face

with God was taken away, and we are now able to enjoy a close personal relationship with God *at all times*!

In the New Testament, therefore, the focus of worship is shifted from a physical temple to Jesus. Believers now worship Jesus, and worship *through* Jesus who indwells them *and* through the Holy Spirit whom He sends (see John 2:21; 1 Cor. 6:19). That is why Paul writes, "Therefore I urge you, brothers, in view of God's mercy, to offer your bodies as living sacrifices, holy and pleasing to God—this is your spiritual act of worship" (Rom. 12:1). Christian worship, then, is not simply the act of praising God in a church meeting—although that is certainly part of it (see Eph. 5:19). Rather, it is to be an ongoing attitude and action of life—a *lifestyle*.

If Christians comprehend that they are ministers and that their labor is indeed worship, the picture will change dramatically. Imagine now a college student serving a hamburger at McDonalds *unto the glory of God*. Visualize a maid cleaning rooms and making beds in a hotel *unto the glory of God*. And further imagine her inviting God to come into that room for His presence to greet guests when they check in. Or a taxi operator "prayer driving" while he cruises for clients, and blessing them as soon as they flag him down. Or a captain of Wall Street submitting his portfolio to the Lord as the Lead Stockbroker. Or a judge invoking the presence of the Chief Advocate over his courtroom every day. If every believer were to do whatever they do heartily "as unto the Lord," then worship would take place 24/7 all over town—not to mention how much the quality of life would be improved by the excellence with which those tasks are performed.

This is not as difficult as it seems, because the issue is not deployment but activation, since the Church *is already* in the marketplace 24/7. The problem is that its members have the *worship switch* in the OFF position, and they turn it ON only when they come to the church building on Sundays. However, if they realize that labor is worship, praise will permeate our cities and the presence and the power of God will flow on the streets, *because God dwells among the praises of His people.*

Worship at Work

What is needed is a shift in paradigms in order to be able to see the sanctity and worthiness of labor, to understand that Jesus has already redeemed the workplace and we have been charged with reclaiming it.

And by this I mean the actual hotel, bank, school, restaurant, etc., where we work.

This is similar to how the members of our body were affected by our first encounter with Christ. In the past we had employed them for all kinds of evil, but when Christ came into our heart, what used to be instruments of iniquity became tools of righteousness. The hand that used to steal is now lifted up in praise to God and is also used to help the needy. As Paul puts it so ably in Romans 6:13, "Do not go on presenting the members of your body to sin as instruments of unrighteousness; but present . . . your members as instruments of righteousness to God." The same needs to be done with our job in the marketplace.

Baptisms in the Court

An excellent example is Barbara, a judge in a region of the world that is run by an atheistic political system. Not too long ago I received a most gratifying phone call from her. She told me, "Ed, we have just baptized one of my fellow judges." Knowing the magnitude of this in light of the restrictive system in which Barbara exercises her judgeship, I asked for details. She went on to tell me that the baptism took place *in chambers*! Oblivious to my amazement at this extraordinary act, she went on to explain that right after the baptism she and her associates laid hands on the new convert for him to be filled with the Holy Spirit and proceeded to engage in praise and worship that climaxed with Communion. *And all of that occurred in the courthouse!*

Barbara became a channel to bring salvation to a place that used to be in darkness and turn it into a place of worship—albeit different from the one we are used to on Sundays. In the courthouse where she performs her duties, there is now a growing group of believers, judges and court employees who bring the presence of God into the heart of the judicial system. Barbara launched this process when she understood that she is a minister and her courtroom is her pulpit. She began by rearranging the furniture since the judge who preceded her practiced Feng Shui, a belief that as part of its ritual "aligns" furniture with spiritual currents to create a corridor for spiritual forces to influence human affairs. Right after the change, Barbara experienced a remarkable improvement in the spiritual climate in her office. Her actions are similar to what Elijah did when he "repaired the altar of the LORD which had been torn down" (1 Kings 18:30), since she saw her courtroom as a ministry that had been defiled and was in need of repairs.

Next, she dedicated her courtroom to the Lord and invited Jesus to set up residence in it. She also makes it a practice to pray for every case that comes before her; and since then, over 50 percent of them are resolved through agreed terms of settlement, as opposed to the winner-take-all approach so common in courts today.

One of the most dramatic experiences in her courtroom involved a wicked person who had forced a number of women into sex slavery. He abused them so much that Barbara feared they would not be able to stand up to him in court. Matters were made more challenging by the fact that this man had hired shrewd lawyers to handle his defense and the women's self-esteem had been depleted by years of emotional and sexual abuse. In order for justice to prevail, it was extremely important that they be able to tell the truth, especially because the defendant had been tried before in a similar case and had been acquitted due to the inability of similar victims to stand up to him in court.

Barbara and some of her prayer warriors activated round-the-clock intercession, and soon miracles began to happen. A motion was made (amazingly, by the defense counsel) and accepted that the witnesses be put behind a screen while giving evidence so that they would not be seen by the public in the gallery. On the application by the defense counsel, Barbara was able to make a ruling that the media could not disclose their names either. This allowed them to give evidence without fear or embarrassment and to disclose the horrific details of what took place. The case was handled in a manner that protected the women. In the end, the defendant was convicted and sentenced to imprisonment and his subsequent appeal was denied on all counts. Justice was served, but above all, righteousness prevailed.

It is impossible not to see how those actions glorify God, how His name was exalted among unbelievers, how worship is conducted and how praise is offered in the marketplace as a result of Barbara's turning her job into a ministry. In the same manner that a pastor would never envision church ministry without worship, when Christians in the marketplace realize that they are ministers, worship is incorporated into their work routine in the most natural form.

Worship is meant to please God and to exalt Him among people. Barbara's actions did both.

Miracles at the Doctor's Office

Dr. Daniel Chen is a health practitioner in Texas. After reading my book *Anointed for Business*, he realized that he is a minister and his patients are his parishioners. Since then, he began to see every appointment as an opportunity to minister and not just as a service to be rendered. One day, he noticed that one of his patients, a new believer, looked troubled. When he inquired about it, the patient explained that due to financial setbacks he would have to lay off many of his workers and his company was going to collapse. Dr. Chen explained to this new Christian that he was a minister and that the blood of Jesus had redeemed his company and now he needed to act accordingly. He showed him how to acknowledge Jesus as the head of the corporation and how to start every workday with company-wide prayer. Furthermore, following the personal example I give in *Anointed for Business,* he told him to set aside a chair in his office as "the Jesus chair" as a place to seek guidance as needs arose. His new disciple did all of this immediately and the spiritual climate and the financial picture changed so much that no layoffs were necessary.

In a subsequent visit, his patient shared that he had submitted a bid for a large deal with Chrysler Corporation but was afraid he would not be awarded the contract because the competition was a much larger firm. Right there, Dr. Chen called on the Lord to intervene. Shortly afterward, he was awarded the coveted contract. But this was only the beginning. He went on to win larger contracts with major corporations like Nike and Nabisco. So much so that it was no longer necessary to pray for strength to get through the unpleasant possibility of layoffs, but for wisdom as to who to hire next. Now he has 89 employees!

This new perspective of labor as worship has also allowed Dr. Chen to turn a personal handicap into a plus. He told me, "Since English is my second language, I feel uncomfortable chitchatting with my Anglo patients. Instead of talking to them, I sing hymns softly while working on them. As I do, the presence of God, resident in me, touches them. In one day alone I had four patients receive the Lord after hearing me sing the praises I have incorporated into my medical procedures."

Turning a medical practice into a place of worship, where the presence of God is firmly enthroned, is bound to have a positive impact, even on those who are reluctant to such spirituality. Dr. Chen reported that a young man named Gary came into his office with a broken nose and fractured ribs as a result of a beating he took at the hands of a drug dealer, for failing to pay on time. He arrived accompanied by his mother. As had become his practice, before doing anything medical, Dr. Chen asked the Lord how he should proceed. This is his report: "The Lord showed me that this young man needed to get down on his knees and repent to his mother for the shame his addiction to drugs had brought to the family."

When Dr. Chen indicated this, the drug addict became very angry. He told the doctor that he had come to be treated medically, not to be preached at. Dr. Chen sternly admonished him, "I am giving you spiritual CPR and if you refuse it you are as good as dead because next time they will break more than just bones." No preacher could have made that statement more convincingly. The young man reluctantly did as he was told, and the doctor proceeded to treat his wounds, after which the patient departed, leaving no doubt that he was angry. Dr. Chen felt certain he would never see him again.

Surprisingly, the next day he received a call from his reluctant patient, asking to see him as soon as possible. When he did, accompanied by his father, he showed Dr. Chen that his nose was healed and that his ribs were pain free, and best of all he wanted to know more about this unusual medicine. Dr. Chen led him to the Lord and instructed him to repent to his father as well, which he did.

As I am sure you can see, this is not what usually happens in a doctor's office, but it gets even more exciting. A few weeks later the young man brought his wife to see Dr. Chen. He was in need of *marital counseling* because his wife was very angry and did not want to forgive his past failures. Dr. Chen instructed the young man, "Well, you know the routine. Get on your knees and repent!" The wife at first was not receptive, but eventually forgave him and their relationship was restored. Shortly afterward they both came to Dr. Chen's church with their children. After the service, the dad knelt before the children (by now the standard procedure prescribed by Dr. Chen) to ask for their forgiveness.

As extraordinary as this story is so far, it gets better. A few months later the young man brought to a prayer meeting a group of friends who were struggling with drugs, and drug dealers and Dr. Chen was able to introduce them to the kingdom of God.

God Receives Glory in the Marketplace

It is very clear that as this human saga with Dr. Chen played out, at every turn God was praised and worshiped, not in the traditional liturgical sense (by a choir, soloists, ensembles and bands), but by the fact that a doctor turned his practice into a ministry that glorifies God. To glorify God means to give, or ascribe, glory to Him. This constitutes worship. This is what angels do day in and day out; as they observe God's mighty works, they praise and worship Him. Dr. Chen's works praise God, but better yet, they cause others to praise Him!

Jesus taught, "Let your light shine before men . . . that they may see your good works (on earth), and glorify your Father who is in heaven" (Matt. 5:16). He demonstrated it when he healed the blind man: "Immediately he regained his sight and began following Him, *glorifying God*; and when all *the people saw it, they gave praise to God*" (Luke 18:43, emphasis added). Notice the cause-and-effect relationship between doing works on Earth and bringing glory and praise to Him. Peter wrote about this also: "Keep your behavior excellent among the Gentiles, so that . . . they may because of your good deeds, as they observe them, glorify God in the day of visitation" (1 Pet. 2:12). Since the works described here impact non-believers, these works cannot be the ones we perform in the seclusion of our religious meetings but in the marketplace where unbelievers abound.

Take Care of Your Garden

Unlike Adam and Eve, we live and work in cities, not in a Garden, and sustain ourselves not with the fruit of trees or plants but with income derived from corporations. In this sense we are different from our First Parents. But we are alike in other aspects. Adam and Eve cared for the creation by tending to the plants and the animals whose health was vital to the common good and the quality of life. Our city is the equivalent of the Garden, and its corporations are comparable to plants. When the First Couple saw a tree damaged or an animal wounded, they took care of that tree or that animal because that was their God-given job, their ministry, as assigned to them by their Creator.

This is the paradigm that needs to shift: Labor is worship when done unto the glory of God. Since every believer is a minister, then his or her job must become a ministry vehicle for labor to be seen as the premier expression of worship—because it ministers to God, to ourselves and to our fellow creatures, thus encompassing the three pillars upon which rest the two greatest commandments: to love *God* and to love our *neighbors* as we love *ourselves*.

CHAPTER 10

Giving the Devil a Heaven of a Time

*Paradigm #4: We are called to take the kingdom
of God where the kingdom of darkness is.*

A landing drill and an amphibious landing are similar except in one key point. The former happens in friendly territory and it does not impact the enemy's position. The latter takes the war to the enemy's territory and is designed to destroy his positions. In order to liberate our cities and nations, it is time that the Church replaces its Sunday parades with all-out thrusts against the kingdom of darkness's entrenchments in the marketplace.

As exciting as worship in the marketplace is, its impact is not designed to be merely inward. Rather, it is intended to have a powerful collateral effect on the devil and his wicked empire. The enemy still holds on to much of what our Lord purchased with His precious blood.

As I elaborated on earlier, human history began with Adam and Eve serving God in a perfect setting where the will of God was fully implemented. When sin entered, fellowship between God and His creatures was broken and the devil gained a free hand to completely defile life on Earth. Very quickly, jealousy caused the first murder, and from that moment on violence has wreaked havoc in what used to be a peaceful world.

However, God has never given up on restoration. In fact, right after the Fall He warned the devil that a rematch would take place and that Satan was going to be the loser—Satan would hit the deck with a bruised head! From that moment on, God is seen all through the Scriptures connecting with people and empowering them to first set, and then keep, a process in motion leading up to the moment when the world turns back to God.

With the stewardship over the earth that God entrusted in the beginning to Adam and Eve came very broad "powers of attorney"—that is, legal jurisdictions over the earth that were, in essence, surrendered to the devil through their sin. Consequently, it became necessary for God to devise a legally binding plan to recover the legal title, a plan that He carried out at Calvary.

The Match of the Ages

At first it looked more like a defeat, with Jesus hanging on a cross, naked, betrayed by one of His own disciples, abandoned by the others and temporarily forsaken by His Father, while the multitude cursed Him. It was a scene of absolute vulnerability for the Son of God, and the devil knew it. What he could not anticipate was that Jesus' moment of greatest weakness was in fact the moment of His swiftest blow, producing the knockout punch of all ages.

Colossians 2:13-15 gives us a step-by-step report of what happened that fateful day. It says that the devil taunted Jesus with what is described as the certificate of debt, a document containing the decrees that were contrary to us (see Col. 2:14). It amounted to a comprehensive list of iniquities committed by every human being, documenting their eternal alienation from God and, as a consequence, certifying the devil's legal title to them. Basically the devil was saying to Jesus, "I cannot have You because You are sinless, but according to the document I hold in my hands, everybody else, including Your mother, belongs to me because Your Father has stipulated that the soul that sins must surely die. And everybody but You has sinned. You are dying alone!"

In these few tremendously agonizing seconds of history, Jesus was bearing the weight of eternity to redeem man and recover what man had lost. If we were able to dissect and capture the fullness of what was taking place, this is what I believe we might see: Having been deserted by His closest allies, Jesus now also had to bear His Father's silence in the hour of greatest need for comfort and companionship. Every single day of His earthly life, Jesus had been able to see the Father and have perfect communion with Him, from His carpenter's shop to the temple and everywhere in between. But now, utterly alone, with the angry crowd hurling curses at Him, the devil was pompously flaunting at Him the files of what he considered to be a bullet-proof legal case.

Jesus then lifted up His eyes toward heaven, anxiously longing to see the face of the Father . . . *but saw nothing.* From the very bottom of the pit of despair He cried out, *"Father, Father!"* But no one answered. *"Why have You forsaken me?"* He painfully intoned. Jesus, who had never done anything He did not see the Father do first, was now staring at a blank screen for the first time. The power was cut off and, as a result, Jesus became totally vulnerable. The devil knew it and he made his move, coming even closer, brandishing his weapon one more time, that certificate of debt, and spitefully shouting, "You are dying alone! Everybody belongs to me because according to the rules laid down by Your own Father, the soul that sins must surely die!"

Yet, at the precise moment when the devil felt so sure of victory, Colossians 2:14 tells us that Jesus seized the incriminating document and nailed it to the Cross, making it possible for His blood to boldly inscribe *CANCELLED!* across its face.

God's Hail Mary Play

Please indulge me as I render some color commentary on the moment of the devil's demise: I imagine Satan, shocked by what had just taken place, sputtering and fuming, "You cannot do that! Every person on that list has sinned and is barred forever from God's presence and is condemned to spend eternity with me in hell, according to the rules established by Your own Father! You cannot break the rules!"

But then I hear God the Father thunder from heaven, "I have just changed the rules. There is a new rule now."

At which the devil, fully cognizant of God's moral immutability and full authority, spits with bitterness and utter confusion, "What new rule are you talking about?!"

"It is called *GRACE.*"

"Why have I never heard of it?" shrieks Satan furiously.

"Because it was hidden in My Son," God thunders back, "waiting for you to hang Him on the cross so that when His holy blood was spilled it would be released to remit every human sin. He who had no sin just paid the debt for everyone who did; and as a result, everybody on that list has been forgiven. That is called *grace.*"

Then suddenly, before the devil can formulate a response, Jesus brings the match to a dramatic finale. Rallying whatever strength that still remains in His beaten body and crushed soul, He cries out in tumultuous victory, "*It . . . is . . . finished!*"

At that precise moment, everybody and everything that had been lost from the time of the Garden onward was redeemed, because Jesus' life was given in ransom for everyone on that list. On that transaction rests the spiritual legitimacy for our mission of those redeemed by that blood (the Church) to repossess everything that Jesus paid for. And that is why we can say with full assurance that the Church has been sent to *reclaim* what Jesus has already *redeemed.*

He took care of the costly part. He paid the full price of redemption for the entire world. Cognizant of that, we must now reclaim it one *institution* at a time. A student needs to know that Jesus died for his or her school. A businessperson should confidently claim his company for God. The same is true when it comes to government officials. The forces of evil love to hang on to government agencies because of the power resident in them, but they have no legal claim. They are spiritual squatters. The price has been paid in full and a new Deed of Trust has been issued certifying that it is God's property. God knows it. The devil knows it. Now we need to know it *and act on it.*

The Church has been sent to reclaim what Jesus has already redeemed.

It is of fundamental importance for us Christians to know that we are entitled to reclaim everything that was lost, and that God will back us up. Very much like a sheriff will enforce an eviction notice, so too will angels—God's deputies—when we serve legally binding notices.

El Cereso Prison: The Devil's Prison Becomes God's Place

Poncho Murguía, a pastor in Ciudad Juárez, Mexico, understood this and put it to good use to reclaim El Cereso, the most infamous prison in his state of Chihuahua. Ciudad Juárez, a city of one-and-a-half-million people just across the border from El Paso, Texas, is the gateway for the North American Free Trade Association (NAFTA). Millions of dollars in goods pass daily through those gates to reach the heart of the USA. Corruption in Ciudad Juárez is not unknown. In fact, most people will say it's rampant, especially when it comes to drugs.

For several years, Poncho was the pastor of a growing and successful congregation with a top-notch K-12 school, a college and a brand-new building. He was loved by the members and could have easily coasted to retirement. But God gave Poncho a passion for city transformation and he could no longer be content with simply growing a congregation to revel in the goodness of heaven while his city each day was moving closer to hell. God directed him to resign his position and then to do a 21-day public fast for righteousness to prevail in Ciudad Juárez. This was no short order, given the prevalent moral decay, but Poncho obeyed.[1]

He set up a tent in a large park at the entrance of the city and for three weeks cried out to God in plain view of his fellow citizens. The media got wind of this and every day sent a journalist with the same question: "What is God saying to you about the city today?" Then the media published what Poncho reported that God had communicated. As the media made the city aware of this unusual prophetic act, and in conjunction with the increasing prayers of the saints on the heavenly places over the region, people began to show up at the site—a few to join Poncho in his spiritual quest, but many to receive prayer. Eventually, up to 4,000 people congregated around his tent. Poncho ministered to them and many were set free. He knew the gates of Hades were in evidence all over, but also that greater is He who was in him than the one wreaking havoc on Ciudad Juárez.

Proof that the balance of power in the heavenly regions had tilted in his favor came at the end of the fast when the newly elected mayor of Ciudad Juárez called on Poncho to request help with El Cereso, a prison housing over 3,000 inmates, 92 percent of whom were on drugs, and where over 80 percent of the security personnel was involved in the drug traffic. In fact, better and cheaper drugs could be bought at the prison than on the streets of Ciudad Juárez.

Many attempts had been made before to clean up El Cereso but they all had failed due to the systemic corruption. But the new mayor recognized Poncho's spiritual authority and called on him to take charge. After securing adequate spiritual covering, Poncho and the mayor devised a plan to reclaim El Cereso. With no prior notice given to the prison staff, 700 troops were deployed to take over the prison, replace the corrupt officials and lock the place down. For the next 30 days nothing went in or came out as thousands of inmates went through drug withdrawal assisted by doctors, nurses and pastors who ministered to them. When the operation was over, El Cereso had been cleaned up and the drug cartel dismantled.

Basically the gates of Hades crumbled because God's people took the kingdom of God to the city. As a result, transformation has begun to take place in businesses with entire corporations, schools, immigration centers and myriads of people coming into the kingdom of God! The mayor now has proof that the Church possesses the power and the authority to eradicate systemic evil and is calling on her to do the same in other areas of the city, with similar results.

Philippines Brothel Becomes Transformation Center

King Flores is a Filipino Christian who, like Francis Oda in Hawaii, holds dual ministerial citizenship since he is both the CEO of an international financial-transfer service in Manila and a pulpit minister. When he was first exposed to *Prayer Evangelism* and *Anointed for Business*, he decided to implement the principles right away. At the time, he was working as a consultant to a person who owned eight businesses, one of which was a motel chain consisting of eight buildings with 1,600 rooms and employing 2,000 workers. However, each room was used an average of five times a day by 3,000 prostitutes who, in cahoots with the management, "processed" around 15,000 "clients."

King brought his boss to our seminar, where the boss realized that he was a minister, his employees were his disciples, his business was his ministry, and his clients were his congregation. He also embraced the truth that salvation could and should come to his corporation in the same manner that it came to him. Soon after the seminar, he walked into his boardroom and proclaimed, "The kingdom of God has come to my business and the gates of Hades shall not prevail against it." Cognizant that his 2,000 employees were in dire need of shepherding, he hired 30 pastors and, under King Flores's leadership, gave them a novel assignment: "I will pay you a salary for you not to preach."

By this he meant that they were to practice *prayer evangelism*, which I describe in its most elementary form as "talking to God about the lost before we talk to the lost about God."[2] Luke 10:2-9 records Jesus' four-step implementation, which I teach in my book *Prayer Evangelism*. The methodology is taken from His instructions to 70 followers whom He had chosen for a special assignment: to *bless* the lost, *fellowship* with them, *minister* to them, and then (and only then) *proclaim* that the kingdom of God has come near them. Thus, what constitutes the four-part thrust is to (1) *bless*, (2) *fellowship*, (3) *minister* and (4) *preach*. Therefore, because preaching is listed at the very end of the sequence, King's boss made the statement about paying the pastors not to preach—meaning that they needed to cover the other steps first.

How serious he was about this became evident when three of the pastors, unable to overcome their training, violated his directive and preached *prematurely*. They were summarily fired and replaced with others who were willing to adhere strictly to the job description. The 30 pastors connected with the 2,000 employees by becoming part of the many task forces that are necessary for the daily running of a motel chain. This placement allowed them to quietly speak peace over the lost. As doors opened up for fellowship, they struck up friendships. As those friendships deepened, employees began to share personal problems with the pastors, who immediately offered prayer. Very soon, answers to those prayers materialized, providing a convincing platform for the proclamation that the kingdom of God had come to the motel chain. So much so that after two years and three months, the majority of the 2,000 employees had received the Lord.

Wherever Satan has taken over an institution, God's children must move forward to reclaim it, knowing that the devil has no choice but to leave.

In the intervening time, the owner invested new capital to upgrade the motels to executive status to make them less accessible to street prostitution. He also built prayer chapels in each motel and recruited intercessors to pray on Mondays, Wednesdays and Fridays for everyone who had spent the night there or was scheduled to do so that day.

The improved spiritual climate was heightened as more and more employees came to the Lord and began to see themselves as ministers, turning their jobs into ministerial vehicles. Can you picture employees praying that the presence of God will greet the guests when they check in? If the new occupants happened to be an illegitimate couple, being greeted by the presence of God as they entered the room must have had a dampening effect on their lustful desires, to put it mildly!

However, the most striking feature was informing the guests that prayer was available upon request, and instructing them how to avail themselves of this unusual hotel service.

The spiritual game plan worked so well that after 18 months, more than ten thousand clients had received the Lord, not to mention many others who were impacted by miraculous answers to prayer. Similar to what took place at the bank in Elk River, once salvation came to the hotel chain, the motels began to do the work of the ministry as believers are expected and empowered to do. The key player here was the owner, someone without formal theological training and who was never ordained and who does not preach from a pulpit. However, when King Flores's boss realized that he was a minister and chose to exercise his pastoral calling in the marketplace, what would have taken a traditional pastor two lifetimes or more and a fortune to accomplish happened naturally and speedily because somebody decided to give the devil a heaven of a time, 24/7, by taking the kingdom of God where evil used to rule unhindered. What was formerly a den of iniquity became a hallmark of God's glory.

These stories and many more like them confirm that the sweeping verdict that was won that day has stood the test of time. Wherever Satan has taken over an institution, whether it be in an industry, a prison or a bank, God's children, deputized and armed with the legal jurisdiction that Jesus' death secured, must move forward to reclaim it, knowing that the devil has no choice but to leave. The kingdom of darkness *will flee*!

CHAPTER 11

Systemic Poverty

*Paradigm 5: Nation transformation
must be tangible, and the premier social indicator
is the elimination of systemic poverty.*

Nowhere is the kingdom of darkness more entrenched in the world today than when it comes to the manifestations of systemic poverty. Systemic poverty is not a peripheral issue in the Bible. The elimination of poverty is central to the gospel message of redemption, and for that reason it is both a by-product and the most tangible social evidence of true, biblically based transformation. In fact, Jesus began His ministry by announcing good news to the poor; the Early Church had no needy people in its ranks (as I will show here in great detail); and the book of Revelation ends with a climactic parade of healthy and wealthy nations bringing their honor and glory to God. The elimination of systemic poverty may sound like a radical statement, but it is fully biblical and, if embraced, will have tremendous repercussions for the Church as we know it today—and even greater and more glorious ones for the world around us.

Our theology today, and particularly our eschatology, has become mystically skewed to the point that we have difficulty considering, much less embracing, this paradigm. Our view of the future tends to focus almost exclusively on escaping this *sin-sick* world to the exclusion of the potential of bettering things on Earth in general and of resolving the plight of the poor in particular. There is nothing wrong with being heavenly minded. In fact, we are told to "set your mind on the things above, not on the things that are on earth" (Col. 3:2). But the intent of this biblical exhortation is to obtain an eternal perspective with which we can effectually deal with challenges on Earth, not escape them.

This tendency is further accentuated by fear of contamination by a social gospel that emphasizes doing good (even excellent) works that address social evils to the exclusion of addressing the eternal issues of the soul—or the so-called *name it and claim it* theology that short-circuits the powerful grace of God available to bring about authentic transformation—by substituting a quick-fix version based on shallow theology and flawed interpretation. To couch this new paradigm in a proper context, three observations must be made. First, I am referring to a *social* indicator, not an ethereal or "spiritual" one. By "social" I mean that which is reflected in the community and can be measured and documented: The crime rate goes down, per capita income goes up, more students are graduating. These are measurable social indicators. Second, the poverty I am discussing is *systemic* poverty, not individual poverty. And third, the causes for *personal* poverty are multiple and usually self-inflicted, such as laziness, addiction or procrastination.

Systemic poverty is different from *personal* poverty in that it is something that most people are born into and their fate is dictated and controlled by it. Those who are not born into it are targets to be brought into it. That is why it must be eliminated—because it reflects a scheme that is diabolical in design and evil in its implementation. It deprives masses of people of their daily bread by stealing the fruit of their labor and keeping them in social misery.

What Is Poverty?

The online encyclopedia Wikipedia defines "poverty" as "a condition in which a person or community is deprived of, or lacks the essentials for, a minimum standard of well- being and life." Thus, the essence of poverty is the lack of resources that are essential for living with dignity.

What then is systemic poverty? It is an all-encompassing socioeconomic structure that keeps people deprived. It exists because of an institutionalized attitude that legitimizes its twin evil premises that (1) some people deserve more opportunity than others, and that (2) there is not much that can or should be done about this prevailing social injustice—similar to how slavery was justified in the past. Because this evil is systemic, it will not be eradicated by simply taking care of individuals at the micro level or providing massive aid at the macro level. It must be uprooted.

For example, prior to emancipation, there were compassionate white people in the American South who took good care of their slaves, but their actions did not eliminate slavery. They merely alleviated conditions for a few. It took the Civil War and the dismantling of the Old South for slavery to cease legally, and an additional hundred years and the Civil Rights Movement for its cultural conditioning and imprint to be ejected from the national psyche.

Let's now look at a definition for the *poverty* side of the term.

There are different kinds of poverty indicators. Economists use the expression "poverty line" to describe the minimum level of income deemed necessary to achieve an adequate standard of living. Populations are then classified as above or below it. However, a simple monetary standard is inadequate because what is considered poor in the USA would easily qualify as rich in most Third World countries. Poverty is also understood as the lack of material resources, such as food, safe drinking water, and shelter, or social resources, such as access to information, education, health care, social status, political power, or the opportunity to develop meaningful connections with other people in society.

For the purpose of this book, I define *poverty* as "lacking our daily bread" and *systemic poverty* as "the structure that perpetuates such deficiency." This definition, extrapolated from the Lord's Prayer, though uncommonly simple, is as comprehensive as the one provided by the editors at Wikipedia. To expand on this point, let's examine each of the core words: "our," "daily" and "bread." The term "our" points to the corporate dimension of life. Provision is necessary, not just for *me* but also for *others* who comprise the community I am part of. Furthermore, this provision has to have continuity; it has to be a *daily* occurrence. The exact words in the Lord's Prayer are "Give us *this day* our *daily* bread" (Matt. 6:11, emphasis added). It is meant to be a *predictable* daily occurrence. The recipient must know, or at least have hope, that tomorrow is part of a continuum and not a crisis waiting to happen. And finally, *bread* speaks of food that has substance and nutrition. The broader context points to a loving God as the source, *Our Father who art in heaven,* and describes provision as a gift ("give us").

Four Kinds of Poverty

From these observations, I see four kinds of poverty: spiritual, relational, motivational and material.

1. *Spiritual poverty* afflicts those who do not know that God is their father.

2. *Relational poverty* encompasses those whose focus is on themselves at the expense of the community they are a part of.

3. *Motivational poverty* is a state of hopelessness that engulfs those who have no adequate way or means (or the confidence) to tackle tomorrow's challenges.

4. *Material poverty* impacts those who lack the basic necessities to sustain themselves.

The flip side of these four dimensions of poverty is spiritual, relational, motivational (hope-filled) and material *wealth*.

Why would our Lord make food (bread) such a central point? Because the food supply is the most volatile component of the marketplace. As I state in my book *Prayer Evangelism*:

> Almost anything can go wrong in the marketplace—inflation, political corruption, even a natural disaster—and the city (or the nation) will put up with it and eventually recover. But if the food supply becomes critically insufficient, then revolutions happen, rulers lose their heads and chaos ensues until order is restored, first in the food supply and eventually in all other areas of the marketplace. A calamitous disruption in the food supply is the societal equivalent of a heart attack.[1]

This is also true for individuals. People can live without everything but food, air and water; but food is the ingredient that provides the energy needed for vibrant productivity.

Missionaries and inner-city workers know about the difficulty of communicating the gospel to starving people without first addressing their hunger. This same understanding was a critical component of the Spirit-led strategy of the Early Church, which made the regular provision of food for the hungry an integral part of its ministry because it knew that this was the arena where spiritual oppression and its resulting deprivation were most visibly and painfully felt.

This social blight is not abstract—quite the opposite is true: Poverty and the resulting hunger, if left unabated, will result in very real starvation. Throughout the Old Testament the penalty for idolatry took the form of famine, pestilence or drought. The brunt of such judgment was always felt in the marketplace and particularly in the stomachs of the people. Food became scarce and eventually insufficient. On the other hand, 2 Chronicles 7:14 teaches that if we get right with God, He will, after granting forgiveness for our sins, heal the land. The implication is impossible to miss: The land that produced insufficiently will once again produce abundant food.

Two things can cause this insufficiency: (1) a divine judgment as a result of sin, or (2) an evil system that enables a few to hoard resources at the expense of many. This is the difference between self-inflicted poverty and systemic poverty. To resolve the first case requires personal and corporate repentance, which opens the door for God to intervene. The second has to be dismantled by the Church, first within its own ranks where mindsets need to be changed and transforming patterns of behavior established, and subsequently into society until it is transformed. The latter is not only possible but also desirable. God wants it to happen, and the leaders of nations are wide open to it since poverty is not only a bane to those who suffer it, but it is also a blight on those who have not been able to resolve it.

Please note that I am not advocating a socialistic approach that imposes a redistribution of wealth. What I am referring to is the social and spiritual blindness of modern-day "rich young rulers" who fail to enter into the kingdom of God because they have too many idle possessions and no concern whatsoever for those who are utterly dispossessed. They could greatly help others by allowing much of their wealth to flow back into the market capital and thus improve the common good. It was exactly that reluctance that kept the young aristocrat mentioned in Matthew 19:22 from entering into what he, of his own volition, came asking Jesus for: "When the young man heard this statement, he went away grieving; for he was one who owned much property." Note that Jesus had not asked the rich young ruler to sell his possessions and give the money to the poor. He told him, "Sell your possessions and *give* to the poor" (v. 21). There is no "it" between "give" and "to."

How is a rich person expected to help the poor? It is not by he himself becoming poor through self-dispossession, but by moving idle capital (possessions or property) into the marketplace for the purpose of developing products and creating jobs as well as making profits with which to alleviate the plight of the poor. Keeping those assets from entering the marketplace, whether out of fear, selfishness, insecurity or all of those reasons, will negatively impact the economy (and, by extension, those who need help the most) by failing to generate new capital.

The point is this: Poverty is not only the *lack of something* but also the *fear of lacking something.* One reason that poor people are kept poor is because those who control the marketplace live in emotional and spiritual poverty themselves, even though they are materially rich. Enough is never enough for them, and the resulting fear causes moral paucity.

The result is that the rich get richer, through hoarding, but not happier or more fulfilled, and the poor are enchained to hopelessness. As a result, the future of the nation is mortgaged because its main assets—its people—have been bridled.

Could it be for that reason that Jesus' parables and miracles so often touched on issues and circumstances involving money and assets— because He was dealing with systemic issues? It is no coincidence that almost all of the miracles of the Gospels and the book of Acts occurred in the economic sector (marketplace) of the city. God was addressing a new way of doing business.

I wish to submit that the case for the elimination of systemic poverty is so intrinsically woven into the Scriptures that we have failed to see it, much less embrace it as a possibility, basically because it is impossible to separate the two. To address this in an orderly way, in the following chapters I have organized the discussion into four parts: the *biblical basis,* the *Early Church experience, individual examples,* and *emerging corporate prototypes.*

CHAPTER 12

The Early Church and Poverty

When God created the world, He planted a Garden with every provision in it for humans to enjoy life and nourish themselves. Poverty was not part of the original design. Poverty was the first social consequence of the Fall because productivity was diminished by the introduction of sin, resulting in the ground ceasing to yield generous crops, which forced man to exchange the sweat of his brow for the fruit of the ground.

Thorns and thistles were introduced as visual evidence of the invisible sin that brought the curse on the source of their provision, the ground. Whenever Adam and his descendants saw a new thistle sprout, they were reminded that the curse and its systemic consequences were real, something that would encompass all of creation and become intrinsically institutionalized.

However, at Calvary Jesus wore a crown of thorns on His brow as a sign that His blood was shed to remove this curse. Furthermore, Jesus' opening words at the onset of His earthly ministry, "The Spirit of the Lord is upon me, because He has anointed me to preach good news to the poor" (Luke 4:18, *NIV*), constitute a radical promise of tangible welfare to the needy, since good news to the poor cannot be that only after a lifetime of deprivation on Earth will they then spend eternity in heaven, where there is no poverty. Good news *to the poor* has to at least include that they will be set free to live a life of provision *while on Earth*!

As corroboration of Jesus' words, one of the first snapshots we have of life in the Early Church shows that "there was not a needy [poor] person among them [its members]" (Acts 4:34). Then in Acts 19:10-11 we read that *all the people* who lived in Asia heard the word of the Lord in a context of extraordinary miracles performed by God through Paul's hands. Later on, alluding to at least part of the reason for such massive impact on the totality of the population, Paul explained that dealing with poverty was central to his philosophy of ministry: "In *everything* I showed you that by working hard *in this manner* you must help the weak (poor) and remember the words of the Lord Jesus, that He Himself said, 'It is more blessed to give than to receive'" (Acts 20:35, emphasis added).

When Paul's apostleship was questioned, he submitted himself to being examined by a panel composed of Peter, James and John. I imagine that he spent the night before his appearance coming up with answers to every possible question that this unpredictable board might come up with since his legitimacy as an apostle hung in the balance. However, the examiners were unanimously convinced of his calling, requiring of him only one thing: "Take care of the poor"—something that Paul "was eager to do" anyway (see Gal. 2:10).

Dealing with Poverty Was a Mark of Apostleship

The importance that the Early Church leaders gave to "taking care of the poor" firmly established this as central to the mission of the gospel. It was a qualifying or disqualifying mark of apostolic leadership that today needs to be attended to more carefully.

When we fast forward to Revelation 21:24-27, we find a majestic parade of nations bringing their honor and glory to God. The fact that these nations have such to present to God shows that they are neither poor nor needy. They are saved nations instead, because "only those whose names are written in the Lamb's book of life" (Rev. 21:27) are part of this splendid exercise. They are also healthy nations, since in Revelation 22:2 we read that the leaves of the Tree of Life have healed them. God is their King and *there is no systemic poverty* in God's kingdom. This is conclusive proof that the elimination of poverty is central to the message of both Jesus and the Early Church.

You might wonder, *If Jesus came to destroy the works of the devil and poverty is one of them, then why is it still around?* To answer this we need to understand the difference between sin and iniquity. Sin is the act of disobedience; iniquity is the mark left on what was touched or defiled by it. Iniquity is the consequence of that wrong, like the imprint left by a shoe after it has been extricated from the mud. Jesus removed the shoe but the imprint was left for the Church to erase as part of the commission to teach all things He has commanded (see Matt. 28:20). This is what Jesus had in mind when He gave the Great Commission. He stated that because of the authority on Earth granted to Him, His followers are empowered to repossess what was lost.[1] And when we lay hold of the full scope of that assignment, it leads directly to discipling the nations.

The expression "discipling nations" is at first hard to grasp, but basically it means teaching a nation what Jesus taught us for the purpose of causing it to embrace the goodness of God and to reflect the character of Christ. In other words, the key is to understand that even though the *sins* of nations have been settled at Calvary, their consequences still need to be addressed and reversed. Sin in and of itself is intangible and is dealt with through repentance. However, its consequences are tangible and must be dealt with through restitution and repurposing—elements that fall in the category of discipleship.

■ ■ ■

Even though the sins of nations have been settled at Calvary, their consequences still need to be addressed and reversed.

■ ■ ■

For example, slavery, morally speaking, is a sin. Today the sin of slavery is no longer practiced in the United States, but the iniquities of slavery—the prejudice, pain and resulting politics—are still evident, and painfully so. African and Native Americans struggle under a system contaminated by debasing and flawed social, economic and moral standards that in turn impact other people groups. This is because the mark (the "shoeprint") of the sin of slavery (iniquity) has not yet been fully erased from society, even though Jesus did pay for it.

It is the same with systemic poverty, a far more comprehensive form of slavery since it encompasses the spiritual, motivational, relational and material dimensions of life. Because Jesus' atoning blood stamped a divine "PAID IN FULL" on the promissory note Satan held against humankind, Satan no longer has the rights to what he obtained through deception in the Garden. The note has been *redeemed*. And to make matters worse for him, the very people he held in bondage are now the ones who have been commissioned to *repossess* that which was legally recovered at Calvary.

The Groundbreaking Example of the Early Church

In the book of Acts, we find several instances when taking care of the needy by the Church was followed by spontaneous and extraordinary membership growth due to the favor it generated with the people in the city by erasing the iniquity represented by the social scar made by the fourfold kind of poverty I am discussing.

In Acts 2:44-46, we see an uncommon reconciliation between the rich and the poor, a definite body blow at systemic poverty: "All those who had believed were together and had all things in common; and they began selling their property and possessions and were sharing them with all, as anyone might have need. Day by day continuing with one mind in the temple and breaking bread from house to house, they were taking their meals together with gladness and sincerity of heart."

While studying this passage I was first drawn to the fact that rich people gave extravagantly to the poor, which reflected a dramatic change of attitude on their part: away from using their wealth and stature to dominate and toward using the same to show godly deference.

But the Lord drew my attention to an even greater miracle, the one encapsulated in the sentence "they (the rich and the poor) were taking their meals together with gladness and sincerity of heart." The lines of distinction between the opposing groups ceased to exist and the two went on to comprise a new community described by the word "together," one characterized by *gladness* and *sincerity of heart* in all its members. The fact that they fellowshipped daily and in homes shows that it was part of a lifestyle and not a function they participated in sporadically. This model publicly exposed as vulnerable and assailable the class divisions and oppression that had been considered immutable in the prevailing social system.

Scoring the Rich and the Poor

I have described poverty as being spiritual, relational, motivational and material. It will be helpful to point out how the rich and the poor succeed in the two categories that the other group does poorly at. Generally speaking, the poor score higher on the spiritual and relational dimensions, because faith in God is often the only source of hope available to survive the hopelessness that engulfs them, and relationships are a vital part of that survival mechanism. On the other hand, people of wealth fare better on the material and motivational aspects. They have resources and the attitude and the know-how to leverage them so as not to approach the future with desperation, but they tend to score lower on relationships, and their faith in God is usually more "professional" than personal, most likely due to the fact that they are less dependent on Him to manage their affairs than the poor.

By coming together, both groups were able to minister to each other in their respective areas of need. The rich found fellowship and were inspired by the resilient faith of the poor, while the poor benefited from material things made available by the rich and by their sense of hope for the future. The key to all of this was the heart. They did everything together with *sincerity of heart* giving birth to a new social enterprise that spontaneously and generously reached out to the community at large, sharing their possessions with all, as anyone might have need, which in turn, brought them favor with all the people, and in that climate God was able to add daily to the church those that were to be saved (see Acts 2:47).

By ejecting from its midst a socially accepted (or tolerated, depending on one's status) system designed to perpetuate poverty through class divisions and the resulting oppression, the Early Church impacted a society ruled by such a system, causing many to join the Church *daily* because of hard-to-ignore good news. Undoubtedly the Church was the most popular institution in Jerusalem!

We know this was not an isolated event, because Acts 4:32 states, "And the congregation of those who believed were of one heart and soul; and not one of them claimed that anything belonging to him was his own, but all things were common property to them." Again we see spiritual unity (*one heart and one soul*) and wealth being shared in the freest manner, by making it common property. Consequently, "there was not a needy person among them, for all who were owners of land or houses would sell them and bring the proceeds of the sales and lay them at the apostles' feet, and they would be distributed to each as any had need" (Acts 4:34-35).

However, at the very center of this paragraph is a statement that at first seems to be out of place: "And with great power the apostles were giving testimony to the resurrection of the Lord Jesus, and abundant grace was upon them all" (v. 33). To give witness with great power means that the testimony (that Jesus was alive) was believed because of the strength with which it was communicated. And the source of such power was not only the boldness with which the apostles spoke and the miracles God performed through them *but also* the fact that the rich and the poor exchanged their old social identity for that of people with the same soul and heart. As a result, non-Christians were able to see proof of the resurrection through what they witnessed in the social arena: a new community defined by love and not by possessions, and its resulting asymmetrical social status—a most appealing alternative to those enslaved by material and motivational poverty and the destructive dullness of wealth without faith and relational joy.

It is obvious that the Church in Jerusalem, whose members had a personal relationship with God, rich fellowship with each other, absolute hope for the future and material provision, enjoyed spiritual, relational, motivational and material wealth. It was this fourfold dimension that made it so attractive to the lost.

And it was not a small-scale experiment but a massive example of societal transformation when we realize that the size of the Church in Jerusalem was extraordinary. Even though there is no specific data in Acts of how large the Jerusalem church was, it is reasonable to assume that it could quite possibly have passed the hundred thousand mark. Consider that 3,000 men believed on the first day (see Acts 2:41). Subsequently God added *daily* to their number (see v. 47). Then an additional 5,000 men[2] were incorporated (see 4:4), and soon afterward *multitudes* of men and women were *constantly* added to the new community (see 5:14) to such an extent that the sick had to be laid on cots and pallets on the streets to receive ministry, a hint that there was no venue large enough to house them and that the size of the group dictated a shift from personal to mass methods (see v. 15).

This new community, in which there was no needy person, was large enough to rock the establishment, as suggested by the deep apprehension and borderline panic with which the religious rulers processed these developments and began to search for ways to squash it (see Acts 4:13-18). The picture of what is really happening here becomes even more astounding when we get to Acts 6: "Now at this time while the disciples were increasing in number, a complaint arose . . . because (the Hellenistic) widows were being overlooked in the *daily* serving of food" (v. 1, emphasis added). Here we see a large number of people being fed and cared for by an untested leadership that was operating within an inadequate infrastructure that led to a crisis: Gentile widows were being neglected in the daily distribution of bread. Please note that the distribution of food to the needy was a *daily* activity and what triggered the crisis was *an additional increase in membership.*

Peter's statement, "It is not desirable for us to neglect the word of God in order to serve tables" (Acts 6:2), does not mean that he considered this a secondary issue. The opposite is true. The fact that the leadership acknowledged the problem, summoned the multitude and outlined a process to deal with it shows how *important* the daily distribution of bread was. In fact, Peter's proposal found immediate approval with the whole congregation (see Acts 6:5), thus confirming it as an integral part of the spiritual DNA of the emerging Church.

Before going any further, let's not miss two very important points. First of all, what we have here is a partnership between God and His Church, since the Lord's Prayer instructs us to ask for our daily *bread*, not our daily *Manna*. The former is the result of cultivating, harvesting and processing the fruit of seeds provided by God (see 2 Cor. 9:10). The latter is a handout from heaven that requires minimum effort, basically just a matter of gathering it every morning. In times when we find ourselves in the wilderness, God may rain Manna on us, but those instances are going to be exceptional and not normal.

Second, there is no mention in the book of Acts of the Church in Jerusalem going into the baking business. Based on what we read, they did not build warehouses for the flour or construct large ovens to bake so much bread, nor was anyone hired to work in church-run bakeries. What went on happened at the grass roots level. It was a people-to-people movement in which everyone shared enthusiastically, house to house. The intervention of the Twelve was required to *organize* things at a more efficient level, not to consolidate the myriad individual initiatives. Notice that Peter did not exhort the assembly to give more; he merely outlined a more efficient system to manage the provision that was *already* part of the Church lifestyle.

And this was not a Jerusalem occurrence only, because many years later Paul provided a wonderful snapshot of how his disciples did something similar. Writing to the Corinthians, Paul described them as eager to share with strangers. So much so that he was able to boast about their bountiful gifts because they practiced the principle of abundant sowing and reaping. They knew that God loves cheerful givers, and having become such, they had sufficiency *in everything* and knew how to use that abundance for good deeds to benefit others.

In this passage, Paul makes reference to God as the role model by quoting Psalm 112:9: "He scattered abroad, He gave to the poor, His righteousness abides forever" (2 Cor. 9:9). The picture here is of someone scattering seeds "abroad," the term implying "away from the immediate sphere of influence, for the benefit of the poor, in a context of enduring righteousness."

Please note the choice of words: "Scatter" suggests the opposite of tightly controlled giving. So often, giving to the poor is stingy because it is perceived as wasting seed. But Paul is making an exactly opposite and much deeper point: When we scatter abroad—beyond the boundary of our own fields, obviously with the intent to benefit *others*—we provide the poor with seeds to turn into bread, a possible inference to the Leviticus 19:9 command *not* to harvest the corner of the fields in order to leave something for the needy: "Now when you reap the harvest of your land, you shall not reap the very corners of your field, neither shall you gather the gleanings of your harvest." And because God's righteousness and generosity is thus put on display, He in turn promises to multiply our own seed supply so that we will be enriched in everything with all liberality.

According to Paul, the tide of thanksgiving to God produced by such righteous deeds will also elicit abundant praise, not only among the saints but also among strangers. Even though Paul speaks of seed and bread, the passage suggests that when generosity is expressed at such a basic level, prosperity takes place at the higher ones: "You will be enriched in everything for all liberality, which through us is producing thanksgiving to God" (2 Cor. 9:11). Paul ends his paragraph with the exuberant words "Thanks be to God for His unspeakable gift!" (v. 15, *ASV*) to remind us that as disciples of Christ we must emulate the One who gave the very best He had.

Clearly, the Church in the New Testament had a *lifestyle of giving* and took very seriously the issue of eradicating hunger—the most tangible manifestation of systemic poverty—from its midst and beyond. And the way in which they went about it reversed the system and left a vibrant model that needs to be emulated once again as part of the discipling of nations in this generation.

Really Good News to the Poor

A line can be traced connecting two pivotal New Testament events: (1) the moment when Jesus announced good news to the poor (see Luke 4:18), at the very beginning of his earthly ministry, and (2) the climax portrayed in Revelation 21 and 22 when wealthy nations will bring honor and glory to God at the very end of human history. This is when the will of God in heaven will become fully reflected on Earth. There is no poverty in heaven, and on that day there will be no poverty on Earth. (I am using the term "poverty" to express not just material lack but also the fourfold dimension of poverty described in the previous chapters.)

How do we get from one to the other? To answer this question, I wish to provide examples "in process" of transformation in the lives of individuals, industries and institutions. What these examples show is that it is possible to break the spiral of hopelessness that feeds systemic poverty and that, by turning its former victims into protagonists of transformation prototypes, it is possible to receive hope to eradicate it.

Individual Examples

One of the main obstacles in the quest to eliminate systemic poverty is the perception that there are not enough resources to take care of the poor. This could not be farther from the truth. First, a cursory scan of the plethora of articles that address the topic on the Internet from every conceivable point of view reveals that there is an untapped well of resources that could be made available by the creation of new wealth as the result of freeing existing resources from the dungeon of greed and fear currently held immobilized by modern-day "rich young rulers" (see Luke 18:18-25). And second, this perception does not foresee that the vast masses of poor people who at present constitute the problem could turn into the solution—which I believe is going to happen; and when it does, it will be the societal equivalent of cold fusion.[1]

I will address in depth the creation of new wealth later on, but for the time being let it suffice to say that God is very intentional about multiplying our assets if we choose to become channels to bless others. Psalm 41:1-4 reveals that taking care of the poor is the social equivalent of acquiring insurance against poverty, economic disaster, hostile takeovers and catastrophic illness. Consider the benefits spelled out in that psalm: "He who considers the helpless," the Lord will:

- Deliver him in a day of trouble
- Protect him
- Keep him alive
- Cause him to be called blessed on the earth
- Keep him from being given over to the desire of his enemies
- Sustain him upon his sickbed and restore him to health

This set of promises covers the past, the present and the future, *if* we take care of the needy. One can never out-give God.

Furthermore, Jesus assured us that there is "no one who has left house or wife or brothers or parents or children, for the sake of the kingdom of God, who shall not receive many times as much at this time and in the age to come, eternal life" (Luke 18:29-30). Please notice that the multiplication of resources that Jesus promises will take place on Earth (at this time) and *in addition* to obtaining eternal life in the age to come. These two passages indicate that new resources will be generated supernaturally by those, and for those, who embrace a vision for the kingdom of God on Earth.

Now let us move on to the more challenging notion that the poor can be the solution to poverty. This is possible because even though poverty is a problem, poor people are not, because according to the Bible they constitute the greatest (albeit still untapped) resource *to eliminate poverty*. The principle is found in Ephesians 4:28: "He who steals must steal no longer; but rather he must labor, performing with his own hands what is good, so that he will have something to share with one who has need." This verse describes the extraordinary social metamorphosis of a thief turned benefactor, a lawbreaker who decides not to steal anymore and chooses instead to work, learning an honorable trade to earn enough to care for himself and have extra to share with those in need. Awesome!

By assigning numerical values to each step in the process described in this passage we can see how the subject goes from −1 to +6, from a taker to a giver, *from a consumer to a generator of resources*:

"Let he who steals" (obviously a negative action) puts the *taker* at -1.

"Steal no longer" neutralizes the negative but does not replace it with a positive, so it moves him to 0.

"But rather let him labor"—the subject, no longer idle, steps up to +1.

"Performing with his own hands" refers to a tool, such as a trade that is always available. He has graduated to +2.

"That which is good"—he is now profitable; we score him at +3.

"In order that he may have something" (surplus)—he now reaches +4.

"To share" gets him to +5 because it reflects selflessness.

"With those in need" is a +6 since it shows a charitable attitude. He has become a *giver*.

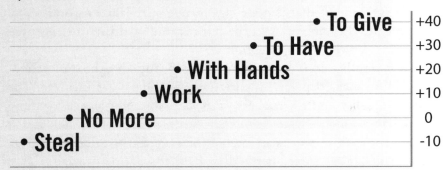

Minus to Plus
Eph. 4:28

• To Give	+40
• To Have	+30
• With Hands	+20
• Work	+10
• No More	0
• Steal	-10

Law enforcement and the justice system can move a criminal from -1 to 0 by apprehending and locking him up for good, but it cannot instill in him a desire to work or learn a trade, much less give him the attitude required to succeed in such a way that when he becomes self-supported, instead of turning ingrown, he develops a charitable lifestyle toward less fortunate folks that cannot pay him back. Only the power of God can do that.

From Drug Dealer to Entrepreneur

Vince is a fine example of a thief turned benefactor. About two years ago he was a drug dealer operating in the sinister alleys of Chinatown in Honolulu, Hawaii. But by December 2006 he owned a restaurant that was featured on the front page of the *Star Bulletin* (one of Hawaii's leading newspapers) because of the uniqueness of his business. He employs recovering drug addicts who he plans to set up with their own businesses.

Married and the father of three children, Vince chose not to live at home, in order to shield his family from his dishonest business in the drug trade. He went home sporadically to shower. One day he decided to significantly expand his operations. He pooled all his resources and borrowed as much as he could to secure a very large parcel of drugs, which he intended to sell at a significant profit. But on a parallel track, he orchestrated a heist to take place at the time of the delivery so that he would end up with both the drugs and enough cash to move into the big leagues as a drug kingpin.

 Consider for a moment that most drug dealers are superb entrepreneurs who have gone morally wrong. They read the market very well. They know how and when to extend credit, when to activate an efficient (albeit cruel) collecting mechanism, how to leverage profits, and how to take risks. None of that is done legally, but in the shifty world where they operate they are kings of the hill because of this entrepreneurial dimension. Vince was no exception.

He carefully selected the time and the location for the transaction, and communicated precise instructions to the parties involved. The buyer, the seller and the robbers, *his robbers,* were in place. Everything was moving along well *until his wife happened to drive by and see him*! It just so happens that his wife is an intercessor who hears from God, and on that particular day He led her to drive by that section of town.

She pulled over and begged Vince to go home. He refused, but she adamantly insisted. An argument ensued and voices were raised. The last thing Vince wanted was a public scene that would attract the police or cause the deal to go sour—or worse. To calm his wife, he informed the various parties that the deal was postponed. Then he rode home with her, where for the next four hours they did nothing but quarrel.

She pleaded with him to mend his ways, but he refused time and again. In desperation she turned to God and began to wail, beseeching Him in the most passionate way to make Vince quit his life of crime. Vince was deeply touched by her commitment to him and by the fervency of her intercession. Even though he did not believe in God (or at least a personal God), he felt totally unworthy of such devotion. To escape a situation he did not know how to handle, he decided to take a shower.

Once under the water, and in a moment of utter despair, he cried out to God, "If You exist, I ask You to change me or to kill me, but nothing in between. I want to be different or I want to die."

The next morning, he suddenly realized that his "ice" pipe, still loaded with drugs, was where he had placed it before going into the shower. This was extremely unusual because the first thing he did every morning was to smoke it to be able to open his eyes. But now the pipe lay untouched and he felt different. The urge to get high on drugs was no longer there!

It was at that moment that he realized that God had changed him, delivering him supernaturally from drug addiction. He decided to look for a job to provide for his family in an honorable way. That was the easy part. He went through countless applications and interviews and was turned down by them all, primarily because of his record as a drug addict and his police rap sheet as a dealer. In desperation he again cried out to God for direction, and God told him to start a restaurant. Vince argued with God, telling Him that he didn't even know how to cook, but God insisted. "Do it," He said.

Vince had neither the capital nor the means to secure any. But God led him to a Christian brother who, unbeknownst to Vince, was a lending official; this man gave Vince a loan for which he signed as guarantor.

Vince had never run a restaurant, but his entrepreneurial side, plus the newly found power of prayer, came to the rescue. God showed him what to do and when to do it, and the restaurant was opened. Soon thereafter, a local newspaper picked up his story, reporting that it was not easy to find a free table at his place. Vince, who used to steal (and worse), steals no more but works with his hands doing something good in order to provide for his family and to help others.

Not everybody begins at the –1 level (since most people are not thieves), but the majority of those enslaved by systemic poverty never reach +4 (to be able to make enough money to have a surplus). Basically they are permanently trapped in survival mode and are bound to remain there *unless poverty is eradicated from their minds and hearts first.*

Vince overcame the four dimensions of poverty: spiritual, intellectual, relational and material. He has faith in God. He acquired knowledge that is marketable. He is rich in relationships, and he has bread to share with others. And he is not short on hope and vision either. He said to me, "My goal is to start as many as 100 businesses to see people and downtown Honolulu transformed." He is a classic example *in process* of how the poor can become the solution to poverty.

From Kitchen to the Chamber of Commerce

Another powerful source of untapped solutions are housewives, especially in cultures where it is the social norm that the day-to-day wellbeing of the family is relegated to them, often with the added burden of inadequate or zero income from their husbands. This cycle of limitation can be broken.

Jennifer Mwesigyee was neither a criminal nor unemployed. A housewife in a village in Uganda, she worked at home as a seamstress to supplement her husband's income, but ends never seemed to meet, placing her at the +2 (working with her hands) level on the scale where Vince rated a –1. Then Jennifer was given a loan of $171 through Opportunity International, the premier Christian micro-lending institution, that enabled her to buy a sewing machine, which dramatically increased her efficiency by allowing her to do more and do it better and faster. Soon she was able to hire others, and she began to make her mark in the wedding-dress market.

Poor people are not the problem; systemic poverty is!

With her confidence strengthened, she then identified a need for affordable and reliable transportation in her community. Beginning with one motorcycle and one driver, she progressively built a fleet of vehicles and, in so doing, created much-needed jobs to support other families. Since then, she has invested in rental property, purchased real estate, and entered into farming with a fine herd of 50 cows!

According to Opportunity International, "Jennifer's journey from seamstress to land owner to farmer to community leader shows . . . the power of poor entrepreneurs when given the tools for their own transformation. But the passion for Jennifer and so many others arises from a central core—the desire to provide for their families. And that passion goes beyond Jennifer's husband William and their seven children. It extends to the four

AIDS orphans she has taken into her home and, of course, to the families of her employees. In all, Jennifer's businesses support 57 people."

Like so many honest hard-working people enslaved by *a system of poverty*, Jennifer was stuck at +2 just working. However, the empowerment that the loan gave her enabled her to purchase the sewing machine that increased her effectiveness (+3), yielded greater profitability (+4), and gave her the ability to share (+5) with those who were indigent (+6). She moved from needy recipient to generous giver—all from a seed capital of just $171! She has become the solution not only to her own poverty but also to many others'.

I repeat, poor people are *not* the problem; systemic poverty is!

The Systems of this World

Social experts tell us that one billion people in the world live on a dollar a day or less. The next two billion live on slightly more than a dollar. This means that half *the world's population* survives on less than two dollars a day. The bad news is how little money people make. The good news is how easy it would be to increase their lot since the bar is so low.

If we define poverty as lack of resources that are essential to survival, then we can safely conclude that there are no poor nations in the world today. The reason is very simple: A poor nation would not be around for long, because it would be doomed to vanish peremptorily, like a patient on life support at a hospital where the electricity is cut off. What we have today are nations with a *system of poverty*. They have enough food (or the potential to have it) but the management and distribution of resources, including infrastructure, is not designed for the common good but for the benefit of a few at the expense of many.

Would you take just a moment to reread the previous paragraph, slowly this time, and let the meaning seep in deeply? It is the foundation and the anchor point for some challenging comments I am going to make later on.

We need to understand that, generally speaking, capitalism in and of itself *has no intrinsic social conscience*. I am not saying that capitalists cannot have a social conscience, because many of them do. I say that *capitalism* doesn't, because while it provides the structure and the means for creative entrepreneurs to generate wealth and get ahead, it does not have as a core value the priority *to rid society of its social evils by actively improving the lot of the disadvantaged through the intentional elimination of systemic evils.* When it does, it happens indirectly, as a sort of trickle-down effect. To the degree that the ones on top benefit, those below will get *some of it,* but capitalism, by definition, is meant to benefit *primarily* the capitalist.

Capitalism Pluses and Minuses

One of the reasons President Theodore Roosevelt's image appears on South Dakota's famed Mount Rushmore (a tribute to his character and presidency) is because he stood for "the little guy" when he took on the greedy marketplace barons of the nineteenth century. If left unchecked, these capitalists-gone-amuck would have perverted the fiber of America by socially enslaving the masses of newly arrived immigrants through exploitation, rendering them or their children extremely vulnerable to the Marxist hurricanes that ravaged the world in the first half of the twentieth century.

When Communism, that evil and flawed system that pretended to have a social conscience, was at its apex, capitalism had to work harder in the social conscience department in order to counter Marxism's worldwide appeal to the dispossessed masses. Those expressions of social conscience manifested themselves on the one hand as investments into the community at large in the form of hospitals and schools. On the other hand, it provided certain services for the workforce, such as preferential loans, affordable housing, and medical care for employees of corporations. The catch was that most of these benefits were available *only as long as people continued to work for the corporation,* or only if those acts of philanthropy improved its public image.

However, this did not come naturally to capitalism, evidenced by the emergence of labor unions that brought on an onslaught of fierce battles fought with management to secure *basic* pay and services that otherwise would have been hard, if not impossible, to come by.

However, once Communism was weakened (after the Soviet demise in 1989) and no longer served as a counterbalance in much of the world, capitalism in the Third World became more unguarded in its drive for profits at the expense of the welfare of the workers, the community at large and even entire nations. Like gangsters who filch cars to disassemble and sell their parts, some powerful multinationals would often acquire traditional industries in undeveloped nations and, under the guise of improving operations, break them up, sell or keep the most profitable divisions and shut down the others. Without care (much less *foresight*!) they contentedly pawn every removable part, and then leave behind the rusting cannibalized and too-bulky-to-move frame.

Capitalism and Biblical Values

Personally, I agree with many Christian thinkers, such as Ken Eldred, who believe that "like no other economic system in the history of mankind, capitalism is producing needed goods and services and improving the world's standard of living"[2]

Eldred goes on to assert, "Capitalism rests on the biblical principle of personal freedom and responsibility. Man is free to use his gifts in the manner in which he chooses; he is free to pursue the vocation to which God leads him. Capitalism also fulfills more effectively the mandate God issued in the Garden of Eden 'to work it and take care of it' (Gen. 2:15)."[3]

However, when capitalism becomes devoid of its biblical moorings, it can turn destructive. Eldred explains, "A nation's business practices can be characterized by three possible moral attitudes: immorality, amorality, or morality."[4] Immoral business practices are those that blatantly operate against that which is part of a body of universally accepted moral principles. The most fragrant perversions will be drug cartels, prison labor, the commercial exploitation of children as sex slaves, and the sale of human organs. But even when those immoral business practices proliferate, they do not pose a major *immediate* threat because their raw moral deformity makes them generally repulsive.

However, the danger looms in the area of *amorality* in business. Eldred again enlightens us: "Amorality is an attitude often found in Modern Western business. Its mantra may be summed up as follows: maximize profits. Amoral business remains unconcerned with moral principles. The question is not 'right or wrong' but 'legal or illegal.' The rule of law takes the place of morality."[5]

Eldred goes on to observe, "In many respects, the United States is adopting a standard of amorality." In other words, capitalism, without the moral backbone provided by the Judeo-Christian culture—from where it drew its ethical compass—ends up abdicating its social responsibility as well as the biblical mandate to "take care" of the world (see

Gen. 2:15). Under those circumstances, what it does is legal, but it misses the higher moral standard. It will be successful but not relevant.

This uncaring and alarmingly fast-growing expression of capitalism—free from any pretense of social conscience since the demise of Communism—and with a mantra of "maximum return on investment" is having devastating and very dangerous effects, especially in Latin America, by creating and feeding massive resentment against anything Western in general and against capitalism in particular. As a result of the groundswell of social rage today (2007), leftist leaders have been *democratically* elected to head the *majority* of Central and South American nations.

They are—in varying degrees—against the United States, and these leaders, even though popularly elected, embody a muscular style of political and economic leadership, which represents a dangerous departure from the safety of checks and balances that are an intrinsic component in true democracies. This is a very unfortunate development in light of the *unprecedented* progress that democracy made in the region during President Reagan's terms in office. When Reagan assumed the presidency, only a handful of Latin American countries had democratically elected governments. By the time he left the White House eight years later, the vast majority of nations was led by progressive, free-market, democratic leaders, and capitalism was welcomed and practiced in the region.

Latin America Turning Left
Unfortunately, today a growing number of Latin leaders are overly anti-Western, the standard bearer being Hugo Chávez, the volatile president of Venezuela, who has become a thorn in the side of Western interests. He is erratic, explosive, rude and blunt, but unfortunately he has also become the strident expression of an underlying issue that is the rallying point of most nations in the region. The issue is encapsulated in their perception that in Latin America, every nation but Cuba has tried unhindered capitalism for the last two-and-a-half decades, only to end up poorer than when Communism was around.

Chávez is not my hero, nor is he or his brand of state-funded socialism the solution to this dangerous dilemma. But bear with me as I engage his position on this issue, because it shocks us into understanding that heretofore no known political system, including both Communism and capitalism, is capable of resolving the challenge of systemic poverty, especially if capitalism operates in an amoral context that could suddenly turn immoral for lack of the moral ballast provided by Judeo-Christian ethics.

Chávez errs in describing the current state of affairs as "made in the USA." The truth is, it is a sin issue of global proportions whose roots go back to the dawn of human history; but its trunk can be found in the worldwide colonization scheme of European empires.

The Empires' Dark and Bright Sides

On the positive side, European empires brought significant and much-needed progress in health care, literacy, and economic infrastructure. In the case of England, as documented by Winston Churchill in his landmark four-volume work, *History of the English Speaking Peoples*, it introduced to its colonies, and to non-colonies by social reflex, a love of liberty and the rule of law, making possible the emergence and establishment of democracy in nations and even continents that neither culturally nor historically had the potential or the opportunity for it if left on their own. Most important, in my opinion, it became the channel for the most extraordinary missionary movement ever that brought salvation to hundreds of millions of people and inserted Christian values in traditionally pagan nations.

But on the dark side, and by deliberate design, the empires co-opted, colonized and created nations, allowing them to be, or to become large enough to survive, but they kept them sufficiently weak so as not to be able to compete against them, making it "necessarily advantageous" for the colonies to enter into a lopsided commercial contract with their masters.

Central to this scheme was the design and development of *modern* (as in *Western*) local infrastructures to "facilitate" (the intention being to "obligate") the colonies to export their materials to the European continent to be manufactured *and then to subsequently sell back to the colonies the surplus* at prices advantageous to the empires' merchants. This, in turn, created a class of *European*-minded *native* administrators, who by social gravity moved into positions of national leadership but whose interests were in the empire, not in the colony, thus adding the harvesting of minds to that of the land.

The American Revolution represented an astounding rebuttal to this scheme. After securing independence from England, the Founding Fathers fought for and achieved an ideal balance between autonomy for the individual states on the domestic arena and a corporate front in international affairs, making the new nation strong enough to resist and overcome repeated attempts by the British to keep her commercially subjugated to its well-established control of the markets as well as the shipping channels.

But the rest of the world did not fare so well. Even today, the ex-members of the British Commonwealth are mostly pitifully poor. They did not become poor because they left the empire. *They were already poor when they became independent*, and became poorer afterward, because the intention all along was to develop them as suppliers, not competitors.[6] Consequently, they were never given the means or the training, much less the encouragement, to become self-reliant. When they finally broke away after the political and economic exhaustion that overtook the empires following World War II, they were unable to succeed because their economic infrastructure had been corrupted by *a system of poverty*. Political independence was not a guarantee of national stability without economic freedom, nor was it a means to obtain it.

Africa: Two Case Studies

Though still a work in progress, South Africa's continuing transition from brutal apartheid to democratic government run by the black majority seems to be making progress, because during the international isolation leading up to that dramatic transition, South Africa was forced to hone and improve its *internal* economic strength. When the black leaders were democratically voted into office, they, unlike their peers in other colonies in Africa, got more than just political freedom; they also gained access to economic viability, or at least to a system designed for and capable of self-reliance. Sustainability, not to mention additional progress, depends on the new South African leaders' embrace of Judeo-Christian values and ethics, instead of the existing drift toward amorality and the emerging push toward blatant immorality, as evidenced by the recent legalization of homosexual marriage.

Uganda: The Heart of Africa
Uganda is a nation that is courageously struggling, and making progress, against the remnants of colonialism. Two stories reveal how potential for change can be activated when people with faith decide to wrestle to the

ground the system of poverty enslaving a nation or, as in this case, its prime natural resources.

Andrew Rugasira was born into a wealthy entrepreneurial family in Uganda. Educated in London with degrees in law and economics, he decided to return home instead of living comfortably in the U.K. With abrupt changes taking place in the school chalk business in which his father had succeeded, Andrew looked to new investments in Uganda's Rwenzori Mountains, where he spent two full years studying the plight of the coffee farmers.

Uganda is a rich coffee-growing nation, but Ugandans do not own a single processing plant. Rather, international brokers buy raw coffee beans from middle men and ship the beans overseas for processing, only to send it back to Uganda as finished product at premium prices with the profit going to the international concerns. Economists term this process "extraction."

The local middle men made small cash advances to each farmer, which the farmers quickly consumed. As a result, the farmers became obligated to sell their crops at a price that did not allow for the farmers to get past the survival level.

Andrew decided to change all that.

Trekking the length and width of the rich coffee-growing region in western Uganda, he organized over 14,000 farmers into 280 co-ops and guaranteed them the best price for their product. Instead of shipping the coffee bean overseas, Andrew set up the processing system to clean, roast, grind and package the coffee in Uganda, creating more jobs for less cost and returning 50 percent of the profit to the farmers in the form of grants for projects that the local co-ops could choose. As the co-ops generate sustaining income, the grants make available start-up capital for interventions in healthcare, education and community development.

Most businesses have only one bottom line: the shareholders. Andrew's has four: the farmers, the communities in which the farmers live, Andrew's employees, and the shareholders of Andrew's business. His employees get 10 percent of the company profits in addition to their salaries. This means that the shareholders (in this case, Andrew's family) get to keep only 40 percent since the farmers and their communities are slated to receive 50 percent through community grants.

Andrew uses a GPS system to track the condition of the coffee fields, in order to help the farmers improve their yields. He also monitors their social evolution through a management information system by which he can tell how many who lived in thatch-roofed huts last year now dwell under sheet-metal roofing, and how many were able to buy their first bicycle or upgrade to a motorcycle. And it is happening!

Andrew is now seeking to resolve another flaw in the system. In the old days, the coffee brokers paid the farmers in cash, which was subsequently and rapidly squandered. One of the most challenging propositions for people who live from hand to mouth one day to the next is the concept of *saving money*. To people who for generations barely subsisted from one crop to the next, the notion of setting money aside is as foreign as rain was to Noah's audience before the Flood. Andrew tried as best as he was able to communicate the idea, but to no avail. Finally, realizing that he was dealing with a mindset that blinded them to the notion of saving, he decided to demonstrate it so that once it became tangible it would be more easily assimilated.

To that end he plans to pay the growers another 10 percent above what he is paying them (which would come out of his 40 percent), but he will deposit the increase in a savings account in their name in their own village bank. Andrew has already developed banks in six areas of the region. A solar-powered ATM system will employ a "smart card" supplied to each farmer onto which the payment for the crop will be loaded. The village banks will then make these funds available as loans to their fellow farmers at a reasonable rate, with a large portion of the net profit going to the investing farmers. By reasonable rate, Andrew quotes 15 percent a year, as opposed to the prevailing rate of 35 percent to 45 percent. By doing this, not only would the farmers benefit, but also many people who presently are being systematically subjugated by such atrocious rates will instead be empowered in the form of affordable loans and in the process will have witnessed a solid example of a fair practices business system.

Andrew's coffee enterprise (named Good African Coffee), while still in its beginning stages, is already an exciting and inspiring example of what can happen.

Not only is progress being made in the private sector, but it is also taking place inside government agencies, in this case the entity in charge of tax collection in Uganda. So often poverty is made worse by the government's inability to provide essential services due to insufficient tax revenue caused by deficiencies or corruption in the collection mechanism (or by both, as was the case here).

Allen Kagina, a committed Christian, joined the Uganda Revenue Authority (URA) in 1992. For 14 straight years, URA was ranked the second-most corrupt institution in the nation, right behind the police. During that time, the agency underwent three major reform programs supported by the International Monetary Fund (IMF) and the central government. The president of Uganda made deliberate efforts to recruit born-again Christians in an effort to increase integrity in the department. Expatriates believed to be skilled and above corruption were brought into management positions; substandard salaries were increased to match those in the private sector; errant staff was dismissed and others were prosecuted. A judicial commission was instituted to investigate and make recommendations on how to rid URA of corruption, and the Board of Directors was changed three times.

None of the changes seemed to make a significant impact. The gap between management and staff remained unbridgeable, and unfair human resources practices went unchecked. As a result, there was no job security, and staff morale was at an all-time low, causing good and skilled employees to leave the organization. Revenue collections took a nosedive. Allen Kagina asked the question that was on the mind of so many: "With so many Christians working in the organization, why is there no impact?"

In the year 2002, things could not have gotten any worse, and Allen contemplated resigning. Fortunately, she sought counsel from the right person, her brother-in-law James Magara, who told her that the only way to bring change to URA was to raise a prayer altar on site and to convene intercessors to pray non-stop until change took place. He trained Allen and a few others on spiritual warfare. Allen and her team raised an altar to the Lord in her office and prayed for two years.

Even though the Lord was working and moving things and people behind the scenes in response to prayer, they did not see evidence of it until they had travailed in prayer for two years. But when the change came, it was like a tsunami. Allen and her team could hardly keep pace with God and what He was doing at URA. God even gave them a foundational Scripture of what was to take place: "Thus Joseph stored up grain in great abundance like the sand of the sea, until he stopped measuring it, for it was beyond measure" (Gen. 41:49).

Through a series of divine interventions, Allen was appointed to the head of URA and was given free hand by the Minister of Finance

and the president to reform the department. With the help of two people and the backing of the prayer team at the altar, she drew up a radical
new structure for the organization that was immediately approved by
the Board. She then had to face what to her was the most difficult thing:
As part of the reform plan, she had to lay off over 2,000 people working
in the national system, including the management staff and the two
persons helping her with the new structure. However, she allowed them
to continue to collect revenue while applying for jobs in the new structure. The process was phased in over six months.

All this time, the prayer team, whose members had also been laid
off, was praying and fasting for each new position in the new structure,
asking God to send angels to protect it against the wrong people. The
spiritual and physical opposition, including attempts to interfere with
the turnaround, were intense—Allen felt very vulnerable and was often
scared. But the presence of God and the prayers were intense. Allen tes-
tifies, "God raised a prayer cover like I had never experienced in my
entire life."

By June 2005 the restructuring was completed in record time and the
new URA was totally transformed, with no resemblance to the old URA.
The first miracle was that during the transitional months, tax revenue shot
up so sharply that the authorities could not find a human explanation for
it. Subsequently, heads of corporations have called on Allen so that they
could repent for unpaid taxes and regularize their fiscal situation. Allen
and her team have received extraordinary favor with the government, the
public, the taxpayers and even the media, which has become their best ally.

The changes delivered a blow to systemic corruption (which is always
the backbone for systemic poverty). To put it in perspective, tax revenue
in Uganda grew from 44 billion Ugandan shillings in 1986, when
President Museveni first came to power, to 2,230 billion Ugandan
shillings in 2005, the first year after the reorganization of the URA. This
monumental increase attests to the fulfillment of the promise Allen
received that "provision would be stored up in great abundance like the
sand of the sea." The fact that Allen, as head of the URA, officially welcomed the presence and the power of God into the agency provided
an entry point for transformation at the highest possible level, which
has now resulted in the establishment of prayer altars in every URA
department and in every region of the nation. As Allen put it, "Prayer
continues to be our foundation."

What took place at the Uganda Revenue Authority is a prime example of how a key governmental department can undergo transformation as part of the discipling of a nation.

Egypt: A Garbage Dump Becomes a Transformational City

However, the point of inception for transformation does not necessarily have to be as high as it was in Uganda. In fact, it can be as low as a garbage dump and still work its way up. A dynamic example of this upward social lift is found in the outskirts of Cairo, Egypt.

Father Samaan is a Coptic priest today, but sometime back when he was an average Christian holding a job in the marketplace, he befriended a Christian garbage collector who kept insisting that he visit the dump. Eventually he did, and God got a hold of him and, through a series of divinely orchestrated steps, led him to become a priest and move to the dump!

When he first visited the place, there were no permanent buildings. Thousands of people literally lived in rudimentary cardboard huts erected inside the garbage piles strewn on the hillside of what is known as "Garbage City." There were no pathways, much less roads. There was no electricity or running water. Diseases wreaked havoc on the inhabitants, primarily the children, who shared sleeping cots *as well as meals* with pigs, dogs and goats. Rats had the run of the place. It was the most hideous desecration of human dignity imaginable!

In February 2007 my wife and I, along with a group of marketplace ministers, visited the now legendary "Garbage City of Moqattam" and witnessed the unbelievable changes. Today, most of the 7,000 garbage collectors profess to being Christian. They still bring Cairo's garbage there, to the tune of 17 tons a day, and the rancid odors and squalling of pigs are part of the environment, but nowadays there is a fine hospital, an excellent school, a recycling center with shops to sell its products, and several churches, called "cave churches," which are carved into the side of the mountain, including one that seats 20,000 people.[7] There is electricity, a sewage system and running water. And the people live in still humble but permanent structures, most of which have a recycling facility on the bottom floor and family quarters on top.

Graham Power, the South African marketplace leader who introduced us to Father Samaan, describes him as "the closest thing to Mother Teresa I know." In fact, Mother Teresa visited Moqattam and held a meeting on the premises. Father Samaan loves his people and is dearly loved by them in return. As he showed us around, they kept coming to him for ministry, and without missing a beat he laid hands on them, spoke comforting words and directed them to the right person or place for additional assistance. With great satisfaction he walked us through the brightly lit and superbly equipped workshops that occupy entire floors in newly erected buildings, where mothers learn how to provide for their children, sewing beautiful dresses for sale. At the school, he introduced us to the kindergarten classes of immaculately dressed children who now have a future, thanks to Father Samaan's obedience. He showed us a fully equipped hospital, where doctors and nurses told us about the pleasure of taking care of so many patients.

How the hospital was built is an example of how God uses bad things to generate something good. In the late 1990s a tourist from Finland hit a child with his car in the vicinity of the dump. In desperation he carried the injured child to Father Samaan's nearby church where he was given assistance, and the child's life was spared. The visitor, impressed by what he saw and noticing that there was no medical facility, offered to raise funds to build one. He was as successful raising funds as Father Samaan and his team were at administering them, so much so that there was plenty of money left to build a five-story school building with space for workshops.

There is plenty of work still to be done in Moqattam, but hope has been injected and is gradually dismantling the system of poverty that once ruled supreme. Little by little, new open areas are displacing old piles of rubbish. In addition, God chose to "create" new space supernaturally when a cave, dating back to the pharaohs, was accidentally discovered. Father Samaan claimed it for the Kingdom and today there are four church facilities in that cave, plus a modern community center. God even provided a sculptor who has carved larger-than-life biblical scenes and Bible verses on the surrounding hillsides. Where once people saw nothing but raw garbage, today biblical representations and inspiring pieces of Scripture liven the landscape and inspire the observer.

All of this is a tribute to the power of prayer. Father Samaan is simply a man of prayer. He spends the bulk of his time asking God for provision and breakthroughs, and God honors that devotion. He has an excellent team around him that is nurturing a new generation pregnant with hope that is literally "sprouting up" from the newly carved streets in Garbage City. They believe that the future will be better than the past because they have seen what God has done and they understand that this is *just the beginning*.

God uses bad things to generate something good.

That these garbage collectors see their work as their ministry, and the transformation of Cairo as their ultimate objective, is the fuel that causes this extraordinary transformation fire to burn white. A process is in motion to bring transformation to Cairo and eventually to Egypt. Not unlike the Rome of Paul's days where the gospel first flourished in the catacombs, Garbage City may well transform the land that opened its arms to Jesus and His parents when murderous King Herod tried to kill Him.

The New Breed

In the past, we have witnessed individuals become freed from poverty after coming to the Lord. Subsequently, we have seen their families improve their social standing as the favor of the Lord found channels to impact its members. In such context, an illiterate person who had just come to Christ would feel the urge and develop the ability to learn how to read and write. His children would attend and most likely graduate from high school, giving his grandchildren a good shot at becoming professionals, something that was unthinkable two generations earlier. This is what has provided the backbone for the strong Church we see in lands where three or four generations ago there was none. The missionaries taught passionately that nothing is impossible with God. People believed it and they changed their personal environment. They left no doubt that God can change people.

Building on that foundation, a new breed of *marketplace missionaries* is emerging: men and women who dare believe that the same salvation that transforms the soul can also change society, beginning with their sphere of influence. This is why the paradigms described in this book are pivotal. They provide focus and sustainable momentum. The Bible is clear that poverty is not part of God's kingdom, and that His glory will fill the earth, nation after nation. Jesus came to redeem us from the curse of the system of poverty that resulted from the Fall in the Garden. The example of the Early Church is diaphanous. What has begun to happen in places like Uganda and Egypt gives us solid reasons to believe that it can happen at regional and at national levels.

We still don't know *precisely* how to get there, but we surely understand the directions in which we need to go and we are biblically persuaded that we shall overcome (see Rev. 21:24–22:5). Men and women who have already attained success and are now searching for significance are leading this new army of marketplace transformers. Very close behind them, listening to every conversation and watching their actions, there is a younger generation. They don't have the baggage of the old. They are forward looking. To them, the new is the norm.

Anytime now God will pour out His Spirit upon all flesh. For that to happen, it will have to take place in the marketplace, where the masses dwell, live, work and strive. When it does, our sons and daughters will prophesy. They will stand in the river of God's revival declaring and welcoming the new order. On that day young and old will join hands; the old with their dreams of the past will be energized by the visions of the young. I will sketch my perception of how this will play out in the next chapter. I believe and am fully persuaded that the outcome will be awesome, majestic, splendid, and the whole earth will be filled with the glory of God as His Spirit is poured upon *every flesh* so that everyone who calls on the name of the Lord shall be saved (see Acts 2: 16-21).

CHAPTER 14

Integration

An automobile has five critical components: a frame, an engine, a transmission, a steering mechanism and wheels. Other parts can be mentioned, but these five are the foundational ones. Properly connected, they provide you with mobility; in fact, self-mobility, since this is what the word "automobile" means. It may or may not be a particularly attractive automobile, but it will take you places!

However, if you take the automobile apart, leaving the frame in the street, the engine and the transmission in the driveway, and the wheels and the steering mechanism in the backyard, even though the components are nearby, because they are no longer connected, you will not be going anywhere in it.

God has ordained that we, His Church, be His instruments to transform the entire *world*: to disciple, teach and baptize *nations*. That is a daunting, incomprehensible task unless we understand that God has placed in each of us, and in the world we inhabit, connection points that when properly linked will provide the vehicle for transformation to take place. These points are like the rails of a railroad track that, once laid down, huge trains can run upon. But without these tracks, the trains remain immobile no matter how powerful their engines are.

In the transformation process, there are five critical *connection points*:

1. You
2. The Church
3. The kingdom of God
4. The marketplace
5. The city

When these five components are linked as concentric circles, the divine DNA resident in each one is activated and God's transformation begins to flow like a terraced pond, from a source pond at the top, down to ever-widening pools. The connection and interdependence between these components is the key to achieving and sustaining transformation.

It is in seeing them as connected where we usually miss the mark. For example, when we ask someone, "Who are you?" their reply is, "I am so and so."

"Where do you go to church?"

"To such and such."

"When will the kingdom of God come to Earth?"

"When the New Jerusalem descends from heaven."

"And what about the kingdom of God coming to your city?"

"I am not concerned about that since I am awaiting new heavens and a new earth."

Though simplistic, this hypothetical conversation sadly reflects a widespread and unhealthy attitude in many believers, which causes them to miss out on the greatest journey of life because *they have no "vehicle."* It is the *integration of the critical parts* that triggers transformation. We are members of the Church at all times—not just on Sundays, but 24/7—and have been entrusted with spiritual authority to take the kingdom of God to the marketplace in order for cities to be transformed.

To find out how this works let us take a closer look at each one of these five key components.

You

Who are you? Understanding our identity—how and why God made us—is critical for the transformation process to begin. According to Ephesians 2:10, you are "His workmanship, created in Christ Jesus for good works, which God prepared beforehand so that we would walk in them." This verse provides one of the best summaries of your identity: You are God's handiwork, something that is true of every person on Earth. But as a Christian, you have also been placed *in* Christ Jesus, granting you access to His power; and you have been set apart to carry out a plan with divinely orchestrated good works.

These good works are defined by the two greatest commandments: to love God with all our heart, and to love our neighbor as ourselves. We believers generally do a decent job loving God, but we fall short when it comes to loving our neighbors. The reason for this, in most cases, is that we do not love ourselves the way we should and we can only love others to the degree that we love ourselves. This anomaly occurs because we do not understand or appreciate the fact that God made us the way we are—and He does *not* create junk. Unless we understand and accept that we are *His* workmanship, we will never have the confidence needed that allows us to extend unselfish love to another.

I often encourage people to do something a bit peculiar when they get up in the morning. I suggest that they write on the mirror in the bathroom the words, "I am wonderfully made" (see Ps. 139:14), and to recite them every day until they become a conviction. Of course, we are all "a work in progress." That is why we should stand in front of that mirror every day—hoping to improve a bit on the outward appearance of what God created so that we can turn our present condition into a constructive process by first acknowledging what God has already done for us. In that way, we can move on to the next level.

Connecting Her Cubicle to the Kingdom

Jessica Austin is a single, self-supporting Christian woman who has always been grateful for God's provision in her life, but some time ago she grew dissatisfied with her "secular" work at a well-known manufacturing company in Tennessee.

In early 2000, she attended a weekend seminar, led by Tod Bell, called New Vision for the Marketplace.[1] What she heard there swept over her like a fresh breath from God. Tod kept using the phrase, "Your job is not your *problem* but your *platform* for the kingdom of God." It was an eye-opening and life-changing experience that made Jessica aware of how much good she can do for those in her sphere of influence. From that point on, God opened her eyes to His call to love and to minister to others *in the workplace*. She voraciously read literature on what God was doing in that area, including Rick Heeren's book *Thank God It's Monday* and my book *Anointed for Business*.

As her new perspective became enriched, so did her prayer time. She added the needs of others and the company to her intercessory times, rather than just asking God to do things for her. For the next two years, every Thursday she prayed on the phone with a friend at 6:00 A.M. She also turned her sphere of influence, which was a cubicle in a large room of workstations, over to Jesus Christ. It wasn't much, but it was the thing she had direct authority over, and she made it an outpost of His kingdom and a point of intercession for others to pray for those around her. To her surprise and satisfaction, in a short amount of time her coworkers took the initiative to suggest forming

groups to pray about everything from sick people and troubled families to broken equipment.

For several years the company had been losing money and management often spoke of "giving it one more year" to turn things around.
It was a dismal time, but Jessica and the others took on the burden of
the corporation and began to intercede with intensity and faith. When
business hit a new low, she went to the vice president to inquire if she
could pray for a recovery miracle. He said, "I believe in the power of
prayer. So I am open to whatever works." Jessica organized three teams
to prayer-walk the company grounds.

We can turn our present condition into a constructive process by first acknowledging what God has already done for us.

By that time she and a coworker decided to ask a group of men
from the machine shop if they would join them during their lunchtime
Bible study. Jessica began to share about *Who* the real owner of the company was and to cast the vision for transformation.

The group found itself discussing how to welcome and enthrone
Jesus as the Sovereign Lord over the corporation. Finally, one summer
day at lunch, with everyone in agreement, three members of the group
were shown by the caretaker how to get to the rooftop. While the rest
remained in prayer below, they took anointing oil, poured it on the
rooftop, claimed the 100-year-old company for the Lord and invited
Jesus in. It was an overcast day, but right after they prayed, the sun broke
through the clouds as though it was a visual confirmation that their
prayers had been heard! Jessica felt that *the Son* was shining on them.

From that moment on, amazing things began to happen very quickly:
The men's machine shop gathering grew so much that it had to move to
a larger room. A coworker who had worked in the plant for 18 years was
saved on a Friday and on the following Monday started a lunchtime
Bible study. Jessica met with her, and almost overnight God's vision for
the company was downloaded to Debbie. She became like a piece of dry

wood ignited with passion to pray for the company, moving boldly among the workers in the plant, urging them to believe and to intercede. Soon "prayer points" (the equivalent of a "canopy of prayer") were organized over the company, each point consisting of two to three people who would pray during breaks.

Today, the company has fully recovered financially and has more business than it can handle. After three years of no salary raises, every worker received generous bonuses and pay increases, and the company has experienced its best revenues in the corporation's history.

Jessica's testimony shows that it is not necessary to own a business in order to become a vehicle for its transformation. The turning point was when Jessica, who already loved God, began to focus on loving her coworkers and the management in ways that met *their* felt needs. When she did, the journey of good works promised in Ephesians 2:10 got underway. Even though it began small—two years of brief early prayer with one coworker every Thursday—it eventually expanded to encompass the whole corporation. There is no doubt in the minds of those with whom Jessica works that she loves God and her neighbors, and there is even less doubt that He heard and answered their prayers!

When you and I stand before the Judgment Seat of Christ for that final examination, everything will revolve around two themes: (1) Love God, and (2) Love your neighbor. Consequently, we would be wise to plan the rest of our lives around these two commands. They are the road map for a journey that leads us to discipling nations, beginning with our own sphere of influence, just as Jessica did.

God will be pleased, many will get saved, and we will grow in our understanding of how wonderfully made we are!

The Church

Jesus was strolling with His disciples through the countryside of Caesarea Philippi when He engaged them in a conversation about who the people were saying He was (see Matt. 16:13). The answers were multiple, but Peter went to the head of the class when he responded, "You are the Christ, the Son of the Living God" (v. 16). Jesus commended him for getting his revelation from the right place (the Father) and proceeded to give him the next piece of the revelation. He said, "I will build My church; and the gates of Hades shall not prevail against it" (Matt. 16:17-18, *ASV*).

When Jesus first spoke of the church, He did not coin a new word but instead borrowed a Greek one that described a well-known institution of the time. The word was *ecclesia*.

Today we attach religious significance to the term, but in Jesus' day, ecclesia was simply a secular forum, a gathering or assembly of people entrusted by the emperor with authority to apply his decrees. For instance, in Acts 19:41, when the proconsul dismissed the *assembly*, the word "assembly" is the same word that everywhere else in the New Testament is translated as "church." *Ecclesia* literally means "the gathering," but one with a purpose and a corresponding binding authority to fulfill it.

From this we can deduce three key characteristics of what the church is meant to be and to do. First, it consists of *people*, not buildings. Second, it is *entrusted with authority to implement God's will*. Third, it is *meant to be on the offensive*, not the defensive, since Jesus stated that the gates of Hades would not prevail against it, and gates have never attacked anyone. On the contrary, in war, enemy gates are to be stormed.

The Issue of Quorum

Since the church is an assembly entrusted with authority, a quorum is required. Quorum is the minimum number of persons needed for decisions to be binding. For our Board meetings at Harvest Evangelism, for example, the quorum is four people. If only three directors are present, no binding decisions can be made, but if four or more are participating, any resolution becomes binding. Even though the difference between three and four is only one person, the issue is whether or not we have a quorum. The decisions made when the four are present are just as binding as when all seven directors were present.

Jesus established a relatively low quorum for the church: two or three. He said that if that many are gathered in His name, He would be there, assuring us of His ruling presence and affirming that the decisions made would be binding. If two or three meet, they get the same Jesus and the same authority. If two or three thousand meet, they get . . . the same! If two or three hundred thousand congregate . . . they get the same. The point is that we can never improve on what we get with two or three, because it's not how many of *us* are in one place, but whether *Jesus* is present: "Again I say to you, that if two of you agree on earth about *anything* that they may ask, it shall be done for them by My Father who is in heaven. For where two or three have gathered together in My name, I am there in their midst" (Matt. 18:19-20, emphasis added).

This low quorum requirement empowers the church to operate easily, fluidly and spontaneously because wherever that many believers connect for a purpose, whether in a home, on a street corner, between classes at school, or during a coffee break, Jesus has promised to be there, and they can conduct Kingdom business with authority. In fact, *they can have church in the marketplace!* This is precisely what took place in the marketplace gatherings described in Acts 2:42-47—they discussed the doctrine of the apostles, broke bread (had a meal together), fellowshipped, and prayed. These types of church (ecclesia) meetings were the *norm* in the book of Acts.

Doing Church in the Marketplace

Can you imagine the positive impact on the quality of life in the marketplace if believers turned every lunch break into an opportunity to establish Jesus' presence and exercise His authority in their spheres of influence? It would be like a spiritual air, land and sea invasion, only much simpler to mobilize because we are not talking about deployment and all the myriad of logistical detail involved. No, the "troops" have already been deployed and are in position. We are talking here about *activation.* The *ecclesia* is already in the marketplace 24/7. All it needs to do is turn the switch to the ON position during the week.

On a recent ministry trip to South Africa, we had the joy of taking two days out of a very hectic, cross-continent schedule to enjoy a wild game park. From the very first meal, we thanked the Lord for those who were serving us our food. With every meal, their off-color jokes and conversations began to diminish. For many, the great pain and deep hurts they were feeling began to fall away and be replaced by an atmosphere of love and trust.

On the last day, we let it be known that we would like to pray for the waiters and waitresses. One of them "escaped" to go tell all the cooks, housemaids and tour guides that prayer was happening on the dining porch, and soon we were having church right there in the lodge. As we ministered, the presence of the Lord filled the whole place. Tears began to flow from many of them as the Lord ministered healing, hope and restoration. As we left, they formed an impromptu choir and began to sing songs of praise from their hearts. What had started out heading toward being a carnival appealing to flesh had turned into a festival of praise in the Spirit—church happened in a non-church setting.

In Hong Kong, I once used a dinner occasion to demonstrate how to have church in a restaurant. We invited Jesus to sit at the head of the table and enjoyed His presence as we partook of excellent Chinese food. As different subjects came up, we would turn to Jesus for guidance as needed. It was a sublime moment! Suddenly I received a frantic call from one of our associates who was at the airport, informing me that he had lost the bag containing his documents, money and airplane ticket. He was stranded in an unfamiliar place with no means to get out.

I told him not to worry because we were having dinner with Jesus; I was confident that He would remedy the situation. "Stay put," I said, "while we ask Jesus to look into the matter." We did so and continued to enjoy the succulent Peking duck on our plates.

A few minutes later we received a second call from our associate, but now he was exuding excitement. A bus driver found his bag and, seeing the airplane ticket in it, drove back to the airport and looked for him at the airline counter where he was stranded. Not a penny was missing! And key to this outcome was that we had church around the dinner table in a restaurant.

Churches vs. Congregations

The term "local church" never appears in the Bible, nor does the term "parachurch." Those are man-made phrases that often (and sadly) have created some kind of class distinction within the Body of Christ. "Church" in the Bible is rather presented as a divinely orchestrated movement of people in a region responding to the stimulus of the Holy Spirit and the direction of the Son. The focus is always on what the church *does*, versus what it is.

What we today call *local churches* in reality are *local congregations* that make up "the" one church in the city. In biblical times as it is today, many of those congregations were different from each other culturally, in degrees of spirituality, and even in doctrine. God in His infinite wisdom allowed for these myriad of *local* expressions. But He also made it crystal clear that there is only one Church in the city or region. So much so that when Jesus, the head of the Church, dictated His letters to John in the book of Revelation, He addressed them to "the" (singular) church in Ephesus, Pergamum, Thyatira, Sardis, etc. Likewise, the elders we read about in the Bible were citywide elders, not just overseers of a local group.

The church has been defined by writer A. T. Robertson as "the unassembled assembly."[2] That's a great definition. It speaks of order, coordination and fluidity. It alludes to it having legislative power or authority. And being unassembled, it can operate in dozens or hundreds of places about the city in a coordinated way under the direction of the Holy Spirit. That is consistent with Jesus' statement that any time two people, or more, gather in His name, *they constitute a genuine expression of the Church.* The authority, the anointing, the gifts, the fruit of the Spirit, the doctrine of the apostles, all that and much more is available to them and ready to go into operation *because the ecclesia is in session.*

Whether it is a gathering of the board of directors of a Christian school, a soup kitchen run by the Rescue Mission, a retreat for evangelists, a coffee break in the marketplace, a Bible study on campus, a mass crusade, or a staff meeting at a local congregation, they all qualify as meetings of the *church* according to Jesus' definition of *ecclesia.*

When the Church finally gets a handle on operating 24/7 all over the place, its priorities will become clear. Leaders from both the marketplace and the pulpit, praying and planning together, *will be the norm,* not the exception. Pouring resources into joint projects will be standard procedure. And the axiom, "It will take the *whole* church to present the *whole* gospel to the *whole* world" will *just happen.* Let the Church arise!

The Kingdom of God

Despite the obvious importance of the church, Jesus did not spend a great deal of time teaching about it. In fact, He touched on the subject only twice, in Matthew 16 and 18, using the word "church" a total of only three times in the four Gospels. And when He did, He said, "It is *my* church and *I* will build it." The implication seems to be, *Please, get off the property, but on the way out pick up the keys to the Kingdom* and go look for the gates of Hades.

Even though Jesus did not talk much about His church, the subject of the kingdom of God was ever present in His teaching, which He either mentioned himself or was used in connection with Him a total of 69 times. On the two occasions when He discussed the *church*, He also spoke of the Kingdom, linking them from the very start: "Upon this rock I will build My church; and the gates of Hades will not overpower it [and] I will give you the keys of the kingdom of heaven" (Matt. 16:18-19). Not only did He link the Church with the Kingdom, but He also connected heaven with Earth, for He continues, "And whatever you bind on earth shall have been bound in heaven, and whatever you loose on earth shall have been loosed in heaven" (Matt. 16:19; 18:18).

This is significant because of the imagery in the context of *keys* and *gates*. Binding and releasing describes the function of a key in a gate and, in fact, could be translated as *"locking* and *unlocking."* Therefore the keys to the Kingdom entrusted to members of the Church are to be used on the gates of Hades. Gates are only as secure as their locks, and if we have the key, they become vulnerable. The believer's mission is to take the kingdom of God to where those gates are (meaning: *demonic entrenchment*) to render them powerless.

Building the Church is what Jesus does; taking His kingdom all over the earth is what He commanded us to do. Why is this still necessary if He died victoriously on the cross and rose majestically from the tomb? Because there is an evil empire still entrenched all over the earth that needs to be dismantled using the keys entrusted to us. Satan and his minions no longer have the authority in the heavenly realm nor the right on Earth, but like stubborn spiritual squatters, they refuse to relinquish their position, and this is why Jesus has deputized His Church (His army) to evict them.

When Jesus stated that whatever we bind or release on Earth *shall be bound in heaven,* He introduced a principle that has perplexed theologians. On first read, it appears that we have been entrusted with the means to take actions on Earth that determine how things are to be done in heaven. There is no qualifier to this word in the context.

Can humans make decisions on Earth that become binding in heaven? Well, that is exactly what the verse says; but such a notion leaves us perplexed. I believe the perplexity is caused by the assumption that the heaven mentioned here is where God has His abode, when in reality it is not what is being referred to. We can safely suppose that there are at least three heavens, since Paul mentions that he was taken up to the third heaven (see 2 Cor. 12:2). Even though the Bible does not elaborate on where those heavens are, the mention of the third heaven as "paradise" in 2 Corinthians 12:2-4 suggests that the third heaven is God's dwelling, the second heaven would then be the place where the principalities and powers operate (including angelic beings on a mission; see Rev. 12:7), and the first heaven would be where human life takes place.

With this as our background, we can now return to Matthew 16:18-19 to zero in on two words: "gates" and "keys." Jesus stated that we are entrusted with the *keys* to the Kingdom and that the *gates* of Hades shall not prevail against His Church, that is, His people. By word association we can deduce that the keys Jesus is talking about are designed to lock (bind) and unlock (release) the gates mentioned in the same passage, that is, the gates of Hades.

■ ■ ■

Building the Church is what Jesus does; taking His kingdom all over the earth is what He commanded us to do.

■ ■ ■

Therefore, if that is the case, then Jesus is teaching that whatever we bind on Earth (the first heaven) will become binding in the second heaven where the gates of Hades are located, since the devil rules the world from a spiritual base, as Paul taught in Ephesians 6:12: "For our struggle is . . . against the rulers, against the powers, against the world forces of this darkness, against the spiritual forces of wickedness in the heavenly places." In such context it is then logical to conclude that we have authority to bind and release things in the heaven *where the devil operates.*

This becomes clearer when we consider it against the backdrop provided by Luke 10:17-20: "The seventy returned with joy, saying, 'Lord, even the demons are subject to us in Your name.' And He said to them, 'I was watching Satan fall from heaven like lightning. Behold, I have given you authority to tread on serpents and scorpions, and over all the power of the enemy, and nothing will injure you. Nevertheless *do not rejoice in this, that the spirits are subject to you, but rejoice that your names are recorded in heaven*'" (emphasis added).

In this passage, the disciples returned amazed by the fact that demons submitted to them, most likely in light of the setbacks suffered by the apostles in their dealings with demons in the previous chapter. Jesus explained that the reason for this breakthrough was that Satan had fallen from heaven. The logical conclusion is that he was no longer in command, leaving his troops in disarray and making surrender or submission their best option. This is the equivalent of sacking the quarterback in American football. When he goes down, the offensive players no longer run their patterns. The players still pose a threat, but they are rendered inoperative for the moment.

Next, Jesus instructed them to take advantage of Satan's fall and tread upon his evil infrastructure (on Earth) until it has been dismantled. But it is the next statement that at first seems like a contradiction. What I am referring to is His admonition *not to rejoice in the ability to exercise power over the devil*, but to instead draw joy from the fact that their names are recorded *in heaven* (see Luke 10:20). Some interpret this as a caution against becoming involved in spiritual warfare. The heart of their message is for you to be glad you are going to heaven because they take "written in heaven" to mean "written in the book of Life." However, Jesus had not died yet for the sins of mankind. Consequently, the book of Life was not able to record any names because Jesus had not yet cancelled the certificate of decrees against us (see Col. 2:14).

So what did Jesus mean then by His statement in Luke 10:20?

Once again, to find help with the interpretation we need to look at the context. Jesus implied that the reason for the demons' surrender was Satan's fall from heaven (see v. 18). And once Satan and his demons are down, Jesus says, "I have given you authority to tread upon serpents and scorpions [an allegorical reference to demons], and over all the power of the enemy, and nothing shall injure you" (v. 19).

It is in this context of active, intentional warfare directed at the devil that Jesus made the statement that causes some to reach the opposite conclusion: "Nevertheless do not rejoice in this, that the spirits are subject to you, but rejoice that your names are recorded in heaven" (v. 20). What does it mean to have our names recorded in heaven? By word association we can find the answer. Satan fell from *heaven*. The disciples went out in Jesus' name, and demons became subject to them because Jesus is a name that the demons surrender to. As a result, the names of the disciples became known in the *heaven* from which Satan fell as having authority, and now Satan and his demons *must submit to them* as they do to Him. The Lord is instructing them to focus on the principle of *authority* instead of on the simple exercise of *power*.

A police officer standing at an intersection is no match for the tons of steel of a vehicle in motion, but he is able to stop a car with just a wave of his arm because he or she possesses the investiture not of greater power but of greater authority.

Likewise, accomplishing something similar to what the 70 did makes our names (identity) known (recorded) to the devil and his demons as people with authority *over them*. A biblical example is the dramatic event that took place in Ephesus where Paul was casting out demons with riveting authority. His success tempted some unbelieving exorcists to emulate him and they "attempted to name (invoke) over those who had the evil spirits the name of the Lord Jesus, saying, 'I adjure you by Jesus whom Paul preaches'" (Acts 19:13). The result could not have been more disastrous: "And the evil spirit answered and said to them, 'I recognize Jesus, and I know about Paul, but who are you?' And the man, in whom was the evil spirit, leaped on them and subdued all [seven] of them and overpowered them, so that they fled out of that house naked and wounded" (Acts 19:15-16). The demons *knew* who had authority over them: Paul did, but his imitators did not.

Therefore, what Jesus taught in Luke 10 is that once we've tread upon and destroyed the power of the devil in a particular region, we become known to him and his demons, forcing them to recognize us as people who have authority over them *everywhere else*.

This is particularly evident in the area where we are most effective spiritually in terms of our gifting or calling. Some people are consistently effective when it comes to faith, city transformation, marketplace miracles, deliverance, or similar operations. However, in order to attain that level of effectiveness, they have had to go through struggles, at times so fierce that defeat looked imminent more than once. But God, time and again, delivered them until they destroyed the devil's stronghold in that particular area. As a result of such decisive victory, the evil one has come to recognize them as superior to them. Their names (that is, their identity) became recorded in the heavens from where they dislodged those evil forces. And when they go to other locations, evil forces in that area know them and have no choice but to submit. This is what Jesus taught in Luke 10 and Matthew 16.

I have found this to be true in our own ministry. As reported in my book *That None Should Perish*, Resistencia, Argentina (pop. 400,000), was the first city reached for Christ in modern times. From the handful of 5,143 believers who were in the evangelical church population in 1988, the number has since grown to over 100,000 in the entire city. The ominous control the devil exercised over the region has been replaced by open heavens, and the Church is impacting the city, the government, the media and the schools.

Key to this transformation has been the work of pulpit and marketplace leaders who mobilized the church to do what the 70 disciples did in Luke 10: They systematically lifted Jesus up all over the city, established hundreds of Lighthouses of prayer, adopted all of the 400,000 inhabitants, prayer-walked every street and visited every home with good news and, better yet, demonstrated the power of God by taking care of the needy and praying for extraordinary miracles, of which they got plenty.

It was our privilege (the Harvest Evangelism team) to be present at ground zero, inspiring, equipping, supporting and partnering with the local leadership in this first of its kind city-transformation thrust.

Unless we move our base of operations to the marketplace, what we do will be nothing more than a spiritual parade, never the amphibious landing needed to decide the outcome of the war.

We were there when demonic powers used to run the city, and we were there when they came crashing down as a result of prayer evangelism. In fact, we facilitated the step-by-step follow-through that eventually turned the city to Christ. As a result, our names, along with those of the local leaders, have been recorded in heaven where evil forces operate, making us known to them as people with spiritual authority. It is not our own authority, but the authority Jesus has delegated to us.

Having learned this, when we come to a city the first thing we do is to praise God and exalt His name and speak peace over the area. But then we say to the principalities and powers, to the rulers (usurpers) over the darkness enveloping that metropolis, "We don't know you, but you know who we are. What happens next can be clean or dirty, easy or mean, quick or slow. It is entirely up to you. You know that we have authority because it is recorded in heaven and one way or the other you are coming down!" This is not bragging; it is merely stating a fact that emanates from a biblical principle enunciated by Jesus Himself in Luke 10 and in accordance with Ephesians 3:20 about "making known to the rulers and authorities the multiform grace of God."

This is what makes the development of transformation *prototypes* key because those who establish them become known in the heavenly places and set in motion a spiritual chain reaction that rapidly expands beyond its original perimeter. The stories in previous chapters of King Flores's leading the reclamation of a motel chain in the Philippines and Ken Beaudry's initial breakthroughs in Ukraine, are prime examples of this. At first it took them a season of intense warfare to get the first victory. But once it was accomplished, an indication of the devil's falling from heaven, they proceeded to systematically tread upon the remaining manifestations of evil power in motels, neighborhoods and prisons. The subsequent explosive growth, leading to the conversion of so many in the Philippines and the planting of so many churches in Ukraine, and beyond, in such an unusually short time, is evidence of demons surrendering to believers they know have authority over them.

This one-two punch combination by the Church and the Kingdom, as two sides of the same coin, must have as its main target the marketplace. Unless we move our base of operations there, what we do indoors will be nothing more than a spiritual parade, never the amphibious landing needed to decide the outcome of the war.

The Marketplace

When it comes to the inception and propagation of ideas, the marketplace is the most fertile environment because it is designed for networking. The moment a breakthrough takes place there, its ripple effects are immediately felt all over. All through the Bible, God's activity has been focused in the marketplace.

The Old Testament records two monumental moves of God that thoroughly transformed secular societies, one in Egypt and the other in

Persia. Both nations constituted the leading world empire of the day. Neither one had a Jewish background nor was the Lord of Israel part of their worldview, religious or otherwise. The detonator in both cases was of revelation entrusted by God to His servants that solved serious problems in the marketplace.

In the case of Egypt, Joseph received insights to overhaul the nation's economy, and the anointing to devise and implement a plan that averted famine and made Egypt the leading power in the region. In Babylon, Daniel's answers to the king's dilemma catapulted him to the number one position in the empire, from where he served three rulers with distinction, administrating the affairs of the state. As a result, two leading world powers, their population and scores of neighboring nations were impacted because God's power was channeled into and demonstrated in the marketplace.

God is focused on the marketplace because it is the heart of the city and the nation, and He is after nations. The list of heroes of the faith provided in Hebrews 11 consists of people who received a call *in the marketplace* and fulfilled it *in the marketplace*. None of them left the marketplace in order to do God's work elsewhere.

A prime example is Abraham, the father of the faith. One can hardly go any higher up the ladder when it comes to influential leadership over nations than him. He did not come home one day and announce to Sarah, his wife, that because he had received *the call* he would sell the animals, lay off the workers and quit his job in order to buy a mountain where they would spend the rest of their lives learning how to become the father of the faith. On the contrary, he learned it by integrating his faith into undertakings in the marketplace day after day.

Jesus was born and educated in the marketplace, where He was recognized as a carpenter, a highly respected occupation at the time. His parables and teachings all have to do with marketplace issues.

In *Anointed for Business*, I list the subject of those parables, *and they are all marketplace related*:

- Construction (see Matt. 7:24-27)
- Wine making (see Luke 5:37-38)
- Farming (see Mark 4:2-20)
- Treasure hunting (see Matt. 13:44)
- Ranching (see Matt. 18:12-14)

- Management and labor (see Matt. 20:1-16)
- Family-owned businesses (see Matt. 21:28-31)
- Hostile takeovers (see Luke 20:9-19)
- Return on investments (see 25:14-30)
- Futures market (see Luke 12:16-21)
- Crop yield (see Mark 13:27-32)
- Management criteria (see Luke 12:35-48)
- The value of research (see Luke 14:24-35)
- Misuse of money and bankruptcy (see Luke 15:11-16)
- The advantage of leverage (see Luke 16:1-13)
- Venture capital in high-risk situations (see Luke 19:11-27)[3]

Furthermore, Jesus recruited His disciples in the marketplace. Also, the Church was born in the marketplace when the Holy Spirit fell on the disciples in a private residence and the first 3,000 members were saved and baptized in the heart of the city. Consider that 68 out of the 69 divine interventions recorded in the book of Acts took place in the marketplace. In fact, everything we call "church" today was deeply embedded in and disseminated all over the city. It was uncomplicated and natural, and at the same time so prolific that it changed the city and beyond because its members took the presence and the power of God to the marketplace 24/7. This is why in my definition of marketplace (the combination of business, education and government), I do *not* include church as a fourth entity. Doing so will reinforce the misbelief that the Church is an organization instead of being the organism created by God that needs to permeate the marketplace.

How to Pastor Bars

Let me illustrate with the refreshing story of Joey, a Filipino taxi driver. Joey was a brand-new believer when he attended our seminar on transformation in 1999. There, he fully understood that he was a minister, that his job was his ministry, and that his clients were his congregation. He left the seminar determined to make an impact in his sphere of influence.

However, being a practical person (and marketplace people have to be practical or else they cease to be in the marketplace, because they go bankrupt), he realized that turning a taxi into a ministry had some serious limitations: He could only minister for a few minutes to small groups since most rides are short ones. This led him to ask the Lord for further guidance.

God drew his attention to a bar he used to frequent seeking sensual pleasures, and told him to go back, but as its pastor. The name of the place was Sweet Moments, but there was nothing sweet about it. The manager was a homosexual who doubled up as the pimp for 35 prostitutes. He was also a drug user and drug dealer, the latter a practical necessity to subsidize the former. Obviously this bar was in dire need of a pastor.

Joey, being new in his faith, did not want to be disobedient to the Lord, and having understood the message, he took it to heart. Such is the beauty of new Christians—they are sufficiently naïve (and innately wise!) to believe everything they read in the Bible. Consequently, Joey began to take his lunch breaks there, practicing "close range" prayer evangelism on the management, staff and patrons.[4]

Every day, Joey walked into the bar quietly declaring, "The kingdom of God has come to this place and the gates of Hades will not prevail against it." Day after day, he ate his meal in a corner while speaking peace over the gay manager, the prostitutes, their clients and anyone who walked into the place. I can only imagine the demonic confusion at this holy intrusion as Joey confidently declared, "Greater is He [God] who is in me than the one [the devil] who is in the world [the bar]."

What we have seen consistently is that the implementation of prayer evangelism creates spiritual momentum from one step to the next. When a Christian speaks peace over the lost, the spiritual environment improves and leads to constructive fellowship that eventually creates the climate for the sinner to feel free to share personal needs for which he is offered prayer. And this is exactly what happened here.

The manager began to gravitate toward Joey, first stopping by his table for a greeting or a brief chat, and eventually sharing a meal. Then one day he shared a personal problem. Joey told him about the power of prayer and offered to pray for him.

He said to Joey, "But I do not believe in prayer."

Joey replied, "It's not a problem, since I am the one who will pray, not you, and I believe in prayer."

"But I do not believe in Jesus."

"Don't worry. I do, and once I am done, you will, too," said Joey.

Jesus basically used the same approach when people did not believe in Him: "Believe . . . otherwise believe on account of the works [miracles] themselves" (John 14:10).

Sure enough, a few days later the manager approached Joey's table totally perplexed since the prayer has been answered. In a friendly tone he demanded to know, "Who is this God of yours who granted a petition for someone who does not believe in Him? What is going on?"

Joey explained, "The kingdom of God has come near you. Would you like to get in?" Right there the manager invited Jesus into his heart.

■ ■ ■

The implementation of prayer evangelism creates spiritual momentum from one step to the next.

■ ■ ■

What happened next is amazing, and to fully grasp it you need to keep in mind that Joey had a major disadvantage. He had no formal theological training. But he had a counterbalancing advantage: He lacked formal theological training! This meant that Joey was free to believe everything he read in the Bible as current and relevant without the smothering suffocation that traditional theology tends to place on it. Joey saw that in most cases in the book of Acts, the one who led people to faith baptized them right away. Consequently he took his new convert to the beach and immersed him three times, once for each person of the Trinity since he had also read that it had to be done in the name of the Father, the Son and the Holy Spirit.

As soon as the now ex-gay man came up from the waters, he was struck by the power of God, evicting the demonic forces that had controlled him for so long and rewiring his psyche correctly to enable him to feel like a man again. Full of joy and wonder, he asked Joey, "What do we do now?"

Joey, in his childlike and literal understanding of the Scriptures, told him, "Now we need to invite Jesus to come into the bar, something I was not able to do before."

"Why?"

Joey elucidated, "Because it takes two or three people gathered in His name for Him to show up. Now that we are two, He will come." So they invited Jesus in and began to pray peace over the prostitutes, and as the doors opened, to intercede for their felt needs. Before long the prostitutes also came to the Lord. And now, Joey, the manager and the ex-prostitutes began to intercede for the owner of the bar, a lawyer who was hard to approach.

To overcome this problem, what Joey and his spiritual confederates did next is something that can only be understood as an expression of childlike faith. I can neither validate it as being biblical nor can I recommend it be repeated, but in the purest desires of their hearts for the lost, they baked a cake, anointed it with oil, laid hands on it, prayed for the owner, wrapped it up as a present, and sent it over to the law firm!

As the owner shared later, no sooner had he taken a bite of the cake than he experienced a totally unexpected power encounter. The presence of God touched him, and he began to shake. It was a pleasant experience but a perplexing one too. Not knowing what was happening to him, he made a beeline for the bar where he asked Joey and his budding congregation what was going on. They happily explained that the kingdom of God had come to the bar, and they invited him to receive the Lord, which he did.

Next, the lawyer turned to Joey, by now the resident theologian, and asked, "What should I do with the bar?" Joey suggested that it should be turned into a church, not just to shelter believers, but also to reach sinners. As you can imagine, when a bar becomes a church there is not much need for advertising since sinners gravitate naturally to the place. Many came to the Lord and six months later two other bars were turned into churches!

As extraordinary as this is, there is more. New converts were taught to prayer-walk the streets around the bar praying for the neighbors. Two years later over 50 percent of the neighborhood had come to the Lord and the bar manager had been sent to his hometown where he planted a church with 300 members!

This is unusual and extraordinary, but it should not be so. If more and more believers were to master the basic principles, as Joey did, we would see more cases like this because God has already deposited the imprint for transformation into the human heart. What we must do is align and connect the components correctly—that is you, the church, the kingdom of God, the marketplace and the city.

Joey learned that he was a member of the church, the unassembled assembly, at all times, and that as such he had been entrusted with the keys to the Kingdom to go to the marketplace where the gates of Hades are entrenched to bring them down so that the city would experience transformation.

South Africa: From a Company to a Continent

Half a world away and in an entirely different context, I observed the same principles at work in the life of a very successful businessman. Graham Power is the owner and chairman of the Power Group of Companies, which includes the largest privately owned construction company in South Africa.

In 1999, Graham had an encounter with God and received Jesus into his heart. At the time, his hometown, Cape Town, as well as the rest of the nation, was going through severe social upheavals (22 bombs exploded in 18 months). Not a week went by without at least one bomb going off. Apartheid had crumbled but the subsequent switch to black rule had put the nation in a challenging position. South Africa stood on a threshold that led on the left to social upheaval, on the right to economic chaos, and ahead to moral disintegration.

Graham understood the power entrusted to the Church and, inspired by a video produced by George Otis Jr. (showing how drug-cartel-instigated violence had abated in Cali, Colombia, following all-night prayer meetings in stadiums), he challenged all denominations to a day of repentance and prayer. As a result, in March 2001, 45,000 believers from the most varied denominational backgrounds cried out to God at the Newlands Rugby Stadium in Cape Town. The bombs and the violence stopped immediately. Changes became so evident that the following year eight stadiums were packed to intercede for a region encompassing eight provinces in South Africa. In May 2003 it expanded to include simultaneous gatherings in 77 South African regions and 27 African countries (66 cities) for a total of 143 venues.

In May 2004 I had the privilege of being the keynote speaker at the continent-wide prayer gathering that linked over 1,000 venues via radio and television in the 56 countries to make it *the first continent-wide prayer meeting ever*. I cannot come remotely close to describing the exhilaration and the magnitude of the spiritual power that was released when millions of Africans held hands and prayed in unison, from South Africa to Tunisia, from Senegal city to Somalia, and every country in between. A spiritual highway was formed from Cape Town to Cairo.

In 2005 Africa passed the torch to the world and hundreds of millions of people in 156 of the 220 nations produced the first global day of prayer; in the following year (2006), 199 nations participated. Starting in Tonga in the Pacific and moving west through Asia, the Middle East, Africa and Europe, crossing the Atlantic Ocean, sweeping the Americas and climaxing in Hawaii, believers representing every tribe and nation, using hundreds of languages and dialects, raised the most majestic worldwide canopy of prayer ever. It was awesome!

■ ■ ■

The Gospels record two incidents when Jesus wept, once for a friend, and another time for a city. His tears show how deeply He loves individuals *and* cities.

■ ■ ■

But it all began with the work of God in one man, Graham Power, making him understand that he is a minister in the *ecclesia*, called to take the kingdom of God with authority to where evil is still entrenched, namely in the marketplace of the world for cities and nations to be saved. Graham's pilgrimage began in his own heart by first discovering who he truly is in Christ. He soon realized that he was also a minister, but in the marketplace. To that effect he dedicated his group of companies to the Lord, made prayer *an integral part* of staff meetings, and brought intercessors on board to pray at construction sites as well as in a chapel at headquarters. His business was never the same after that.

Shortly thereafter, he connected his faith and his company to the vision for transformation. Using his company as the administrative hub, many of his directors as field managers, and the rugby stadium on whose Board he sat as the venue, he took the point to facilitate the first prayer gathering that grew year after year until it encompassed the entire world. Because Graham integrated the five components, in a manner of speaking, transformation *just happened.*

Cities

Integrating the first four components in our sphere of influence as Joey and as Graham Power did provides hard-to-ignore evidence that God can use us to impact our city.

Cities are important to God because He is going for nations, and the backbone of a nation is its cities. What would the United States be without Washington, D.C., Los Angeles and Peoria? What would Japan be without Tokyo and Osaka? Or Brazil without Rio de Janeiro and Brasilia?

God refers to Jerusalem in endearing terms, and His love includes other cities also, even sinful ones such as Nineveh, which the prophet Jonah wanted destroyed (see Jon. 4:1-11). And Jesus spoke of cities, comparing them to baby chicks in danger, and referred to Himself as the mother hen spreading her wings to provide much needed protection (see Matt. 23:37).

Jesus' choice of this analogy is not casual. The absolute commitment a mother hen has for her chicks is a most moving phenomenon. She is fearless and readily despises her own life for the sake of the ones under her care. I have seen these fragile birds face coyotes and snakes, without the slightest chance of overcoming them, but never turning tail, fiercely clucking warnings to their young to take refuge under the mother hen's wings. As a child, I was moved by the story of a farmer who, after a fire, found the charred remains of a mother hen *with the baby chicks still alive under her wings!*

The Gospels record two incidents when Jesus wept, once for a friend, Lazarus (see John 11:35), and another time for a city, Jerusalem (see Luke 19:41). His tears showed how deeply He loves individuals *and* cities. Now we need to understand that He also loves everything in between—the school systems, the business communities, the government agencies, everything.

Cities have spiritual gates, and in the psalms we are told to speak lovingly to a city, inviting her to open those gates for her King of glory to come in (see Ps. 24:7-10). Proverbs 11:11 states that by the blessings of the righteous the city is edified. We must bless our city as a manifestation of our love for it and do everything in our power for the kingdom of God to take up residence.

As I discussed in chapter 6, Stephanie Klinzing, the mayor of Elk River, Minnesota, understands this perfectly well. During one of the weekly prayer meetings she holds to intercede for the city with pulpit and marketplace ministers, she officially invited Jesus to come into Elk River and proceeded to turn its keys over to Him. And Jesus did come in, because He has stated clearly in Revelation 3:20 that if *anyone* opens the door He will come in, much more so when the highest-ranking official does the inviting.

Once He is *inside* the city, Christians have the home-court advantage. This becomes evident every time ungodly but still legal enterprises try to set up operations in Elk River. It would have been procedurally impossible for the mayor to oppose them on moral grounds at City Hall but on Tuesday morning, when she and her fellow elders meet with the Lord, they are able to *bind and release*, to *lock and unlock*, and from the heavenly realms prevent them from moving forward.

This principle was also put to work for the benefit of the school district in Elk River whose campuses stood dilapidated for lack of funds. A bond issue to raise money for the schools had been repeatedly turned down every time it was put before the voters. In desperation, the issue was brought by the School's Superintendent to the Tuesday prayer meeting and followed by a thorough prayer walking and dedication of the schools to God. At the next election the bond issue passed and today Elk River has a new high-school campus.

In Cedar Hill, Texas, Mayor Robert Franke and Alan Sims, the City Manager, host regular prayer breakfasts for pulpit and marketplace leaders to intercede for the city. As they spent time together, a genuine concern for the city began to develop among the participants, leading the mayor to ask the pastors to adopt every school in town in prayer and in material support and to provide tutors for students who had fallen behind, which they did. Also, when neighbors are cited for code violations such as sidewalks in disrepair, broken-down fences or graffiti, pastors are notified and the congregations see that the repairs are done for free or at cost, a tangible blessing, particularly for indigent families.

Aware that many visitors to Cedar Hill are prospective residents and that they get their first impressions from what are known as "front line service providers" of the city (the reception hosts at restaurants, attendants at gas stations, clerks at food stores, and so on), the mayor, with the leaders of the Church of the city, has designed a values training course saturated with biblical principles to help them be people of blessing. All this has brought a marked improvement in the spiritual climate over the city because Christians are beginning to see the city the way Jesus does.

Mr. Cahyadi Kumala, an Indonesian businessman, came to full faith in Christ in 2005. Shortly afterward he understood his role as a minister in the marketplace. Mr. Cahyadi Kumala, however, was the majority shareholder in a corporation that had built a city, so what he was talking about was dedicating the entire city to the Lord!

After we spent a week with Mr. Cahyadi Kumala, his wife, Stella, and their children, sharing about transformation principles, he asked us to officiate at the dedication, something we had the privilege of doing in August 2006. The place was originally called Bukit Hill (Sentul Hill), but the developer-now-turned-marketplace-minister made the executive decision to change it to Sentul City (God's City).

This is no ordinary place. It's one of the most upscale communities in Indonesia, less than an hour south of Jakarta, the capital. It is built with excellence—I was told that close to half a billion dollars have been spent *in infrastructure alone*. It has shopping centers, golf courses, a nearby Formula One racetrack, and a polo field. The average price of a home is into the hundreds of thousands of dollars. But the most important feature is a prayer tower provided and built by a large evangelical congregation, with meeting facilities for 11,000 people being erected at the very center of the project. Pastor Niko, the leader of the project, made it clear from the very beginning that the tower will be available to every church in the country to pray in—and to pray not just for the city but especially for the nations.

Sentul is not a city *for* Christians, it is a *Christian city*. The former would be a place of seclusion that by perception (if not definition) would restrict the entrance of non-believers. On the other hand, a Christian city is an entity that has received salvation and, like a mother hen, provides protection for those who dwell in its midst. For that reason, on the day of the dedication, a covenant was signed by leading pulpit and marketplace ministers pledging to work in unity to make Sentul City *a city on a hill* to project spiritual light over the entire nation and beyond. Realigning the corporation to embrace the new paradigms and incorporating prayer evangelism to the culture of management are an integral part of the working out of that covenant.[5]

On the day of the dedication, Ruth and I were flown by helicopter from our hotel to a landing strip near the gates of the city. The moment we entered the airspace over Sentul City, we sensed tremendous angelic activity overhead, and I heard the Lord say, "Legally she will be known as Sentul City, but I have given her a nickname. To me she will be known as Bethel." When I shared this with Mr. Cahyadi, his mouth dropped. He motioned the general manager over and asked him to recount a conversation they had had a few days before. His associate related that his boss had told him that he felt that somehow *Bethel* should be part of the name. What a confirmation!

As we stood in a beautifully landscaped field, flanked by the clubhouse, a lake, the golf course, and five hills outlining a majestic perimeter in the distance, we sensed God's pleasure at what was taking place. We poured oil in the shape of a cross and, with a *shofar* blowing over and over again, a procession of pulpit and marketplace ministers planted a stake in the ground with the inscription *Sentul City—God's City,* symbolizing a land claim for the Kingdom of heaven on Earth. The dedication ceremony was the equivalent of its water baptism because somebody understood that he and his family were part of the church charged with taking the kingdom of God to a site that used to lay in darkness but now was set aside to become God's city. Salvation had indeed come to one of the most beautiful cities in the world.

Let it be clear to the reader that all of the stories that I am telling are works in progress, and necessarily so, for we have not gotten to the parade of nations before the throne of God yet. Nevertheless, the facts remain that from Elk River, Minnesota, to Cedar Hill, Texas, to Sentul City, Indonesia, Kingdom-minded children of God have taken informed and irreversible steps in the process to bring their cities and nations to the party.

The road ahead is likely to be long and, because this is the first of a kind, I am sure at times it will turn bumpy. Victories may be temporarily reversed by setbacks. The devil will do everything possible to derail the emerging transformation. But the fact remains that it is always better to aim for a star, even if we miss, than to aim at a skunk and hit it instead.

Yes, integrating you, the Church, the kingdom of God, the marketplace and the city provides a spiritual pathway for *supernatural* transformation to happen *naturally.*

CHAPTER 15

The Healing of Nations

The health (or lack of health) of a nation always reveals itself in the marketplace. If a nation is sick, the government is inefficient and most likely corrupt. Business is poor and powerless to provide adequately for the needs of the population, and education is anemic, unable to come up with solutions. It is like a combination of cancer, heart disease, diabetes and having to be on dialysis, all at the same time.

We know today that most, if not all, of the nations of the earth are seriously unhealthy in some area. The question now is, *How* did those nations get healed? The answer comes with an understanding of the purpose and operation of the "tree of life."

In the first verses of Revelation 22, where John gives us one of those "flash forward" descriptions of the scenario, the scene is presented in such a way as to appear to answer the very question, *How did the nations get healed?* Here it is: "He showed me a river of the water of life, clear as crystal, coming from the throne of God and of the Lamb, in the middle of its street. On either side of the river was the tree of life, bearing twelve kinds of fruit, yielding its fruit every month; and the leaves of the tree were for the healing of the nations" (Rev. 22:1-2).

The River, the Fruits and the Leaves

John describes here in Revelation 22:1-2 a river that runs in the middle of the street, flanked on both sides by the tree of life, which bears 12 kinds of fruits and yields those fruits every month. Please note that the verb tense used here is progressive tense, which denotes an *ongoing process*. It does not indicate that the tree of life bore (past), or will bear (future), but that *it is yielding* its fruit as part of a process scheduled to take place month after month.

However, when Revelation 22:2 talks about the leaves of the tree, most versions, including the *New King James Version* and the *New American Standard Version* translations of the text, say that the leaves *were* (past tense) for the healing of the nations. Now, the Greek text itself does not contain the past tense verb *were*; however, the context of Revelation 22:2 clearly suggests that the healing was something that happened in the past and that the leaves are no longer used for such healing. The context for this conclusion is provided by the description in Revelation 21:24-27 of healthy nations, and by the statement that the curse (and its resulting infirmities) is no longer around, as found in Revelation 22:3. However, when those nations were under the effects of this curse, without the honor and the glory that characterize them in that majestic parade, it was the leaves of the tree of life that provided the cure for them, making it clear that healing came through those leaves.

Later on, I will provide a rationale and a biblical foundation for my conclusion that the leaves mentioned here represent scientific, social and economic breakthroughs orchestrated by God to provide solutions (healing) to problems afflicting the world. But for the time being, please, bear with me and allow me to make this statement for background purposes.

The twentieth century, the most expansive century in the last 2,000 years of world history, was shaped by two discoveries (vaccines and antibiotics) and four inventions (the transistor, the computer chip, the automobile, and the airplane). Without these groundbreaking breakthroughs, this period would have been similar to the more injurious and far less progressive nineteenth century. Instead, millions of lives were saved, life expectancy grew exponentially, commerce of every kind expanded to global proportions, man made it to the moon, and powerful computers were developed to manage and track with outstanding efficiency much of what goes on around us. These six innovations created domino-effect breakthroughs far superior to any prior century and the lives of billions of people were improved.

However, even with all this progress, nations are still sick and unhealthy, only in a more sophisticated and complex manner. How can that be? With all the creativity unleashed on the world, it seems that Christians, operating more effectively in cooperation with the Holy Spirit, certainly could have taken advantage of these innovations to obtain more comprehensive benefits than what we currently have. Why has that not occurred?

I am gripped by the observation that in the past, God had to entrust breakthroughs like these to non-Christians or to people who professed to be Christians but did not see the connection between their "secular" breakthroughs and the spiritual destiny of nations. Could it be that in the very same age when such tremendous innovations were taking place, much of Christendom was caught up in a "rapture mentality" that distracted us from actively being on the cutting edge for making the world a better place? By "rapture mentality" I mean that believers did not have a working theology for discipling nations, nor did they pursue one, for two reasons: (1) They considered them beyond redemption, and (2) they erroneously looked at the rapture as *the* way of escape from a world that they perceived was rapidly being taken over by the Antichrist.

Because of that, and certainly along with that, we have not adequately addressed the immense opportunity before us to bring healing to the nations.

In the context of our present circumstances, it becomes absolutely essential to access new ideas, concepts, procedures, inventions and discoveries capable of making right all that is detrimental at the systemic level (and usually on a national scale). Such is the role of the leaves of the tree of life.

The Role of the Tree of Life

To see how this works, we need to do a survey of *the Tree of Life* in the Scriptures. There are only three books in the Bible that mention the phrase "tree of life." The expression "*the* tree of life" appears in Genesis and Revelation. The slightly different phrase "*a* tree of life" is found in four references in the book of Proverbs.

The first occurrence in Genesis (chapters 2 and 3) suggests that the tree infused life into the Garden. Up to that point, Adam and Eve simply *tended* the garden and the soil bountifully *yielded* its fruit. Because the tree was right there at its very center, there was no need to *toil* over the land. However, when sin entered, the land was cursed and God positioned a cherub with a flaming sword to prevent humans from accessing the tree (see Gen. 3:24). From that moment on, the entire Garden became off limits to humans, and soon Eden was lost altogether.

Originally the Lord had placed Adam in the Garden (see Gen. 2:15) to freely receive the flow of God's life. It is clearly inferred from Genesis 2 that as long as Adam and Eve interacted with the tree of life in the context of "tending and guarding" the Garden, life emanated from that interaction. When tending and guarding were separated from the tree of life, its life ceased to flow into Adam and Eve and onto the earth, as spelled out by God Himself (see Gen. 3:16-24).

In this context it is helpful to remember that the veil to the holy of holies, both in the tabernacle and in the temple, featured the cherubim guarding the entrance to God's presence (see Exod. 26:31; 2 Chron. 3:14). When Jesus' death on the cross cancelled the power and the consequences of sin, including its curse on creation, the veil in the temple was rent in two (see Matt. 27:51) and thus the cherubim were also removed, opening again the way to the tree of life. Humans were able to approach God and partake of His blessings, not only for themselves but also for all creation, because "the Son of God appeared for this purpose, to destroy the works of the devil" (1 John 3:8; see also John 10:10).

--- ■ ■ ■ ---

Wisdom expresses itself in the form of new insights, concepts, revelations and procedures designed to improve the quality of life.

--- ■ ■ ■ ---

The presentation of the "tree of life" in Revelation is consistent with what we have already seen: It produces and sustains life (is nurturing), and as such it brings healing to the nations.

John's statement in Revelation 22:19 confirms that this healing dimension is for the present age, and that we who are living now are partakers of it. He writes, "If anyone takes away from the words of the book of this prophecy, God shall take away his part from the tree of life and from the holy city, which are written in this book." The only age when "taking away from the words of the book of this prophecy" can occur is during the time frame in which we are living, thus the "his part in the tree of life" also applies to today.

So the question is, What are those leaves and how do we access them? The book of Proverbs sheds the necessary light. Proverbs is a book on the virtues and power of wisdom, and in that context it contains four references to "a tree of life": *Wisdom* "is a tree of life to those who take hold of her" (3:18); "*The fruit of the righteous* is a tree of life" (11:30); "*Desire fulfilled* is a tree of life" (13:12); and, "*A soothing tongue* is a tree of life" (15:4) (emphasis in each verse added). Everything that is mentioned in these four passages—wisdom, the fruit of righteous actions, desires fulfilled, and a soothing tongue—suggest attributes, attitudes and actions that, when activated, have the resident ability to bring about every kind of transformation—political, spiritual, social, intellectual, emotional, and so forth.

The cornerstone for this "tree of life" process is set in Proverbs 3, a section that extols the wisdom of God and details the benefits of possessing it. Verse 5 highlights wisdom's exclusionary dimension by stating that we are to trust the Lord with *all* our heart and not to lean on our *own* understanding. In verse 13 we read how blessed is the person that finds such wisdom and gains understanding: "For its profit is better than the profit of silver and its gain of fine gold. She's more precious than jewels and nothing you desire compares with it." And finally, in verse 18, we read, "She is a tree of life to those who take hold of her." The word "she" here refers to wisdom, which is described as a tree of life.

I wish to suggest that, according to Proverbs 3, this wisdom expresses itself in the form of new insights, concepts, revelations and procedures designed to improve the quality of life, since this would be consistent with what the tree of life did in the Garden as a sustainer and dispenser of life. AIDS was a totally unknown scourge until the last century. Nations, particularly in Africa, are being devastated by this out-of-control plague and are crying for their health to be restored. In the same fashion that it came into being through the combination and activation of destructive elements, there are still untapped productive and constructive resources that this type of wisdom will access to develop a cure for it. Because of the access that Christians have to the tree of life, they should be the pioneers in the search for this type of breakthrough.

A Candid Self-Evaluation

Allow me to condense these observations into five concise statements:

1. We, the post-first-century Church, generally speaking, have not had a theology that proactively embraces the healing of nations, as Revelation 22:3 shows is God's will.

2. Consequently, we have not nurtured our faith to believe it could happen.

3. As a result, we are not people who intentionally strive intellectually, scientifically or in other helpful ways to pursue such breakthroughs. Too often, when confronted with contemporary problems on Earth, we have taken an ethereal and mystical tangent and have called it "spiritual," but we have not become transformational.

4. But God, who is infinitely merciful, as part of His "general grace,"[1] has released creative, transformational ideas into the world using many non-believers who see the need for and apply themselves to becoming channels for those extraordinary advances.

5. As the end times draw near, with its anticipated increase in evil and promised outpouring of divine countermeasures, God will pour down even more grace, both personal and general. The latter will result in new breakthroughs to counter new or greater manifestations of evil. The only real question is, What role will the Church play? Will it be participant, leader, or idle spectator?

God designed His Church to lead in the struggle against evil and its consequences; but in order to see the need *for us* to lead, we must fully realize that the Great Commission is *ultimately* about discipling, teaching and baptizing nations. I am not referring simply to evangelistic or ethereal activity, but to transformational earthly undertakings as well, for which it is essential to access wisdom from on high. And when we do, we will be the bearers of *good news* to the world because, in addition to a sure hope for the future, we will become channels of blessings for the present.

Wisdom and the Healing of Nations

But, in order for us to get the job done, we need to discard old patterns, including the pseudo-biblical dichotomies. For instance, when we read Proverbs 3:14-15 through the old paradigm, "For [the] profit [of wisdom] is better than the profit of silver and the gain better than fine gold. She is more precious than jewels," we dichotomize and conclude that we'd rather have wisdom than gold, jewels or profit. But the next verse specifies that wisdom will bring "long life in her right hand and riches and honor in her left" (v. 16), with *riches and honor* being consistent with what the nations offer to God in Revelation 21. In other words, what we have in verses 14 and 15 is not a dichotomy but an exhortation *to align wisdom with its fruits*. It is saying, don't go for gold, riches or jewels in opposition to wisdom but instead go for wisdom from on high first, and then you will get those things *to benefit nations*.

We can assume that nations are the ultimate beneficiaries because verse 18 ("she [wisdom, the leaves of the tree of life] is a tree of life to those who take hold of her") sets the stage for verse 19 in suggesting why this wisdom (tree of life) has to be applied to care for matters on Earth: "The Lord [in the beginning] by wisdom founded the earth, by understanding he established the heavens. By his knowledge the deeps were broken up and the skies dripped with dew."

The text describes the pristine condition of the world at the dawn of creation, but when access to the tree was blocked, what was established (on Earth) by wisdom became defiled. Now, on this side of the Cross, we can once again access the tree to restore the earth, and its nations can obtain honor and glory, which we can bring joyfully to the Lord in the parade described in Revelation 21:24-27.

Babylon: Capital of the Evil Empire

To fully grasp *why* the leaves of the tree of life are necessary for the healing of the nations *in this present age*, we need to understand the role Babylon plays in the Bible and in the world today.

Look with me at chapters 17 and 18 of the book of Revelation. The subject is Babylon, and in chapter 17 we get a description of her as the "mother of harlots and of the abominations of the earth," represented by a woman who is drunk and with whom the kings of the earth have committed adultery (see Rev. 17:2,5; 18:3). As a result, she has seduced them and has established her control over them. It is impossible not to see that those nations are unwell as a result of Babylon's seduction. This is indeed a very sad and tragic picture.

But then, in chapter 18, we are introduced to an angel (see v. 1) coming down from heaven and vested with great authority, and the earth is illuminated with the glory the angel reflects as he announces with a mighty voice, "Fallen, fallen is Babylon the Great!" (v. 2). This is no ordinary pronouncement, as attested by such a magnificent context. It is very much like *the* climactic moment in a play. Babylon is no longer great. It has been deposed. The villain has been brought to justice.

This Babylon is nothing less than the infamous global system ruling the world in general and the marketplace in particular today. The phrasing in the passage describes Babylon as having "a dwelling place of demons. And a prison of every unclean spirit and a prison of every unclean and hateful bird," revealing the intensely evil nature of this kingdom. The power behind the Babylonian system is demon driven and focused on world control, and it has been successful in its quest: "for all the nations [plural] have drunk of the wine of the passion of her immorality, and the kings of the earth have committed acts of immorality with her and the merchants of the earth have become rich by the wealth of her sensuality" (vv. 2-3).

This picture is universal and all encompassing in scope. The narrative moves from the spiritual ambit (Babylon, as a dwelling place for demons and unclean spirits) to the material realm (nations, rulers and merchants, enriched by the wealth of her sensuality). The Greek word *dunamis* in Revelation 18:3 means "wealth," and can also be translated as "power." The Greek word *strenos* is the word that is translated as "sensuality" or "luxury." The words used here suggest excessive wealth employed to seduce nations into slavery to the system.

In the same fashion that an adulterous relationship is driven by illegitimate enslaving passions that hurt the people and the marriages involved, the merchants and rulers have been seduced by a system that gave them power and pleasure in exchange for a treacherous and defiling relationship in which their nations became the casualties. This is the structure that will eventually be brought down by the saints accessing the leaves of the tree of life to bring healing to the nations (as I will explain in great detail later on), which the angel announces in such a sonorous and majestic way (see Rev. 18:2).

Trade and Satan, a Deadly Combination
To shed light on how this system came into being and how it operates today, we need to review Ezekiel 28, which, according to some

theologians, provides insights into how the devil was cast down from God's presence.

When reading Ezekiel 28, keep in mind that this is Hebrew, not Western, literature. The latter is linear in its structure, with a clear beginning and a plot that builds to a climax, whereas Hebrew literature contains overlapping circles. Ezekiel is talking about the human king of Tyre in one circle (see Ezek. 28:1-10) and about a spiritual ruler in another (see Ezek. 28:11-19), and we see that at times the descriptions of those circles overlap. I believe that both refer to Satan, the former in an allegorical form and the latter in direct reference to him.

Verse 2 states, "Because your heart is lifted up and you have said, 'I am a god, I sit in the seat of gods in the heart of the seas,' yet you are a man and not God, although you make your heart like the heart of God. Behold you are wiser than Daniel, there is no secret that is a match for you." Most biblical scholars agree that this is a description of a demon-inspired human king, which reflects the essential profile of the devil before his fall. He was in a high place and he had great knowledge and wisdom, but he fell down because he exalted himself by embracing the lie that "I am a god."

The interesting *and perplexing* thing is that not once but three times in this chapter it is stated that this fall was precipitated by his craftiness (his perversion of wisdom) *in trade*! The first allusion is in verse 5 (emphasis added): "By your great wisdom, *by your trade*, you have increased your riches and, therefore, your heart was lifted up because of your riches," which were the result of his success in trade. Verse 16 expands on this, saying, "By the abundance *of your trade* you were literally filled with violence and you sinned" (emphasis added). The cause-and-effect relationship is hard to miss. The central figure of the passage had a very positive trade balance that filled him with violence that led to sin.

The third reference is in verse 18: "By the multitude of your iniquities, in the unrighteousness *of your trade*, you profaned your sanctuaries" (emphasis added). Please notice that it is a perverted form of trade that brought defilement in the form of profanity (blasphemous behavior) to his sanctuary (a safe place of service and worship).

I never noticed these obvious references to trade until I saw the centrality of the marketplace in Scripture, and even more particularly in God's redemptive plan. I had seen theologians expound on the reasons for Satan's fall—most of which are mentioned in the passage: pride, self-centeredness, misguided heart, rebellion, mounting iniquities, unrighteousness, and profanity. But I never heard them make reference to the environment in which those evils took place: trade.

Satan involved in trade? It is absolutely mind blowing, but we cannot deny that this passage specifically mentions *trade* in connection with his fall, not once but three times. So, *why* trade? And *how* and *when* did the devil fall?

The How and Why of Satan's Fall

As to why and how it happened, we have *some* information here as well as from other parts of the Bible stating that the fall was because of pride, misappropriated wealth and insubordination, among other things. But because we have not factored trade into the equation or found a context for trade and the devil, we have been at a loss to determine the *when* with any kind of precision.

I have asked theologians at what point in time Satan fell, and those I talked to thought that it happened before the creation of man, most likely in that nebulous period when the earth was "without form, and void; and darkness was on the face of the deep" (Gen. 1:2, *NKJV*). But they also acknowledged this to be an assumption, since the Bible does not specify when it happened.

However, in Ezekiel 28 we have some unusual insight as to the timing. Verse 13 states, "You were in Eden the garden of God," placing this character at the very beginning of life on Earth; and, "Every precious stone was your covering," dressing him in valuable rocks and describing him in an honorable position. Verse 14 speaks of someone "placed . . . in the holy mountain of God," a position of honor, "(who) walked in the midst of the stones of fire (rocks)." This can be cross-referenced with Genesis 2:12: "The gold of that land is good; the bdellium and the onyx stone are there"; and possibly with Genesis 3:1: "Now the serpent was more crafty than any beast of the field which the LORD God had made," a passage that rates the serpent/devil as superior to others in craftiness and subtleness. This, in turn, seems to fit with the description given in Ezekiel 28:3-4: "Behold, you are wiser than Daniel; there is no secret that is a match for you. By your wisdom and understanding you have acquired riches for yourself and have acquired gold and silver for your treasuries."

Granted, this is a most perplexing possibility, that prior to his demotion Satan was somehow, somewhere, engaged in trade, and even more so that his trade must have taken place with other angels assigned to oversee portions of the earth as suggested in Deuteronomy 32:8.

In this verse, we read that God set up boundaries for the future nations according to the number of the "sons of God (angels),"[2] and that the angels assigned to Earth existed before God created man and nations, something that is also corroborated by Genesis 2:1, which mentions that God had already created the heavenly "hosts" (see 1 Kings 22:19 and Ps. 103:21). If Satan influenced other angels to rebel against God, which is clear from Revelation 12:4 and 7, and if trade was a major component of Satan's rebellion, as Ezekiel 28 indicates, then it follows that trade could have been part of Satan's influencing the angels who fell with him in his rebellion.

For the sake of completing the argument, allow me to take you to Genesis 2:10 and the four rivers that branched out of Eden: "Now a river flowed out of Eden to water the garden; and from there it divided and became four rivers." These rivers are described in a manner that alludes to them being used for commerce—by the reference to both the lands they reached and the valuable minerals found there. Study carefully the description of the region/nations and the inference to their use for transportation (see Gen. 2:9-14).

Keep in mind that rivers were the only thoroughfares available for long distance trade and transportation until the land was settled many years later. Trade seems to be the context (or at least part of it), otherwise this specific geo-economic reference in the description of the rivers appears to be out of place since it refers to a time prior to the expulsion of man from Eden and his subsequent migration to the regions beyond.

Also take note that as soon as God created man, the picture is one of plentiful produce: "Out of the ground the Lord God caused to grow every tree that is pleasing to the sight and good for food" (Gen. 2:9). Was there anyone else besides Adam to benefit from it? Such an abundance of food raises a question that seems irreverent but begs to be asked: How much food can one person (Adam) eat?

Granted, animals also consumed food, but they are incapable of appreciating beauty, and the text states that the food-producing trees *were also pleasing to the sight.* Only humans and angelic beings have this capacity. Therefore I want to raise the possibility that angels, who later on in the Bible are reported eating and drinking (see Gen. 19:1-3), were also the recipients of this bonanza (given on the basis of grace, since no labor was required yet) and that Satan oversaw its distribution until he corrupted himself by inserting trade into a system that was operating on grace.

Adam as Keeper of the Garden

To evaluate this possibility further, we need to take a closer look at two slightly different references to Adam in relation to his placement in the Garden. Before the description of the four rivers, we read that God simply *"put* the man whom He had formed" in the Garden (Gen 2:8, *ASV,* emphasis added), but the second time it specifies that God *placed* him there "to cultivate it *and to keep it"* (Gen. 2:15, emphasis added).

The phrase "to keep" carries with it the assignment to *guard,* to *protect* the Garden. Who or what needed to be protected if neither the man nor the Garden had yet been defiled? This is certainly a very interesting question, and I believe the answer is *Satan.* The next verse (in which God instructs man not to eat from the tree of the knowledge of good and evil) contains an indirect reference to the devil, since later on he would both corrupt the Garden as well as life on Earth by successfully tempting Adam and Eve to commit that very act.

It is obvious that by the time Satan is exposed and punished by the Lord in the Garden (see Gen. 3:1-15), Satan had already eaten from both trees, because he possessed knowledge of good and evil and immortality, characteristics that, according to God, are imparted to those that have eaten from both trees (see Gen 3:22).

Definitely there is a *before* (sinless) and an *after* (sinful) in the spiritual status of the devil relative to his presence in Eden. Ezekiel first describes the *before* part. He had a character of excellence revealed in the phrase "the seal of perfection, full of wisdom and perfect in beauty . . . in Eden, the garden of God." He also had a privileged position because he was placed in the garden by God as "the anointed cherub who covers . . . on the holy mountain of God . . . [walking] in the midst of the stones of fire" (Ezek. 28:12-14). In verse 15 he goes on to say, "You were blameless in your ways from the day you were created, until unrigh-teousness was found in you."

Then Ezekiel covers the *after* status: "By the abundance of your trade you were internally filled with violence, and you sinned; therefore I have cast you as profane from the mountain of God. And I have destroyed you, O covering cherub, from the midst of the stones of fire" (v. 16).

This passage and others as well definitely state that trade was a key factor in the devil's downfall. But trade prior to the creation of the inhabited world defies all logic, making it intellectually impossible to grasp. However, if the being described in Ezekiel 28 is the devil, it is not entirely farfetched to suggest that he fell sometime after the creation of life on

Earth and before man's assignment *to keep* the Garden when he became involved in some form of trade, possibly with other angels, as suggested earlier in the context of Deuteronomy 32:8 (concerning the division of mankind and the setting up of boundaries of the peoples).

Now watch this carefully. Genesis 2:1 states that "The heavens and the earth were completed, and *all their* hosts" (emphasis added). Obviously the devil was part of that company of angelic beings that was assigned to *both* the heavens *and the earth*. Next, the focus in the narrative moves on to the earth to specify that the soil did *not* yet produce fruit: "Now no shrub of the field was yet in the earth, and no plant of the field had yet sprouted" (Gen. 2:5).

■ ■ ■

The need to guard the Garden arose because Satan had inserted trade into a system that was meant to operate on grace.

■ ■ ■

It is only after God created man that the ground began to produce bountifully: "The LORD God formed man of dust from the ground . . . the LORD God planted a garden toward the east, in Eden; and there He placed the man whom He had formed. Out of the ground the LORD God caused to grow every tree that is pleasing to the sight and good for food" (Gen. 2:6-9a). And right after this statement, we are introduced to the two trees: "The tree of life also in the midst of the garden, and the tree of the knowledge of good and evil" (v. 9b). Both trees are to play central roles in the upcoming fall of both man and the devil.

To reset the chronology, first Adam is created and "placed" (set, appointed or ordained) into the garden with no instructions (see Gen. 2:8). Next come the trees, including the trees of life and of the knowledge of good and evil (see v. 9), followed by the description of the four rivers. Then Adam is "put" (settle down and remain) in the Garden (see v. 15) with orders *to cultivate it* (dress it and work it) and *to keep it* (keep watch, to guard it), at which time there is a second reference to the Tree of Life and to the Tree of the Knowledge of Good and Evil, with the express divine admonition for Adam not to eat from the latter.

A Bold Suggestion

I'd like to suggest that Satan's fall occurred at some point between the first reference to Adam's placement in the Garden in Genesis 2:8 and the second one in verse 15 when Adam was assigned *to keep* the Garden. And the need to guard the Garden arose because Satan had inserted trade into a system that was meant to operate on grace. Furthermore, it seems that this trade involved other angels, the hosts of heaven *and Earth* mentioned in Genesis 2:1, who, according to Deuteronomy 32:8, provided administration to the earth: "When the Most High gave the nations their inheritance [assignment], when He separated the sons of man [humanity], He set the boundaries [territories] of the peoples [nations] according to the number of the sons of God [angels]," some of whom fell with Satan as well.[3] The subsequent administrative role of fallen angels over affairs on Earth is clearly stated in Ephesians 3:10 (see also 1 Peter 3:19-22).

Apparently, God set up the geographical boundaries of the peoples according to the number of the angels He assigned to the earth at the time He created humanity. The earliest copies of the Deuteronomy 32:8 text (in Qumran texts and in the Septuagint) have "sons of God" rather than "sons of Israel," which is the standard way that the Hebrew Bible refers to angels. "Inheritance" refers to geographical assignment. This is what is reflected in Paul's words in Acts 17:26: "From one man he made every nation of men, that they should inhabit the whole earth; and he determined the times set for them and the exact places where they should live" (*NIV*). "Sons of man" refers to humanity, human beings. "Set the boundaries of the peoples" refers to geographical boundaries because the Hebrew word used here, *gevulot* ("boundaries"), is always used for geographical boundaries.

We don't know precisely when or how Satan's fall occurred, but being certain that trade was a major part of his assignment and a trigger to his demise and that trade could have been ongoing in Genesis 1 and 2, it is possible to conclude that his fall took place in the Garden. However, the most important point as far as how to bring healing to the nations is the fact that, following his deception of Adam and Eve and his subsequent control of life on Earth (including their descendants), he used his evil expertise to set up a worldwide control system based on a perverted form of a trade, one built on greed, deception, control and fear, one that I call the Babylonian System.

CHAPTER 16

The Babylonian System

Like St. Augustine's *City of God* and *City of Man,* the Bible is the tale of two cities engaged in a battle for control of the world. At the beginning of time, neither city exists, but the forces and philosophies behind them are seen in full array from almost the very dawn of life on Earth. In the course of history, though both cities appear on the world's stage, only one of them remains, yet the power and influence of that unseen city is so strong up to the moment of its demise that its name rings fear in the hearts of men. Before time comes to an end, good reigns over evil, but the manner in which it is achieved is most intriguing and captivating. This is the story of the Bible. The players are the peoples and nations of the world—including you and me. The cities are Babylon and Jerusalem.

The story climaxes at the end of the Bible as Jerusalem embodies the glory and the presence of God depicted in the book of Revelation 20 and 21; whereas Babylon, representing a depraved center of world commerce and oppression, is described as "The mother of harlots and of the abominations in the earth" (Rev. 17:5). From the days of old, battle lines have been clearly drawn. God calls Jerusalem, "The city which I have chosen me to put My name there" (1 Kings 11:36, *ASV*), and Babylon—always ruled by pagan kings—hates God and His people.

Babylon's origins are found in the Tower of Babel, when the post-Flood world population committed themselves to an ungodly fourfold goal, as revealed in Genesis 11:4:

- Build a city *for themselves*
- Reach heaven from an earthly platform
- Make their name an object of honor and fear
- Avoid being scattered all over the earth

These four objectives represent the exact opposite of what God has consistently purposed for His people throughout the ages. For example:

- We are never instructed to build our own city, but rather, from the days of Abraham, to look for that city "whose architect and builder is God" (Heb. 11:10). We do not have to strive to get to heaven; we are going there someday.

- The purpose of our lives is to bring heaven to Earth, not the other way around. That is why Jesus instructed us to pray, "Thy [God's] will [not ours] be done on earth as it is in heaven" (Matt. 6:10, *KJV*) and to expect that it will happen.

- As far as name is concerned, it is not our name that should be recognized, for there is only one name, one that is above every name: "Jesus"—to which every knee shall bow and every tongue confess that Jesus is Lord (see Phil. 2:9-11).

- When it comes to our mission, God has designed from the time of Abraham that in his descendants all the nations of the earth will be blessed. And as the Church, we have been sent to go to the ends of the earth to set people and nations free (see Matt. 28:18-20).

No two city-states could have had a more different set of values and operational philosophies than Jerusalem and Babylon. That is why they can never coexist. With that as the background, we now turn our attention to a deep and contrasting look at Babylon.

At the very heart of the thrust that gave birth to Babel is an anti-God scheme to establish a command and control center from which to subjugate the earth. The men described in Genesis 11 were not just constructing a city; they were building a city *of their own*. As such, it was a city with an attitude of arrogance, as far as heaven was concerned, since their objective was to be able to go there any time they chose by making its tower a platform from which to oppose God's command to fill the Earth (see Gen. 1:28) and to spiritually influence the earth.[1] In fact, in the Genesis 11:4 statement, "a tower whose top will reach into heaven," the Hebrew word for "heaven," *shamayim*, literally means "the heavenlies" and corresponds to the New Testament Greek word *epouraniois*, which Paul used to describe the heavenlies, a place where demonic activity is based for the purpose of controlling affairs on Earth (see Eph. 6:12).

Their determination to make *a name for themselves* reveals how absolutely self-centered and humanistic they were, since such a choice was made as an overt act of rebellion against God; and their accompanying goal of *not* going to the ends of the earth was, in addition to being a direct challenge against the divine command to that effect (see Gen. 1:28; 9:1,7), is also an indication of their intent to make nature subservient to them, and not the other way around.

Keep in mind that the Hebrew word *avad*, meaning "to work" or "to cultivate" (and was first used to describe Adam's assignment in the Garden according to Genesis 2:15), also has the meaning "to serve" (*eved*, the Hebrew word for "servant," also comes from the same root). Man was called to serve, to care for and to tend nature, since in doing so there is alignment with God's plans and designs for himself and for the earth. This is so because the command to "subdue the earth" was given in the context of fruitfulness and multiplication for the purpose of replenishing (not depleting) its resources (see Gen. 1:28).

What erupted in Babel is the very essence of Satan's character, who was cast out of heaven because he perverted himself and others through a self-serving scheme of control. At Babel, the devil tried to "jump the gun" on God by taking control of the world population and inciting them to build a city that, by reflecting his ill-acquired expertise in trade, would give him *complete* domination of the human race to preempt the option of the Messiah's advent, since every nation on Earth would be under his *direct* control, thus blocking the way for Israel to come into the picture.

It is interesting that right after God thwarted this attempt by scattering the people over the face of the earth (see Gen. 11:9), Abram (as he was called then) comes into the picture (see Gen. 11:26-32), and shortly afterward, God calls him to be the founder of a nation that would be a blessing to all other nations on the planet: "Now the LORD said to Abram, 'Go forth from your country . . . and I will make you a great nation, and I will bless you, and make your name great; and so you shall be a blessing . . . and *in you all the families of the earth will be blessed*'" (Gen. 12:1-3, emphasis added).

The Unbeatable Formula

That the tower of Babel was indeed a potentially catastrophic move for humanity and that much was at stake is certified by the fact that God came in the form of the Trinity (the "us" in Gen. 11:7) to put an end to it.

Every day, people on Earth come up with and implement plans that are ungodly—even anti-God—yet we do not see God personally intervening to foil them, as was the case here. Two factors made this case very different.

First was the potential for out-of-control evil (in *Prayer Evangelism*, I explain this in detail). What were they doing? They were not building nuclear bombs or developing weapons of chemical warfare. They were baking bricks and gluing them with tar. So what causes the Trinity to intervene, lest they become unstoppable? The answer is in God's assessment of the unlimited potential for evil in the people: "Behold, they are one people, and they all have the same language. And this is what they began to do, *and now nothing which they purpose to do will be impossible for them*" (Gen. 11:6, emphasis added).

In this passage, God lists three factors that, once combined, have the potential to render these men unstoppable:

1. They had a compelling, unifying *common goal*: "this is what *they* began to do." They were not building walls in their spare time but a city. To accomplish this, they had settled down and agreed to dwell together.
2. They had *unity*: "they are one people."
3. They had *communication*: "they all have the same language."

God was saying that when a group of people has a compelling purpose, unity and communication, *nothing is impossible for them*. This is not the hype of an overly enthusiastic evangelist but God's own assessment! This is a very serious and important matter that deserves close scrutiny. It wasn't *what* they were doing but *how* they were doing it—the combination of purpose, unity and communication—that produced unlimited potential.

The second factor that caused God to intervene was that their actions and their fourfold objective unmistakably reflected the DNA of the Babylonian system that later on would take control of the world. At Babel, a triple alignment—involving the totality of the world population, Satan, and a self-contained system—would have preempted the emergence of Israel as God's people and as the vehicle for the Messiah to rescue the world.

Through the ages, the DNA first exhibited at Babel has expressed itself in different forms, but the four-headed monster of *control, disregard for moral absolutes, self-centeredness* and the *exploitation of nature and people* has always been a constant, regardless of how or through whom it had been expressed.

From the dawn of history, domination of one group over another was exercised by raw violence in the form of war. The spoils always belonged to the victor, and what they could not take they destroyed, including human lives, livestock, crops and cities. Wars were waged not to expand civilization but to destroy competing ones and strengthen the victor with the loot.

When a group of people has a compelling purpose, unity and communication, nothing is impossible for them.

The system became progressively more sophisticated but definitely not less cruel. Control was exercised by political domination backed by military might (or vice versa) to extract tributes from subjugated nations. Beaten nations were made vassals instead of being destroyed as in the past, to create a flow of resources from the ends of the empire toward its capital, affirming the premise of a centralized vortex of power. One empire followed the next, leaving a path littered with human debris that remorselessly spanned from one century to the next.

Following the two World Wars in the twentieth century, the issue became ownership of the land, as the oligarchs, challenged by emerging populist movements, unsuccessfully tried to hang on to idle lands needed to abate the hunger of multitudes. Land reform finally took hold, giving more people access to land ownership. However, today the new tool for worldwide domination is the use of trade to control and limit access to markets. Trade, as practiced at the macro level in the world today, can easily be used to subjugate and oppress because trade is basically an exchange—though not necessarily a fair one, since the one with the liquidity usually decides how much is paid for what is being offered. Trade has become the velvet hood over the four-headed Babylonian system, which is still in effect today.

Trade is not evil. Like sex, as part of the human reproductive system, it is divinely designed to energize and multiply what is already present *and latent* in the lives of the participants, in addition to giving birth to new things. In describing the dynamics of the kingdom of God, Jesus Himself told two parables involving trade: the Parable of the Talents in Matthew 25:14-30, and the Parable of the Minas in Luke 19:11-26.[2]

After the Fall

Enron—the now disgraced and defunct energy conglomerate—made it painfully evident that trade can be easily perverted, because the trader's objective is not to give things away but to use them to acquire more in an advantageous manner. When the greed resident in human nature kicks in, it can easily lead to excesses that undermine the welfare of others. In that state, trade becomes the opposite of the system of grace that was prevalent in the Garden, where everything was made available for the *common good*.

I believe this is why in one of the first snapshots of the Early Church we see believers considering their possessions as common property so that everyone would have what they needed, in a beautiful throwback to the way things used to be in the Garden: "And the congregation of those who believed were of one heart and soul; and not one of them claimed that anything belonging to him was his own, but all things were common property to them" (Acts 4:32).

The way world trade is often used (more precisely, *abused*) now and in the past is not a positive exercise because it has neglected and ejected the grace that was such an integral part of its core and purpose in the Garden. In today's world economy, bankers and venture capitalists determine the bottom line (*their* bottom line) by skillfully and shrewdly controlling the cash and writing the rules for the market. Governments provide further momentum by unilaterally establishing tariffs and domestic subsidies with the interests of their own nation in mind, and not those of the rest of the world. The result is a growing gap between the have and the have-not nations and between rich and poor peoples. This is due to a trade system designed to concentrate power in one place instead of using it for the common good. It favors a win-lose rather than a win-win outcome.

The Tragic Scramble for Africa

To see the application of this self-serving expression of trade, it is most alarming to revisit the Berlin Conference of 1884 to learn how the partition of Africa came about. It is a disturbing tutorial on the use of trade to subjugate nations, and in this case an entire continent. The conference was convened by Otto von Bismarck, the German Chancellor at the time, and was attended by the European powers with colonial interests in Africa plus the representatives of the Ottoman Empire. The USA was also a participant, though mostly as an observer.[3] This gathering formalized the division of Africa among the European powers, which included making Congo the *personal* property of Leopold II of Belgium, an infamous act that led to the death of as many as ten million natives.[4] A review of the map of Africa eight years later (1902) reveals that 90 percent of all the land that made up Africa was under European control.[5]

Colonial powers proceeded to unashamedly structure African economies to complement their own. These individual European nations strictly specialized in accordance with the needs and desires of their own individual countries, and subjugated the African economies to engage in exporting their commodities to the cities of Europe.[6] To make the extraction of those commodities possible, the empires made substantial investments in infrastructure, such as railroads, roads, ports, and so forth, *but did not invest in the specialized education and development of people the local population* since it was economically advantageous to the empires that Africa remain a non-industrialized society. This was justified by two premises, one false and one true. The first one, abominably racist, was that Africans were primitive people and unsuitable to live in "developed" societies. The second one was that any manufacturing and processing infrastructure in Africa would hurt the economies in Europe.[7]

As a result of these policies, when African nations finally became independent they found themselves with two fundamental handicaps: a lack of educated nationals, and no industrial infrastructure. Local leaders replaced the colonial rulers but not much changed since the economies continued to be agrarian, with the complication that in the post-colonial era, access to international markets was stacked against them through subsidies and tariffs crafted by some of their former masters.

Subsidy Nonsense

Developed countries spend one billion dollars *a day* to subsidize their agricultural industries.[8] These figures and their impact on Least Developed

Nations (LDN), most of whom are located in Africa, is a matter of active and heated debate; but what is being argued is the magnitude of its impact, *not* its existence.

However, in a press conference given by Mari Robinson, former president of Ireland and the United Nations Commissioner for Human Rights, Ms. Robinson said that the policies put in place by the United States of America, the European Union and Japan concerning subsidies, tariffs and other barriers are costing the developing countries 320 billion dollars per year. Comparing this number with the world budget for AIDS (which is estimated at 57 billion dollars), Ms. Robinson concluded that what the world is losing in productivity is more than what it is paying to address AIDS.[9]

Few acts would improve the agricultural income in Third World nations more than the elimination of government subsidies to farmers in the USA and European Union.

Few acts would improve the agricultural income in Third World nations more than the elimination of government subsidies to farmers in the USA and the European Union, even if done gradually. This program, created in the USA at a time when America was a nation with a large farming population dependent on incentives and protection, is driving farmers in other parts of the world into bankruptcy and pushing non-industrial nations deeper into insolvency because it gives an unfair advantage to the gigantic conglomerates that have taken over most farming interests in America. Additionally, in some cases it gives incentive for farmers of certain crops to plow those crops under, rather than bring them to market, since they're effectively receiving payment for those crops via government subsidy anyway.

The issue transcends the economic dimension when we see that 18 million people per year (50,000 *every day*) die of poverty-related causes such as unsanitary water, inadequate food and lack of basic health services.[10] These conditions cannot be abated at the local level because their economies are in shambles. When the Western world is presented with the staggering cost in lives caused by systemic poverty, many well-meaning people and agencies rise up with a most sincere desire to provide more aid; but in others a deep-seated skepticism (even hopelessness) takes hold, because of how inefficient aid has been until now. That skepticism soon turns to cynicism in the face of the rampant corruption prevalent at practically all levels in the recipient countries.

However, the solution to this horrendous issue is not that difficult. The need is not for more aid but for fair trade, something that can be achieved by opening Western markets to Third World producers. The more precise choice is between massive aid, with its resulting lowering of self-esteem and increased dependency on the part of the recipients, and the opening of markets in the West accompanied by both Western capital investment in least developed nations and a redirection of aid to empower producers in the Third World to upgrade their infrastructure.

People in poor nations are not lazy. They are not loafing under trees, waiting for UN convoys to drop them some food. They labor harder and longer and under much more demanding circumstances than most of us in the West, but at the end of the day they are also left to worry about finding markets for the crops they expect from the seeds they just planted. They are hard-working folks, but the deck is stacked against them. For instance, according to Oxfam, U.S. *domestic* cotton subsidies reached almost five billion dollars—for a crop that was worth only four billion dollars.[11] These subsidies to just 25,000 cotton farmers depressed world cotton prices, hurting developing countries, including more than 10 million people in West and Central Africa who rely on cotton *for their livelihood*. To put this in perspective, cotton production in Benin, Burkina Faso, Chad and Mali accounts for 5 to 10 percent of the Gross Domestic Product and represents an average of 30 to 40 percent of overall export earnings.[12]

The same source contends that the US has paid over 25 billion dollars to corn farmers over the past five years for a crop that would otherwise have *lost* 20 billion dollars over the same period. These subsidies have depressed world prices and caused losses of up to 4 billion dollars in other corn growing countries. Rice farmers in the US receive over 1 billion dollars a year in subsidies, *which equals the total value of the entire US crop!*[13]

Tariffs: The Second Blow

Also, by imposing tariffs on foreign grown commodities, Western nations make it prohibitively impossible for Third World growers to enter their markets. And by selling their subsidized commodities in the international market at artificially lowered prices, due to domestic subsidies, they drive Third World producers out of business, which has disastrous consequences on entire local economies and hundreds of thousands of families.

For instance, the European Union pays its sugar farmers almost three billion Euros in subsidies to produce a crop that exceeds the internal demand and costs more than the international price while *blocking non-EU countries from selling in the continent.*[14] The surplus is sold in the international market and/or given as foreign aid to non-EU countries, some of which are sugar-producing nations themselves! The donated sugar depresses the local economy further, driving local producers into despair.

Many of these figures and the resulting conclusions are the subject of an ongoing debate, but no one denies that better access to world markets will improve the economy of the least developed nations. As an example, consider the plight of this non-Western farmer:

> Njay Coulibaly is an average farmer of Korin, a village in Mali, West Africa. He is the head of a family of 13 able-bodied men, women and children, all who work in the cotton fields. They worked hard for six months this year carefully tending their cotton crop. Yet Njay's total harvest of nearly 2500 kilos sold for only $815, and after paying back the bank and hired labor, he and his family were left with a mere $110 to live off of.[15]

Why? Because wealthy countries are giving huge subsidies to their large producers and then dumping the overproduction on the world market, according to a World trade Organization (WTO) report published by the Harvard Center for International Development (CID). This type of subsidization has caused the world supply to soar while driving prices to all-time lows. A further report states, "Sub-Saharan countries are struggling not due to a lack of aid from wealthy countries, but because their economies are blocked on the world market. For example, according to Oxfam, the country of Mali received 37.7 million dollars from USAID in 2001, yet the country's producers lost 43 million dollars due solely to American subsidies. The obvious solution is to end subsidies."[16]

The World Bank and the International Monetary Fund (IMF) have as their mission to provide aid to nations with troubled economies by providing loans and expertise; but those loans are often contingent on those countries' adhering to their recommendations. For instance, today the IMF wears an ideological hat different from the one it wore when it was created. Its first article states that it aims "to contribute . . . to the promotion and maintenance of high levels of employment and real income and to the development of the productive resources of all members." Interestingly, the IMF today has become a guardian of the type of deflationary measures that the Bretton Woods conference in New Hampshire in 1945 sought to consign to history.[17]

Sometimes the good intentions and well-meaning advice of the IMF and the World Bank collide with local reality with catastrophic consequences for the weaker party, which is always a Third World nation. In 2003, for example, Ghana decided to protect its rice industry from imports (often subsidized) by putting tariffs in place. Almost immediately the IMF demanded that Ghana rescind that decision, and since then "the US now provides 40 percent of Ghana's rice imports. Ghana's own production has collapsed—local rice farmers can no longer make a living. And in countries like Ghana, most people are farmers."[18]

Fair Trade Must Replace Aid
These unfortunate and unnecessary victims of a system of poverty could be spared by eliminating self-serving trade practices on the part of the Western nations. If trade were to be governed by the win-win axiom that is an integral part of grace, instead of by the Darwinian predatory win-lose imposed by the Babylonian system, entire nations would flourish.

I realize that the suggestion to eliminate tariff and domestic subsidies to allow for the development of true free trade is radical and unwelcome in the West, mainly because of the potential losses in standard of living. However, we cannot have the cake and eat it too. If we promote free trade and globalization of world economies, we need to subscribe and submit to the rules of the game. The reason why every meeting of the World Trade Organization faces such virulent protest is because of this inconsistency.

To put this in perspective, let us remind ourselves that when industries in the West that have had a historic advantage came under competition—such as automobile, home appliances, and so forth—the first response was highly reactionary: strict protectionism. But when the West saw the folly of it and engaged in a fair contest with the emerging competition, *everybody won* through improvement in the quality of the products and more affordable prices, in addition to the development and strengthening of the economy in the non-Western nations.

Aid that Does Not Help

In chapter 12, I touched on how empires took advantage of the colonies through a trade system designed to develop them as simple providers of raw materials while actively keeping them from becoming strong enough to be competitors. Though the empires are no longer around, this unfair form of trade has become institutionalized in the domestic economies of the wealthiest nations.

Even laudable things such as aid to poor countries can be perverted. When close to half of the national budget comes from foreign aid, as is the case in several nations in Africa, the resulting dependence compromises their sovereignty. The mere suggestion on the part of the donor nation of a cutback in aid or a delay in its delivery compromises the freedom of local governments—or when aid is given on condition that the recipient country must endorse the donor's foreign policy.

The "Babel-onian" objective lives on: to build *our city* (self-interests) *with a tower* (anti-God systems and procedures) in order to make *our* name (products, activities) so powerful that others will have to come to us *on our terms.*

What can be done to change this situation? A lot!

A Better Way

In Nelson Mandela's last chapter of his autobiography *Long Walk to Freedom*, he describes how he discovered the all-encompassing nature of apartheid when he understood how it enslaved whites as much as it did blacks. Blacks were shackled but so were the white oppressors, by giving up the most pristine expressions of humanity in order to be able to carry the depravation of apartheid. The white man's conscience went into a coma that eventually extended to every meaningful aspect of life.

Mandela eloquently narrates how he came to understand that he would never be free until he had set the white people free, since both were victims of a cruel system. Like master and slave sharing the same shackles, it did not matter if one was educated and had expensive clothes while the other was ignorant and naked, since their destiny was tied to each other through apartheid. By keeping the black man down, the white man prevented himself from rising to the height of his own destiny.

■ ■ ■

Wealthy nations dwell on a planet where the poor, the destitute and the dying cannot be ignored anymore.

■ ■ ■

The same dynamic is at work today with regard to wealth and poverty and the gap between the rich and the poor (whether it be people or nations), because poverty and misery are "in the air." Like a bad odor, it cannot be restricted to a certain group of people. Because everybody smells it, everybody suffers. It does not matter where the odor originates.

Rich people may live in secluded, gated communities but every day when they exit those gates they come in touch with the stark reality of slums and shantytowns around them. Wealthy nations dwell on a planet where the poor, the destitute, and the dying cannot be ignored anymore. No matter how beautiful a nation is, if the world is getting poorer, and as a result uglier, so too eventually will that nation.

Furthermore, poverty affects everybody, even the rich. In chapter 11, I described poverty as being four dimensional: spiritual, relational, motivational and material. I explained that the poor score well on the first two and the rich on the latter two. But to truly eliminate poverty, everybody needs to score well on all four.

To have material and motivational wealth but to lack deep relationships and an active *practical* faith in God creates a debit that sooner or later will cancel out the "credit" of that partial wealth. Newspapers constantly report stories of wealthy people who have died lonely and/or resented by those close to them. Howard Hughes was an extreme version of the many social fugitives that abound in the world of the wealthy. One can have plenty of possessions and still be poor inside.

In the scale discussed in chapter 12, I showed how the progression of the person described by Paul in Ephesians 4:28 can be tracked from -1 to +6.[19] People of wealth can easily reach +2 but they will remain stuck there unless they focus on doing what is good, with the ultimate objective of sharing with those in need. This is the picture we find in Acts 2:46, of rich and poor dwelling joyfully together with gladness and sincerity of heart. *Everybody* there scored +6. Like Nelson Mandela said about the iniquity of apartheid, the rich will never be truly rich until the poor are set free from systemic poverty.

Most Christians, at a personal level, practice Kingdom economics. They are honest, hard-working people. They care for the needy in their own sphere of influence. They donate time and expertise to help the disadvantaged. The world would be a terrible place without such life-giving involvement. However, the question is, What can be done to alter the *systems* of poverty? In other words, can we change the world systems to get rid of systemic poverty?

The answer is absolutely and emphatically *yes!*

What's more, what seems massive and impenetrable from the outside might already be crumbling on the inside. During the Bolshevik Revolution that dethroned the Russian Czar and paved the way for Communism, the turning point was the storming of the Winter Palace. By exposing the fragility of the system, it set in motion a domino effect that in an unexpectedly short time brought down the old system. Reflecting on that event afterward, Lenin mused, "I did not realize how easy it was until it was done." It looked formidable until it was challenged, first in the minds of the people and then at its very gates. Key to this was the discontent not just in the minds and hearts of the peasants but also of key people in power in the old regime.

The same is true regarding systemic poverty. Within the establishment, strong voices are beginning to be raised, crying out for the elimination of poverty *in our generation*. They see the devastation produced by capitalism devoid of Judeo-Christian values, but because they are not aware of the need for those values, they limit themselves to proposals that seldom go beyond providing more aid or forcibly redistributing resources.

Those who don't know the Lord or who lack an eternal perspective see those approaches as the ultimate objective. But we Christians should perceive in this groundswell an *extraordinary* opportunity to use the elimination of *all forms* of poverty as a masterful act of kindness to open the eyes of *billions* of people to the reality of Jesus Christ and His gospel of good news to the poor.

It has happened before (albeit on a small scale) and it should happen now. The principle at work in Acts 4:32-34 linking the elimination of poverty and credibility of our message is powerful. In that passage we read that the apostles' witness of Jesus' resurrection was credible because of two major social breakthroughs: (1) The congregation, which comprised rich and poor, was of one heart and soul; and (2) there was no needy person among them because they had joyfully and selflessly shared with each other.

Governments can bring about the redistribution of wealth to make the plight of the needy less painful at the expense of the rich, but only the power of the gospel can change the hearts of people at opposite ends of the social spectrum to constitute a new order that is held together not by the enforcement of policies and regulations but by hearts and souls bonded around the resurrected Jesus Christ who dwells in their midst.

You can see it as you read these words again: "And the congregation of those who believed were of one heart and soul; and not one of them claimed that anything belonging to him was his own; but all things were common property to them. And with great power the apostles were giving witness to the resurrection of the Lord Jesus, and abundant grace was upon them all. For there was not a needy person among them, for all who were owners of land or houses would sell them and bring the proceeds of the sales, and lay them at the apostles' feet; and they would be distributed to each, as any had need."

However, we will tragically shortchange ourselves and the world if we limit ourselves to the social arena. The context for this passage is rich in the supernatural. In fact *it is dependent on the supernatural*. It begins with corporate prayer triggered by threats and persecution, to ask for boldness, confidence, healing miracles and signs and wonders, all around the word of God: "And now, Lord, take note of their threats, and grant that Your bond-servants may speak Your word with all confidence, while You extend Your hand to heal, and signs and wonders take place through the name of Your holy servant Jesus" (Acts 4:29-30). And it concludes with a two-punch, first a resounding divine AMEN in the form of an earthquake: "And when they had prayed, the place where they had gathered together was shaken;" which is followed by everybody being filled with the Holy Spirit: "And they were all filled with the Holy Spirit," with the end result that they "began to speak the word of God with boldness" (v. 31).

It is this connection between heaven and Earth, expressed in a constant flow in both directions that makes Christianity absolutely uniquely qualified to eliminate all expressions of systemic poverty. Anybody can tackle social issues, but only Spirit-filled Christians can do it by accessing the Tree of Life, filled with the Holy Spirit demonstrating the power of God through signs and wonders *performed through their hands* (see Acts 5:12). Please notice in this passage how the action begins on Earth with the congregation praying a prayer that is heard in heaven, which in turn replies with a sort of "earthquake amen" (see Acts 4:31) that results in the believers speaking boldly on Earth the word first spoken by God in heaven. Awesome!

The Third Axiom of Poverty: Corruption

There are three foundational axioms about poverty issues that we must keep clearly in our minds as we seek to resolve it. We have mentioned two: first, that systemic poverty does not exist by itself but through a system of poverty; and second, that poor people are not the problem; they're a significant part of the solution, because they constitute the largest untapped source of capital.

The third foundational axiom is this: *Corruption* (the glue that holds the systems of poverty together) and *corrupt people* fall into two different categories, which we must keep separated in our minds. Corruption is beyond redemption, but corrupt people are the very object of it. Corrupt people do not love corruption. Like drug addicts (who do not love drugs, but are enslaved by them), the corrupt hate corruption and wish to be liberated, but they don't know how. Jesus clearly demonstrated this reality with Zacchaeus, the discredited tax collector who was desperate for change, and when salvation came *to his house*, he embraced it wholeheartedly. He enthusiastically let it rescue everything that had been lost to corruption, including his businesses and his ill-gotten profits.

Likewise, today multitudes of people in positions of influence and authority are hoping for deliverance. They are crying for an alternative, but because they don't see it, they sink deeper into hopelessness and sell out to the Mother of Harlots—Babylon. This is why it is most imperative that we Christians change paradigms and get into the marketplace *to do business* with Kingdom principles. Babylon has enlisted the most talented leaders in nation after nation to run its corrupt system. We must present these "indentured workers" with an alternative. Case in point is Russia. The country is doing much better economically after capitalism was introduced. But because capitalism arrived devoid of its Judeo-Christian values, sinister forces, particularly the mafia, run Russia today.

What would have happened if, when the Iron Curtain fell, the preachers that flocked by the thousands into Russia would have emulated Paul and taken with them top-notch business people and established their base of operations in the marketplace to bring salvation not just to people but to corporations, political parties, and universities?

Every time a major social shift takes place, like the fall of Communism in the Soviet Union, a vacuum of gargantuan proportions is created. Because we did not have the right paradigms, we missed the opportunity to fill it with transformation principles—*but Babylon did*. This is tragic in extreme because we are the ones who have the anointing, the authority and the power. But because we did not have the right paradigm, we did not show up for the game and lost by default.

Learning from that debacle, a growing number of pulpit and marketplace ministers have been setting up Kingdom businesses in China to avoid a repeat of the Russian fiasco. Flying under the radar, they are investing in and training Christian Chinese entrepreneurs to provide better services and products. In addition they are securing clients and financing to enable them to move up in the emerging economy. This is being done as a ministry, even though the word "ministry" is never used, and since it is focused in the marketplace it is impossible to identify it as such, especially by the political commissars. The intention is to infiltrate the Chinese marketplace with Kingdom companies so that when Communism expires—and it will because it cannot sustain itself in an atmosphere of increasing freedom—those Christian entrepreneurs—who by then will have obtained the greatest return on the "mina" entrusted to them (see Luke 19:12-27) will get the greatest authority in the nation.

This approach is already yielding fruits that are a precursor to the expected breakthrough; it is the emergence, *in the open,* of churches in the marketplace pastored by CEOs and company owners, many of them expatriate Chinese who have returned as business people. This new phenomenon is called "the Third Church," to differentiate it from the other two, the underground church and the official government Three-Self Church.

The Third Church is finding favor not only with Zacchaeus-type influential Chinese—who are becoming believers—but also with government officials who choose to look the other way at this flagrant violation of official Communist religious policy, because of the influence that these Kingdom companies have on the local economy. Given the sensitivity of the subject, it would be unwise to provide specifics, but mass conversions are sweeping some factories as well as the housing complexes where workers live. In one case almost all 4,000 employees have come to the Lord and the owner, very wisely, rather than trying to send them to an underground church, has turned the lunch hour into "informal" services in which miracles take place regularly. In another case, one third of the 12,000 people living in the compound have also come to the Lord.

It is our sacred duty and privilege to demonstrate—not only in China but also all over the world—that there is an alternative to corruption, greed and oppression, that the marketplace can be a pleasant place.

The system of bondage to which they have been subjugated will fall. And when it does, they will no longer be obligated to be its mistress. Rather, once cleansed and purified by the blood of Jesus, they will become part of the glorious solution, when the will of God in heaven will be done on Earth.

CHAPTER 17

The Demise of Babylon

*The secret to win the war does not consist in dying for your country
but rather have our enemies die for theirs.*

General George S. Patton

The bad news is that the Babylonian system is entrenched in the world today. The good news is that it will be destroyed and replaced with God's order. We can be certain of its demise because it has not only been foretold but it has also been described with revealing detail. Its widespread and far-reaching influence will utterly be cut off from the very root it is part of. It will come as a result of a divinely comprehensive strategy involving three successive blows designed to:

1. Terminate its spiritual legitimacy
2. Vacate its position in the heavenlies
3. Destroy its operational capability on Earth

The battlegrounds for these blows are the universe, the heavens, and the earth, in that order.

This epic drama in real life moves from heaven to Earth—and even under the earth. It involves angels and demons, the devil and the archangel Michael, prophets and saints, God the Father, the Holy Spirit, the Lord Jesus, the Antichrist, the Beast and the False Prophet. In fact, the entire universe, including the sun, the earth, the moon and the stars, are all actors in the climax of all climaxes when Babylon is defeated and Jerusalem becomes the permanent center of the universe. All of this makes Revelation 11–20, 10 of the most astounding chapters in all the Scriptures.

As it is the case with so many narratives in the Bible, the script does not always play out linearly. There are clusters of images here and there that reflect back what was just reported or something that is about to take place. Or they provide a glimpse of something that is going on in a parallel track. It is a multiple-screen production. That is why it can be confusing to try to make everything fit into our typical time sequence as so often modern eschatologists try to do.

What the Devil Lost

One of those key clusters of images appears in a short section in chapters 11 and 12. It synthesizes what unfolds and plays out in the rest of chapters 12 through 20 like a two-paragraph synopsis in the program of a three-hour theatrical production. This begins with the Lord's victory over Satan and moves on to a similar outcome at the hands of God's angels to conclude with the saints defeating him one last time—giving us a general outline of what is later on covered in minute detail.

Loss of Legitimacy

The first defeat is the one inflicted by Jesus and has to do with stripping the devil of any legitimacy to world control. An angelic choir proclaims in Revelation 11:15, "The kingdom of the world has become the kingdom of our Lord and of His Christ; and He will reign forever and ever." The 24 elders who sit on thrones before God echo that with, "We give You thanks, O Lord God, the Almighty, who are and who were, because You have taken Your great power and have *begun* to reign" (Rev. 11:17, emphasis added).

This passage seems to describe the precise moment when the atoning death of Jesus gave Him legal title to the kingdoms of the world, for it points to the beginning of His domain as indicated by the 24 elders' statement that He had *begun* to reign. That reign began when Jesus victoriously confronted evil powers (see 1 Pet. 3:19-22) and carried captivity captive (see Eph. 4:8). This sudden change of authority creates a negative but confirming reaction in the earth among the nations that He had just been made Lord over. Rather than rejoicing, they become enraged (see Rev. 11:18).

Why would the nations become enraged if Jesus became their Lord? Because the enemy, knowing that he has received a fatal blow, used every ounce of control over them to make them instruments to attack and squelch the Church, which is the entity commissioned by Jesus to reclaim what was redeemed. This may well account for the fierce, brutal and bloody persecutions that marked the first centuries of the Christian era.

A description of God's temple and the Ark of the Covenant (that suddenly becomes visible in heaven) announcing the beginning of an age of grace, followed by phenomena on Earth that may well be a reference to the beginning Church age, follows the rage of the nations: "And the temple of God which is in heaven was opened; and the ark of His covenant appeared in His temple, and there were flashes of lightning and sounds and peals of thunder and an earthquake and a great hailstorm" (Rev. 11:19).

In this first blow, Satan lost his legitimacy as lord over the world, because Jesus bought it back with His blood. Satan had gotten the world through sin and Jesus now recovered it by atoning for its sins. The battleground for this was the universe.

Loss of Strategic Position

The biblical narrative now moves on to the role of Israel (represented by a woman), as the channel for Jesus' birth and her struggle with the devil and his demons, symbolized by a dragon and a third of the stars under his control. The evil one's attempt at killing the child fails, the child is born to reign and ascends to heaven to sit on a throne from where to rule the nations while the woman is given a place of refuge in the wilderness to protect her from the dragon: "And she gave birth to a son, a male child, who is to rule all the nations with a rod of iron; and her child was caught up to God and to His throne. Then the woman fled into the wilderness where she had a place prepared by God, so that there she would be nourished for one thousand two hundred and sixty days" (Rev. 12:5-6).

In the ensuing interlude, a second cosmic clash takes place: "And there was war in heaven, Michael and his angels waging war with the dragon. The dragon and his angels waged war and they were not strong enough, and there was no longer a place found for them in heaven" (Rev. 12:7-8). The result was a loss of position for the devil and his angels (demons): "And the great dragon was thrown down, the serpent of old who is called the devil and Satan, who deceives the whole world; he was thrown down to the earth, and his angels were thrown down with him" (Rev. 12:9).

Satan and his minions will continue to fight until Judgment Day, but no longer from a position of operational strength. He has already lost the legitimacy at the hands of Jesus in the previous defeat and now loses the strategic advantage of a higher ground at the hands of

Michael and his angels. The battleground here is the heavens, but the next battle for the loss of control is on the ground. These two blows are the modern equivalent of a declaration of war by an international tribunal and the preemptive elimination of the enemy's air force, in that order, confining him to fighting on the ground.

Destruction of Operational Capability

His next fight is with the saints and is again one that he is bound to lose. Written in the past tense from a future viewpoint (as the book of Revelation does), it describes a battle that we the Church are engaged in at this very moment: "and they overcame him [the devil] because of the the blood of the Lamb and because of the word of their [our] testimony, and they [we] did not love their [our] life even when faced with death" (Rev. 12:11).

■ ■ ■

Victory belongs to us Christians; the Gates of Hades shall not prevail against the Lord's people.

■ ■ ■

I have always used this verse as a superb means to obtain personal victory over the devil. In fact, in my book *That None Should Perish*, I included a chapter on spiritual strongholds and employ this passage to teach how to tear down personal strongholds by claiming and accessing what the blood of Jesus did for us, by declaring with our mouth what we believe in our heart and by not being afraid to engage in a fight for fear of losing our lives. All of that is valid as an application of what this passage teaches, but *the victory it describes here is not just personal; it is specifically for reclaiming the kingdoms of the world, since the battleground is the earth.*[1]

All this is to say that victory belongs to us Christians, that indeed the Gates of Hades shall not prevail against the Lord's people.

The question is, How does that victory come about?

With the battlefronts at the cosmic and heavenly levels under control, Revelation 12:11 explains in specific detail the three arenas in which the earthly struggle takes place. The first one has to do with *the act of redemption*. The saints who do the overcoming have understood what it was that "the blood of the Lamb" purchased, and we now know very clearly from the Scriptures that it was much more than souls. It was indeed the whole of creation (including the nations of the world), which is now waiting with bated breath for the manifestation of the sons of God (see Rom. 8:19).

The second arena involves *the act of reclamation*. The phrase "the word of their testimony" is much more than a testimony about "how I came to know the Lord" or about "what Jesus did for me." It certainly should include that, but what is depicted here is not a word about something that has happened in the past. Rather, it is a public declaration about the present and the future by which Christians make it known that they understand that they are empowered to reclaim what the blood of the Lamb has already redeemed.

For instance, in Luke 10:2, Jesus said to the 70, "The harvest is plentiful . . ." How many of us have heard it said, or have been ourselves guilty of saying, "My city is hard to reach." That statement does not reflect what God's perspective is; rather it plays into the devil's schemes. We need to know that what we speak is not only heard by humans but also by the forces of darkness, and when we declare the redemptive purposes that God has already declared, our declaration is paramount to serving an eviction notice on those usurpers to move off the premises that have been purchased by Christ's blood, because the property has been turned over to His deputies, the Church.

The third arena is *the total denial of self*: "They did not love their lives to the death" (Rev. 12:11, *NKJV*). When we are able to say with the apostle Paul, "I have been crucified with Christ; and it is no longer I who live, but Christ lives in me; and the life which I now live in the flesh I live by faith in the Son of God, who loved me and gave Himself up for me" (Gal. 2:20), then we have trumped Satan's best hand when it comes to spiritual power. It is the equivalent of renouncing our citizenship in the Babylonian system, placing us outside of its jurisdiction. We no longer live by its standards. Having no life but Christ's, we are fearless, we are operating completely by faith, and we have the backing of the King of the nations upon us for victory.

How does this play out in our struggle with the Babylonian system?

The four values of the Babylonian system are *control* (*our* city), brazen *immorality* (a self-initiated tower to reach heaven), *pride* (a name for ourselves) and *making the earth subservient to man* (as opposed to tending it).

Of the four, control is the key because it establishes a foundation for the others to develop. The devil garnishes control through hopelessness. For hopelessness to work, it must be absolute, which is what the devil tries to make life look like at every turn, with thoughts like, "It will *never* be any different," "I can *never* change," "It's *always* been this way," "There is *nothing* you can do about it." But the truth is that if that hopelessness can be penetrated with hope—even at the most minuscule level—then, like darkness that has been pierced by the light from a small candle, it will soon succumb.

One First Step

When our Harvest Evangelism team facilitated the first modern-day city transformation thrust in Resistencia, Argentina, in 1988 to 1990, the immediate results were not very impressive. In fact, most observers were not enthusiastic, and some were even critical of it. But the fact that an entire city heard the gospel, that old systemic strongholds were permanently dismantled and that the Church did it in unity, represented a definite first.

A tiny but penetrating hole was punched in the darkness over Resistencia. People were no longer able to say that a city cannot be reached. Now they needed to modify it to the less grievous, "*just one city has been reached.*" As more and more people became inspired by the Resistencia story, a string of cities began to experience transformation. Today, people everywhere attest to cities being reached for Christ. It has become part of the Church's lore. The stronghold of hopelessness with which the devil kept people from even thinking about city transformation had been shattered. Today, the same principle applies to discipling nations, and within that, to the elimination of systemic poverty as the premier social indicator of such discipleship.

What we need to do is to demonstrate somewhere on the earth that a nation, or a strategic portion of it, has been transformed. The prophetic message that will emanate out of that victory will soon impregnate other nations in the same fashion that Resistencia made credible city transformation. Demonstrating this message in tangible ways will shatter hopelessness. And when it does, what was thought impossible due to the prevailing hopelessness becomes gradually possible.

Please allow me to use a negative example to illustrate this principle. In the late 1950s Fidel Castro and Ché Guevara, along with others, sailed from the Yucatán Peninsula of Mexico to Cuba to bring down the dictator Fulgencio Batista and start a revolution to liberate Cuba. Just for the record, so you will know where I stand on this matter, the first two feats they accomplished, but the third one they failed miserably. When their boat reached Cuba it capsized, some of the occupants almost drowned, a great deal of the equipment was lost, and Batista (who had gotten wind of their mission) had troops waiting for them.

The aspiring revolutionaries barely escaped capture by running to the hills. They found refuge in the impenetrable vegetation of a place called Sierra Maestra, where they established a small but secure perimeter. At that point in time, they did not pose any danger to Batista since they and their ideas were confined to a very small and inaccessible region of the country. Batista tried to chase them out but couldn't, and things developed into a stalemate—*that is until the rebels smuggled a radio transmitter into Sierra Maestra!*

It was not a very big transmitter, but it was big enough to broadcast to a vast region of the island nation. They named their radio broadcast, *Radio Cuba Libre* (Radio Free Cuba). Every night they bombarded the countryside with revolutionary exhortations. They did not pose a physical threat to Batista, but the fact that they were able to proclaim that a part—no matter how tiny—of Cuba was no longer under Batista's control, as evidenced through their daily broadcasts, shattered the long-established notion that Batista's regime was in control of all of Cuba. From that moment on, Batista sympathizers and even Batista himself were forced to admit that his control extended to everything *but Sierra Maestra*. It became a matter of time before the regime collapsed and Cuba entered its most tragic period. As sad as the outcome turned out to be, the principle stands: Once a perceived absolute had been dented, it is no longer absolute.

It is similar to the running of the mile in less than four minutes. Until May 6, 1954, the four-minute barrier had stood for centuries, but it has since been breached many times over.[2] Invincibility once shattered makes it possible to accept that it is breakable.

This very principle is dramatically at work today with respect to one of the world's most vile plagues. While most of Africa seems to be fighting a losing battle with AIDS and HIV, Uganda has been able to bring the figures down from 36 percent to an astounding 6 percent. It has done it primarily through the massive education of younger people; teaching Bible-based family values, including abstinence; and prayer. It is one of the most extraordinary, hope-filled and hope-giving breakthroughs in recent times: to be able to reduce the rate of infection from 1 in 3 Ugandans to less than 1 in 16. It is irrefutable evidence that what no one expects to see improved can be improved.

However, on the "*not yet* so bright" side is the fact that the world does not know about this victory—among other factors because the Babylonian systems intentionally prefer to push a futile non-God approach that benefits no one but the manufacturers of condoms, as a Ugandan leader confided to me.

But I believe, like the first crack in the ice of a lake at the onset of spring, that soon the whole mass will begin to crumble, and the threshold that leads to such victories—the fine line that separates hope and hopelessness—will be breached, and the effects will ripple throughout societies around the globe.

■ ■ ■

Once we have punched a hole in the darkness, the inserted light will do the rest.

■ ■ ■

Christians must actively seek a point of inception in the world arena for the discipling of at least one nation (a still unattained objective in modern times) and dismantle the Babylonian system by debunking its four core values of control (control, immorality, pride, and exploitation of nature) *somewhere on Earth*. The procession of redeemed nations featured in Revelation 21 has to begin somewhere, sometime. Why not with us; why not right now, *today*?

We need to take hold of this principle and demonstrate that it is possible to disciple a nation, including breaking the Babylonian systems of poverty. Since none of us is in control of a nation yet, we must begin with our own sphere of influence. Once we have punched a hole in the darkness, the inserted light will do the rest. And we must use whatever victories we have achieved already and turn them into beachheads from which to expand to bigger ground by going from what we have to what we plan to have.

What happened in Resistencia conclusively proved that cities can be reached. And not just one city, but any city, as attested by the myriad citywide transformation models emerging all over the world. These city models establish that the principles are both transferable and—because those cities are in different nations—trans-cultural. Now we must adapt and apply them at the nation level.

From the Known to the Unknown

As in the past, the only way we know to tackle this assignment is to go from the known to the unknown. To see how this strategic transition might happen, we need to take an in-depth look at what we know—how the first city-reaching prototype was developed.

In Resistencia, God downloaded to us the principle of filling a whole city with prayer by praying for the felt needs of the population as a precursor to opening their eyes (and the eyes of the city) to the love of God and to the reality that Jesus Christ is the only way to God. This methodology later came to be known as *prayer evangelism*, which we have described already.

At the very heart of prayer evangelism is an intentional thrust to make peace with the lost as dictated by Jesus' command that we lambs must go to the wolves (the lost) and speak peace over them (see Luke 10:3-5). This is followed by meaningful fellowship, particularly of the kind that they are comfortable with, as outlined by the instructions in Luke 10:7 to eat and drink in *their* homes everything *they* put before us. Next we must take care of their needs by praying for them. Then as God hears those prayers and the ones prayed for become aware of His presence, we are to declare to them, "The Kingdom of God has come near you" (Luke 10:9).

Once a highly cohesive group of pastors in Resistencia embraced by faith the notion that their city should be reached, they equipped and mobilized their members to practice prayer evangelism on the people in their sphere of influence. Six hundred thirty-five lighthouses of prayer were established in as many homes and distributed all over the city to cover the entire population of 400,000 people in prayer 24/7. In the measure that the city filled up with prayer, a dramatic improvement took place in the spiritual climate across the city, and unusual numbers of people began to come to Christ. But this thrust would not have progressed past the point of being a good outreach if it were not for an unusual and challenging opportunity.

Back in the 1980s it was rare that pastors would fellowship with public officials who were not believers—and even less so that they would invest "church money" to take care of city needs. But the improvement in the spiritual climate brought not only hope to the city but also more conscious awareness about the wealth of the anointing resident within the Church. A local businessman had a good relationship with the mayor of Resistencia, who had been a Colonel in the Army and a military governor of the province in years past. This "layman" invited me to meet with the mayor, and I felt that God wanted me to go.

Since my dad had been a politician, I knew the lingo and was able to use it to "talk shop." The more I chatted with the mayor, the more educated I became on how sincere and dedicated he was to his city. A warm camaraderie developed between us and "out of the blue" (God's blue, as I came to realize later on!), I asked him if there were any needs the city had that we should look into meeting. Without any hesitation, he brought up the fact that several neighborhoods were not connected to the city's water supply, lacked running water, and he did not have the budget to fix it.

One thing led to another and I felt led to commit on behalf of the Church to build 16 water tanks as a temporary but real solution. I felt somewhat "ambushed" but I knew that the "Ambusher" was God, and that gave me courage to move forward.

Before parting company, I asked if I could pray for him. Until then I had never prayed *with* a political leader who was not a Christian (remember, this was the late 1980s, and the gap between church and politics was wide and deep). He assented, and as I laid hands on him and prayed, tears welled up in his eyes. It took me by surprise, to put it mildly, since he was a macho kind of a guy, a Colonel in the Army, the city's leading public official and a Catholic, and was being prayed for by an evangelical! Obviously, God was orchestrating this.

The next day at a pastors meeting, I felt the way Peter must have felt when he was trying to explain to the Jerusalem leaders what took place in Cornelius's house. But again, God was in the ambush business and this time His target was the pastors. Just as the meeting was getting under way, the mayor suddenly showed up unannounced.

So much for our meeting agenda, for as the saying goes, where does an 800-pound gorilla sit? Obviously, anywhere he wants! The pastors were momentarily riveted to their chairs by this sudden apparition, then everybody scrambled to welcome him, more like the way we welcome a tax inspector into our shop. But he surprised us by saying to me, "I enjoyed so much what happened to me yesterday when you prayed, *that I came for more*," while stretching his cupped hands, like a child coming for more candies. This time I asked the pastors to join in, and when we prayed, the Spirit overwhelmed the mayor, who fell onto a chair.

By the time of the public outreach, we were able to present to the city 16 tanks that made water available to the poorest neighborhoods, in addition to the donation of an ample supply of medical equipment to the regional hospital. The mayor, who by then had come into the Kingdom, welcomed us and Jesus into the city. Multitudes received the Lord. The number of born-again Christians quadrupled. And best of all, God used all of this to demonstrate that a city can and must be discipled.

Felt Needs Are Key

Meeting the felt needs of the target area is *key*. Years later in Hawaii, that need was embodied in the school systems. Hawaii ranked as one of the worst in the nation. When students and pastors joined hands and resources to reclaim it, public officials and people of influence saw the value of that action and their eyes were open to the reality that the gospel is indeed good news.

Now we are going for entire nations—in fact, for all the nations of the world. And the principle is the same: We must meet their felt needs first, in order to open their eyes to the reality of Jesus Christ.

What is the world's greatest need? Of course it is Jesus, but the world cannot see that, because the evil one has blinded its eyes to the light of the gospel of the glory of Christ: "Even if our gospel is veiled, it is veiled to those who are perishing, in whose case the god of this world has blinded the minds of the unbelieving, that they might not see the light of the gospel of the glory of Christ, who is the image of God" (2 Cor. 4:3-4). To remove that veil we need to meet its most pressing need, and by this I mean what the world *feels* is its most pressing need. Without much debate, I believe we can all conclude that it is the elimination of systemic poverty.

Whoever is able to do this will have the attention and the heart of the world. It will be a repeat of the phenomenal growth described in the book of Acts (see Acts 2:43-47; 4:32-35) *but on a global scale*. With the globalization of communications and economics, once it happens in one place, it will spread like an out-of-control fire to the far corners of the world.

And that process is already in motion!

CHAPTER 18

It's Beginning to Happen

In December 2001, Argentina defaulted on its external debt, sending its 40 million people into turmoil and rocking the international markets. To commandeer financial control, the government appropriated all bank deposits, allowing only one maximum monthly withdrawal of 200 dollars. Deprivation of one sort or another hit everybody. Riots ensued. Supermarkets were sacked. Services broke down. Social order evaporated and the resulting popular uprising forced President De La Rua to resign in disgrace. Four presidents succeeded him in as many weeks. The country was in chaos. No one had the stature to quell the crisis, and the people had neither patience nor hope left to weather the storm.

I was deeply grieved, perplexed and confused over these developments. Argentina had been experiencing the longest running revival in modern times. People from all over the world had been coming to our conferences, as well as other forums, to be blessed. As recently as a month before the onset of the crisis I had visited the presidential palace and ministered to the leaders and authorities, including the president himself.

When I asked the Lord why such chaos was happening in a revival context, especially right after we had brought Jesus into the palace, He instructed me to read Acts 19. Being the optimist that I am, I only read the first part, where everybody in Ephesus and in Asia hears the word of the Lord in a context of extraordinary miracles performed by God through the hands of Paul, resulting in astonishing numbers of conversions.

"I don't get it," I said to God. He reminded me that He had directed me to read the *entire* chapter, not just the first half. When I did, I realized that the extraordinary outpouring of God's grace in the first half of Acts 19 was followed by riots instigated by one of the most powerful unions in Asia, with violence directed against Paul and the Church. With that as the background, God proceeded to explain to me the reasons for the upheaval like the one we were experiencing in Argentina.

No Status Quo

First, we should not expect business as usual once we take Jesus into the seat of government. When ungodly and/or demonic forces drive the economy (such as in Ephesus), God will judge it and it will collapse. Argentina's economy was no exception. However, God reassured me not to worry. He was dealing with the nation. Then He curiously instructed me to pray, not for healing, but for a *funeral* for Argentina! *"The old nation has to die before I will raise a new one from the dead,"* the Lord told me.

The second reason for the collapse, God said, was that the celebrated Argentine revival had been restricted largely to church members, and that even our own transformation thrusts were focused on cities, not on nations. We had not yet seen the transformation of cities as a means to the higher end of discipling the nation.

God then began to open my understanding to the need to disciple nations. The more we read the Scriptures, the clearer it became that we had aimed too low.

In November 2002, as Ruth and I drove from Buenos Aires to our international conference in Mar del Plata with Cindy Jacobs and Omar and Graciela Olier, we received divine download after download. By the time our car pulled into our hotel, we had been given precise instructions concerning launching a movement to disciple nations, beginning with Argentina.

At about that time I experienced a flashback to my childhood, when I used to spend summers with my grandpa in the pampas. On this particular recollection we had been hauling sacks of wheat in the fields since sunup. Grandpa let me drive the wagon and operate the winch while he did the heavy lifting. It was hard work but I enjoyed hanging out with him. However, at the end of the long day I was glad we were heading back to the house.

When we got home, Grandpa sat in the shade, enjoying the breeze. He asked me to get him a glass of water from the well. There was a windmill a few yards away that bored so deeply in the ground that the water was unusually pure and always cool.

I took the water to Grandpa and he drank it with satisfaction, complete with the noisy chuckles that Italians reserve for good food and drink. As pleasure radiated from him, he exclaimed, "I have been thinking about this water all day long. Please, get me another glass."

Suddenly, in the flashback, God replaced my grandpa, and a nation substituted for the glass of water, and I saw myself coming to Him with a nation in my hands. God received it with pleasure similar to my grandpa's and exclaimed, *"I have been waiting so long for someone to bring me a nation! Please, go bring me more nations."*

It was a profound *kairos* moment, a fixed and special occasion in which God impressed on me how important nations are to Him and how much His heart longs for them. I was deeply moved and eager to do whatever was necessary to quench His thirst.

In the past, God, in His infinite mercy, had allowed us to pioneer city reaching, but now He was inviting us to do the same with nations. With a perfect mixture of unworthiness and excitement, we decided to accept the challenge.

This led to the formation of the International Transformation Network (ITN), a network devoted to nation transformation. This network is leading the way in pioneering a hands-on strategic alliance of pulpit and marketplace ministers to build prototypes for nation transformation. Its members have embraced the five pivotal paradigms that are the subject of this book, and are actively involved in developing transformation models within their spheres of influence.

One of the pacesetting features of this unique network is the emergence of what the members are calling the "51 percent circle." This is a group comprised of individuals, corporations and congregations that are actively engaged in a process to continually invest into the community 51 percent of its resources to meet felt needs, with a special focus on the elimination of systemic poverty. The catalytic example that launched this model was that of Myles Kawakami, the Maui businessman who decided to give 50 percent of his business to God. Since then, he and his wife, Joyce, have been using its profit to eliminate systemic poverty in their region. Francis Oda, the architect who led the president of Tahiti to the Lord, was inspired by Myles's example and shared with me his desire to raise the mark to 51 percent as a practical demonstration that God was indeed the majority shareholder.

In April 2006, our annual ITN meeting took place in New York City, the marketplace capital of the world. When we presented this challenge to ITN members, the response was overwhelming as testimony after testimony from marketplace leaders endorsing this idea was made public. But a much greater breakthrough came when it was embraced by churches.

Greg Pagh, a pastor from Elk River, Minnesota, shared his heart and precipitated a chain reaction. "I am a pastor and I have enjoyed pastoring for the past 25 years," Greg said. "I also have a doctorate in Church Growth and I teach on the subject. I intend to be a pastor for the rest of my life. But I would like to be the pastor of a 51 percent church. I want my church, and other churches, to give out more than we keep."

There was such an anointing in the room and God was so powerfully behind Greg's words that everybody was overwhelmed by a sense of awe. It was like walking in the river described by Ezekiel, with water up to our waist and all of a sudden being swept downstream by a current beyond our control.

Since then, numerous other churches have joined in, and the number of 51 percent churches keeps increasing. This is extremely significant because many local congregations, though never selfish, easily drift into self-centeredness. Most of their income is spent on church-related matters, and their ministry focus, attention, resources and time are invested primarily on their own members, rather than on their city and nation.

A Matter of the Heart

I believe that the Babylonian system is so common around us that people often fail to discern how much it has permeated Christians and the *local expression* of Church. We have become conditioned to accept it.

I remember making a call to the pastor of one of the leading churches in central California to ask that an announcement be made to invite his members to be part of a canopy of prayer being raised over the San Francisco Bay area. He is a friend, one to whom I have ministered in times of deep personal crisis, and he and his family had expressed great appreciation for my help. If someone would have gladly obliged my request for an announcement to promote prayer, I thought it would surely have been him. But his reply left me emotionally numb. He said, "Sorry, Ed, I am halfway to my goal of raising three million dollars for my building program and I do not want my people distracted."

This self-centeredness in church leadership easily mutates to selfishness among members. Sadly, I also witnessed the same spiritual complacency in another church elder who is the director for development for the leading religious non-profit NGO (non-governmental organization). His job is to present the needs of the poor to potential donors, and he raises large amounts of money for this organization. However, when it came to selling a house he had been using as a rental, his actions reflected the Babylonian spirit, and not Christ's.

■ ■ ■

As people move in obedience and intentionally challenge the prevailing Babylonian culture, God will give the necessary increase.

■ ■ ■

The house was leased to a couple with young children. They were in financial difficulty due to the fact that the husband was between jobs. When the church elder informed the couple of his plans to sell the house, they inquired if he could extend the deadline in order to allow them to move into a rental that would be available one month later. Oddly, this "man of God" denied the request. When the couple then asked him if he would be willing to inspect the premises right away, to determine if they could count on a refund of their rental deposit to help them pay for transitional lodging at a hotel, he again declined! When he was asked to do the inspection right after the tenants left, he took his time doing so, and then wrote an offensive letter denying the refund—even though there was no proper justification for withholding the couple's funds. All this while going about his job telling potential donors about the plight of the needy and why they should be compassionate and help his NGO! Exactly *whose* side was this church elder on? The Babylonian side—without even knowing it.

ITN is a response to the reality that we the Church have not done enough, that we need to do more, and that we can do it better. As people move in obedience and intentionally challenge the prevailing Babylonian culture, God will give the necessary increase.

Living Examples of Transformation in Action

The Scriptures indicate that Judgment must begin first within the house of the Lord. In the midst of "fiery ordeals" that will be common to all, the flock is to be shepherded "with eagerness" by those who are providing "examples to the flock" (1 Pet. 4:17–5:4).

As a case in point, a businessman I know, soon after leading his partner's son to the Lord, discovered that his partner had falsified his signature in corporate documents that brought him to the brink of insolvency. Rather than protecting his financial position by reporting the fraud, he chose to absorb the loss. When I asked him what motivated him to do that, he replied, "I did not want to give the devil an opportunity to squash the faith of my partner's son." Even though in the natural it had taken him years to work himself out of the financial hole in which his unfaithful partner put him, a soul has been saved and the Babylonian system took a major hit.

The church pastored by Cal Chinen of Honolulu gives 50 percent of its income to ministries and projects outside of its walls and joyfully reports that its members are leading more people to Christ that join other churches than their own church, thus increasing the kingdom of God. Truly, Cal Chinen heads a Kingdom church!

Omar Olier, who has been pastoring the largest and most influential congregation in Mar del Plata, is another example. He could have coasted to retirement on the back of his ministerial success. But he broke free from the influence of the Babylonian spirit when he met with his colleagues to ask for forgiveness for his indifference, something that immediately triggered a reciprocal response. As a result, Omar pledged himself to the other pastors, and they elected him president of the Ministerial Association of Mar del Plata. He proceeded to organize the pastors in twosomes, in which a more successful one was paired with someone who was less successful, and the former pledged not to grow their congregations further until the other had experienced growth.

This meant that if a pastor's salary was inadequate, the other would make up the difference. If one congregation did not have a building, the other would come alongside to secure one, and so on. This arrangement included Omar and his own ministry. He poured himself into the other pastors, spending more time with them than with his own leaders, since they have come to understand that there is only one Church in the city with only one Chief shepherd, a realization that made everybody else an associate of Jesus.

A year later the congregations involved had grown an average of 400 percent. Omar's was the one that grew the least, "just" 130 percent. But the progress has gone beyond mere church growth. The mayor has come in the Kingdom. Similar breakthroughs have taken place among lawyers, judges, business people, doctors and policemen. In fact, Mar del Plata has become known as "God's City." It is no coincidence that it has been the host city for our international conference for the past 12 years.

ITN is a response to the reality that we need to do more and intentionally challenge the prevailing Babylonian culture. And we need to do it diligently and persistently because the Babylonian spirit can deceive even those who do mighty works for God, people of tremendous spiritual stature such as Joseph and Solomon. Joseph, after executing God's plan to protect the Mediterranean world from the effects of a horrendous famine, foolishly forced the entire population of Egypt to sell themselves to Pharaoh in exchange for the food that God had provided through Joseph's management! Solomon, after building the Temple and providing a place for God's presence to reside in, abused his God-given wisdom and built an empire for himself instead of using it to take God's knowledge to the nations of the world. It is key to finish strong. This is why associations like ITN are a definite must for mutual accountability, not just for strategic joint ventures.

When Francis Oda (current ITN chairman) won the architecture competition in Tahiti over other participants, he had every right to "take all the marbles" for his own company—and the profits, too. Instead, he chose to take advantage of the immensity of the project and give participation to those who had "lost" so that the kingdom of God would win and God would be glorified even further.

Lawyer David Monroy brings his faith to bear on every portfolio and legal brief he handles. Instead of pursuing victory at all costs, his objective is to bring peace to all the parties involved, in order to serve the long-term best interests of the clients. His attitude definitely bucks the prevailing cutthroat culture in the legal system.

Graham Power, founder and CEO of the Power Group of Companies in South Africa, saw his business prosper and his influence increase when his business "got saved." He is leading many efforts to meet the felt needs of towns and villages around Cape Town and beyond. In a grass-roots effort to combat systems of poverty threatening his nation and others, he is using his influence to challenge his peers and followers (who include some of Africa's most influential marketplace leaders) to a commitment to be "Ethically Unashamed." Those signing the "Ethically Unashamed" pledge (a standard requirement for ITN members worldwide) commit to the following:

- Be ethical, operating in the highest integrity to produce and deliver quality products and services.
- Refuse to accept or pay bribes.
- Pay taxes honestly.
- Pay reasonable salaries and wages.
- Intentionally invest in the betterment of the workforce and their families.
- Invest generously and sacrificially in the broader community, with the focus on eradicating systemic poverty.
- Purposefully connect with other companies, professions and individuals to impact the world.

Alex Contreras, an Argentine businessman and entrepreneur, has captured the essence of the vision for transformation and is setting out on a goal to establish a 51 percent transformation company in every one of Argentina's 23 provinces and the nation's capital, as a model and an inspiration for others to follow suit.

And the list goes on and on.

ITN members have embraced prayer evangelism and the five pivotal paradigms as central components of their lifestyle, turning them into spiritual Marines, always ready to storm the beaches. During our international conference in Argentina in 2006, God availed ITN with a tremendous opportunity to comprehensively implement the principles we have been teaching.

Attending the conference as an honored delegate, the First Lady of Uganda shared with our network how her heart, and the hearts of many African leaders, is so broken during times of famine. She portrayed in vivid detail the scenes of huge sacks of food supplies—dropped from helicopters—bursting upon impact, forcing the people to forage like animals for comestibles now contaminated with dirt and mud. She explained how rich Africa is in people and in raw materials, yet how undeveloped it is regarding infrastructure. She closed her speech with a plea: "My people do not need fish. They need to learn *how to fish*."

The delegates, deeply moved, started making sincere commitments to aid. Capturing what was in their hearts, I sensed something more from the Lord bearing on the equation. I respectfully stated, "Madam, teaching your people to fish is key, but even more important is for them to own the pond, or else somebody will be making a lot of money selling you fishing permits!"

Subsequent conversations seeking an integral solution in such context led to the conclusion that the best point of inception for a transformation prototype in Uganda would be the district that the First Lady represents in Parliament. It has a population of approximately 250,000 people and is rich in produce but poor in basic infrastructure. Pledges were taken that came to three-quarters of a million dollars, including the donation of construction equipment, as an act that sealed the network's commitment to Uganda.

■ ■ ■

Teaching your people to fish is key, but even more important is for them to own the pond, or else somebody will be making a lot of money selling you fishing permits!

■ ■ ■

Subsequent visits to the district to assess needs and to envision the best strategy resulted in a plan to build roads and to provide the machinery and training for locals to maintain them. Portable drying units were donated to dry and package fruit for export (fruit is abundant but rots on the field due to lack of processing capability). Commitments were made to expand an existing medical clinic to improve the quality of healthcare. The establishment of a faith bank for micro-loans was included. The cost for all this came to one million dollars, all of which was subscribed by ITN members *with no strings attached*.

On a parallel track, ITN members are working with the Transformation Network of Uganda (TNU) on an even more comprehensive plan that will eventually impact every district in the nation. Alex Mitala (the pineapple farmer mentioned in chapter 1 and also the chairman of the 15,000-member Fellowship of Churches) and Andrew Rugasira (the coffee grower described in chapter 12) co-chair the group, which also includes Uganda Tax Commissioner Allen Kagina and many other pulpit and marketplace leaders. Transformation groups are emerging all over Kampala, the capital of Uganda—in banks, shopping malls, schools, and even at the First Lady's office.

It is too early to say for certain, but just as Resistencia opened the eyes of our understanding to reach entire cities, Uganda stands a very good chance to be the nation that provides the point of inception for Christians to demonstrate that a nation can be discipled. Meeting a nation's felt needs is proving to be a great door opener.

Other ITN members are actively pursuing similar initiatives in other nations. (Because of the sensitivity of the projects I am withholding names and locations.) Here are just a few examples:

- One member has become the international purchasing agent for a Third World nation to handle contracts worth millions of dollars, with the bulk of the profit being donated to rebuilding the country. Since making that decision, God has entrusted this person with additional deals worth hundreds of millions of dollars, which will be used in an identical manner.

- Another has landed long-term projects worth billions of dollars and has stipulated that 51 percent of his profits be reinvested in the development and upgrading of infrastructures to better the lot of the needy.

- A third colleague owns patents for technological developments worth millions of dollars, all of which will be used for Kingdom purposes.

- The owner of a cutting-edge highly successful corporation and his CEO have set up a mentoring program for promising young people to teach them everything they know and to offer to set them up with their own company once they graduate from the program. This is a radical departure from what is normative in the industry, since mentoring programs usually require that the graduates work for the company. Even more extreme is setting them up as potential competitors!

- Similar engagements are taking place outside of ITN also. On a recent ministry trip to a Muslim nation, a very wealthy Christian businessman shared with me that he has purchased several hundred hectares of land, on which he plans to build the infrastructure necessary to adopt and nurture with excellence 10,000 orphans. But in addition to food and shelter, he plans to provide the absolute best kindergarten-to-university education in a state-of-the-art campus so that these orphans can become leaders in key fields and bring transformation to the world at large.

- An international broker is planning to recruit and train hundreds of Christians, who graduate from business schools, as brokers who will pledge to practice Kingdom principles and donate 51 percent of their profits for nation transformation.

- Recently, Ruth and I had dinner with people who hold patents to energy-generating breakthroughs that have the potential to revolutionize the transportation industry. Both of them are pledged to nation transformation.

I received the following narrative from my friend Dave Seeba that reflects how much is going on in other sectors of the marketplace:

In an upscale resort hotel, 120 bright, successful businessmen are gathering to discuss strategy not on how to beat the competition, or on how to get a new product to market, but on how to focus on things that make life *significant*, rather than just making people successful. Many of these businesspeople have realized that they have given up too much in exchange for the success they've achieved. Others are seeking to integrate success with significance so that their lives can be an influence to establish God's kingdom on Earth.

A Glorious Vision

These marketplace Christians are trying to live their lives in a manner that recognizes that God gifted and positioned them in a particular way for a specific reason. To a person, these people are entrepreneurial problem-solvers. They see opportunities and encourage each other to take risks.

A roundtable sharing of what they're involved in is both inspiring and challenging. Here are a few highlights from the conference:

- One leads a group of businesspeople to underdeveloped parts of the world to share their business knowledge with local entrepreneurs in developing economies. They also share what motivates them to care for these countries: their love of fellow man, as Jesus taught.

- Another CEO travels worldwide, encouraging businesspeople to use their businesses to express the message of Christ, but also to be a *blessing* to those in their community.

- A high-powered attorney talks about how God pulled him from being a workaholic and gave him compassion for AIDS orphans in Africa. This has reenergized his relationship with his wife and two daughters, who have joined him in this outreach.

- Over dinner, the son of a strict missionary couple describes how observing the profound effect that music and film were having on his peers lead him to a career in Hollywood, producing music for films.

- After dinner, a singer, also working in Hollywood as well as on Broadway, performs his own unique creations. These songs are written to bring biblical situations to life for secular audiences. Between songs he shares about godly men and women working in Hollywood on positive projects and also about their key role in keeping to a minimum the more destructive interpretations that find their way into films.

- The next day, this high-powered group piles onto busses to go to an advance screening of the film *Amazing Grace*. This movie tells the life of William Wilberforce, who led the successful fight to outlaw the slave trade in England and who is generally recognized as sacrificing his political career in the English Parliament in order to catalyze a movement that brought an end to slavery throughout the British Empire. This particular film strikes a deep cord with the group because a fellow Christian who shares many of the group's aspirations is the one who commissioned it.

- The next day, during morning and evening sessions, a well-known pastor speaks about the marriage and parenting problems that most driven, type-A personalities experience. It's unusual for leaders of religious organizations to see these successful people as anything more than a means to fund their own programs. But the speaker's genuine concern for their unique personal struggles is greatly appreciated and his advice is soaked up like water on parched ground.

- During lunch on the last day, the scion of one of America's best-known families describes how God led him away from a career in the family business to run a significant company. At the same time, pursuing his wife's desire to adopt children has resulted in a doubling of their immediate family into an international ministry serving people in Africa.

- Punctuating the dinner break, a top-level executive in a Silicon Valley high-tech company, shares about his prayer life—not what many might expect from someone in his position, but this group knows that such a connection to God is vital in what they seek to do.

- The final evening of the conference is shared between a world-famous pastor speaking about renewal and a former high-tech CEO sharing about how God can effectively use business. The group doesn't see any dichotomy here. They listen intently to the personal change required of them and the life-changing message that their businesses can bring and demonstrate.

Is God able to work through businesses done right, businesses that create jobs, reinvest in communities, and exhibit biblical values within the workplace? These entrepreneurs think so. And this type of gathering is also happening in other places.

For example, I recently conducted a seminar in a rich nation that is also rated among the top five most corrupt in the world. At the close of the teaching, representatives of 47 marketplace groups enthusiastically came forward to sign a public pledge that included working in unity for the transformation of the nation, beginning with the corrupt marketplace culture. To that effect they also pledged *to pay taxes and not to take or accept bribes.*

Recently, 137 Christian captains of industry with businesses in China met for three days to compare notes and lay the foundation for "spiritual joint ventures." They too climaxed their meeting by signing a pledge to pay taxes, provide decent salaries, care for their employees *and stay away from bribes!*

Because corruption is the lifeline that sustains systemic poverty, I have chosen examples that include a valiant public stance against it. Since systemic poverty is *the* felt need of the world that we are called to reach with the gospel, we need to ask the question, *How long would it take to bring down such deeply entrenched mammoth evil?*

■ ■ ■

We are fast approaching the tipping point in terms of generating and/or accessing substantial resources for the kingdom of God.

■ ■ ■

In such a context, it is encouraging to be reminded of a similar worldwide deeply entrenched systemic evil—slavery—that *in a relatively short time* was eradicated: "By the end of the eighteenth century, well over three quarters of the world population was in bondage, subject to various forms of slavery and serfdom. Yet even more astonishing than the extent of slavery was the speed with which it died. By the end of the following century, keeping slaves was officially outlawed almost everywhere. The anti-slavery movement had achieved its goal in little more than one lifetime."[1]

In my estimation, five factors made this swift elimination of wholesale slavery possible:

First, people who did not own slaves but saw the evil of it spoke out against it.

Second, those who could have owned slaves refused to do so.

Third, those who owned them opted to set them free.

Fourth, these three groups joined hands to actively pursue the freedom of slaves among the holdouts, either by moral pressure or by outright purchase of them.

And fifth, the system collapsed when the antislavery movement's momentum—captured the higher moral ground and exposed unashamedly and relentlessly the evil nature of slavery.

In those five steps, there are applicable parallels to how systemic poverty can, and I dare say *will*, be eliminated. ITN members and similar groups have already taken the first three steps. The other two will soon follow, and the current globalization works in our favor. It is just a matter of time if we persevere.

The Final Breakthrough

Now that a significant number of marketplace ministers have embraced or are aware of the pivotal paradigms, we are fast approaching the tipping point in terms of generating and/or accessing substantial resources for the kingdom of God—not just financial resources, but also new ideas, concepts and inventions that can provide a cure for the societal illnesses that feed systemic poverty. No one loves systemic poverty. Everybody wants to see it eliminated, but so far no one has come up with the solution. This is our greatest opportunity as Christians.

In Resistencia, as well as in subsequent models like Elk River and Hawaii, the transformational impetus from God came in three successive waves. The first wave convinced His people that transformation was doable. The second showed them that the world was anxiously awaiting their manifestation as peacemakers and problem solvers. This made them aware of the need to earn the right to be heard by serving the lost first. The third wave turned the enemy's stronghold into the foundation for God's transformational model through the meeting of felt needs. For instance, the lack of water in Resistencia and the crisis in the schools in Hawaii became opportunities for the Church to display in the most tangible way the love of God in action.

I foresee that the breakthrough that will make possible the discipling of nations, and in the process bring down the Babylonian system, will have five components:

1. Christians who have embraced a transformational lifestyle along the paradigms discussed in this book will be led by God to coalesce in different parts of the world in order to develop models of *biblically based social entrepreneurship.*

In the same fashion that we have grown comfortable asking a mayor what we can do to help with city problems, we will soon do the same with world leaders. The principle is the same, except that the answer will have more zeroes. And these Christians will deliver in the name and in the Spirit of Christ, *with no strings attached!*

2. Christians who have learned how to access the leaves of the Tree of Life will come up with discoveries, inventions and new formulas to solve major world problems in at least four key areas: energy, commerce, food and medicine. And when they are offered the financial rewards that such break-throughs customarily bring, these Christians will astound the world by emulating Christ on a worldwide platform as givers and not takers by redirecting that revenue toward entrepreneurial charity to deal with systemic evils. They will be true disciples of the One who said, "It is better to give than to receive" (Acts 20:35). By doing what amounts to a slap in the face to the Babylonian system, they will debunk its greed and control.

3. Christians who have been called to serve in government with a transformational anointing, either as elected offi-cials or career civil servants, will be entrusted by God with supernatural insights to solve perennial social problems that have baffled world leaders. And they will do it with the same generous spirit that Daniel did. As you may recall, when the king ordered the execution of the pagan magi-cians, who were heavily immersed in occultist practices, Daniel interceded with the king for himself *and for the diviners.* Later on, Daniel was made head of them all (the equivalent to being appointed chairman of the witches and warlocks union of Babylon). Daniel not only accepted, but he also ruled the union efficiently since he was 10 times more knowledgeable than all the magicians and conjurers in all the arts and sciences of the Caldeans (see Dan. 1:20).

What money is to business, influence is to politics. These modern-day Daniels will not use the influence resulting from their extraordinary insights to lord over others, but to *serve* them instead. Thus, they will debunk two other manifestations of the Babylonian system: immorality and pride.

4. All of the above will take place in the context of extraordinary miracles, signs and wonders performed by God through the hands of true apostles who will be recognized on account of the anointing for miracles entrusted to them and on account of their devotion to and dependence on prayer. These astonishing divine interventions through human vessels will have exponential influence because they will take place in the context of threats, persecution and even martyrdom (see Matt. 5:12; John 15:20). The purpose for these extraordinary miracles is threefold: to embolden the Church, to open the eyes of the lost, and to trump the Babylonian system. These were then, and will be now, transformation miracles indeed!

5. God will also provide "human accelerators" through the dramatic conversions of highly influential and catalytic leaders, as was the case with Crispus in Corinth (see Acts 18:8) and Saul of Tarsus. None of them were on the Church radar. In fact, in the case of Saul, he was the most dangerous enemy of Christianity, but God saw him as "a chosen vessel unto me, to bear my name before the Gentiles and kings, and the children of Israel" (Acts 9:15, *ASV*).

What these five streams have in common are players who are precise and pure channels for God to touch the world (not just the Church) and the lost (not just believers) through the miraculous meeting of deeply felt needs that will tangibly reveal the majesty, the power and especially the universality of the good news of the gospel—the Gospel of the Kingdom, the only thing that can make the world believe.

Jesus said, "The Law and the Prophets were proclaimed until John; since that time the gospel of the kingdom of God has been preached, and everyone is forcing his way into it" (Luke 16:16). Transformational Christians, without denying or neglecting the Law and the prophets, will actively focus on, and convey boldly, the gospel of the kingdom of God in every place where the Gates of Hades are still standing (*the Babylonian system*). And when they do, those gates will crumble and *everyone* will *force* their way into the Kingdom.

Yes, victory is beginning to rise over the horizon. Let us press on!

CHAPTER 19

God's Faith in You

"Saddle up," said my grandpa while keeping a stern gaze on the eastern pasture. "Saddle up and go get 'em." He was staring at a herd of cows that had broken out of their corral during the night and were having the time of their lives eating what they were not supposed to have.

This particular herd was notorious for its propensity for mischief, which is why it was always locked up at night. It was led by a young bull that, if it had been born a human, would have launched a successful revolution in some South American country. It had an extraordinary capacity for leadership, coupled with a keen ability to spot weaknesses in the system that he quickly turned into opportunities. Whatever it did, the others in the herd followed unquestionably.

Rounding them up was not going to be easy. It never was. During the summers that I usually spent with my grandpa, I had ridden with him on similar occasions and it was always a challenge. But this morning he told me to go and do it *by myself*!

I could not believe my ears. The "old man" believed that I, a little eight-year-old *me*, could do it? Part of me was almost terrified at the prospect of facing that cunning bull and its gang of "illegals" who broke through the fence. But another part of me felt an exhilarating surge of pride, knowing that my grandpa believed I could do it.

Grandpa was not the touchy-feely type. He was born at the end of the nineteenth century and was part of a generation that, rather than saying "I love you," demonstrated their love by working hard to make sure there was food and provisions for everyone. He was also a man of very few words. His facial muscles did not add much to his words. But his eyes did. He never raised his voice, but with his eyes he added the necessary emphasis to what he wanted to say. And that morning there was a glint of "something" in his blue eyes. I sensed it was confidence. He was communicating to me, *"You can do it.* I believe in you. Now go and prove me right."

Seeing that glimmer in his eyes was all I needed. It conveyed to me that Grandpa believed in me, and that was all it took for me to tackle the task he had assigned to me. Besides, there was no recourse to challenge his command. I had received a direct order.

I sprinted toward the small corral in the back of the house to saddle Manchado, my pinto horse, the one Grandpa had given me a couple years earlier as a birthday present. When I mounted and pointed Manchado in the direction of the pasture where the bovine rebel leader and his confederates were setting up camp, I felt like a combination of Zorro, Superman and Captain Marvel, my three cartoon heroes. I was fully energized by the faith Grandpa had shown in me. On my own I would have never come up with the confidence to do it, but Grandpa's words, framed and accentuated by the glint in his eyes, had energized what little faith I had, and here I was, riding to do what I had never done before.

Surprisingly, everything went well. It was not easy, but after a while I had the entire herd where it was supposed to be. When I rode Manchado back to the house, I felt like a victorious Roman general returning from a successful campaign. But I knew better than to expect an accolade from my non-touchy, reserved Grandpa. He was a man of very few words, but his eyes . . . that's what I was going to concentrate on.

By the time I unsaddled Manchado, Grandpa had already hitched another horse to a buggy, the kind of vehicle used for short runs. He did not comment on my triumphant expedition to put down the bull's rebellion, but with an approving glint in his eyes he said, "Let's go to town."

Once in town, a small pueblo, we went to the cantina where he ordered drinks for both of us. That was not unusual. He had done it before. He normally had a glass of wine, or he and I would each get a glass of grenadine. But what was different this time is *what* he said and *how* he said it. In a louder than usual voice, intended for others to hear him, he intoned, "Bring the usual, for me *and my partner.*"

He called me *partner* in front of his friends! That morning, his show of faith in me electrified the faith I had in me and empowered me to perform a task that until then I had viewed as impossible. What triggered this breakthrough was *his* faith *in me.* And now he had just announced that we were partners! Awesome!

When it comes to faith in God, we are often buffeted by similar feelings of inadequacy because we mistakenly root our faith in *our* capacity to believe. We measure faith by how much faith in God *we* have. And we often end up discouraged because we fail to factor in *how much faith God has in us*. We seldom think of that possibility. However, the truth is that God uses *His* faith in us to prime the pump for *our* faith in Him to grow. All through the Bible, in book after book, He eloquently states how precious, holy and victorious we are. These statements come to the rescue when we find ourselves stuck in feelings of unworthiness, sinfulness and defeat. Reading how assuredly He expects us to win provides us with the second wind necessary to pursue it and attain it.

This issue is eloquently illustrated by the story of Gideon, in Judges 6–8. Usually when we think of this Old Testament hero, we picture a brave, fearless man who knew nothing but an unending string of victories. However, Gideon lived at a time of tragic national devastation. Year after year, when harvest time arrived and God's people were ready to enjoy its fruit, their enemies the Midianites descended on the land like locusts, overrunning the crops, trampling through the vineyards, slaughtering animals and raping the land. They came to devastate and subordinate a nation and they did it with an impunity that drove God's people to hide in caves in nearby hills from where they helplessly watched the fruit of their labors being plundered.

On one such occasion Gideon was hiding wheat inside of a wine press before taking off to hole up in a cave. Gideon was not planning to fight, not even to passively resist the invaders. Overcome by fear, he was hiding some grain to have something with which to plant a new crop that surely his enemies would return to steal next year. It was not a very uplifting picture.

It is at this juncture that an angel visits him and declares, "The Lord is with you, mighty warrior" (Judg. 6:12, *NIV*). This was a strange salutation since it did not match the facts at hand. Gideon was certainly not a warrior; he was a fleeing civilian seeking refuge. And by no stretch of the imagination could he be considered mighty. On the contrary, he was crushed inside and devoid of hope. However, this was the angel of the Lord speaking, so we cannot doubt his credibility and integrity in delivering such a message from God, whom we know cannot lie. How then can this declaration, so at odds with reality, be true? The reason why Gideon could be truthfully called a mighty warrior is because *God has a better opinion of us than we have of ourselves*.

God's opinion of us, like my grandpa's, is determined by victories still in the future, whereas our assessment of our own capabilities (or lack thereof) is shaped by past failures and by what we have *not* done. God *saw Gideon as the general he was going to be*, and not the fearful young lad he was when he was groveling in the wine vat.

Like the Israel of those days, many Christians today often become prisoners in caves of resignation and fear. They have worked hard at building a home, a marriage, a career, a relationship, a family, and when they were ready to enjoy the fruit of their labor, tragedy struck, perhaps not once but many times. Like Gideon, they have fallen into a cycle of failure, riding a merry-go-round of defeats until hope has vanished and faith has been discarded as an option.

God has tremendous faith in us because He sees what we are capable of, and to that effect, He is willing and eager to invest in us.

If this is your case, you need to make a decision: Whose report will you believe, God's or the enemy's? God has tremendous faith in us because He sees what we are capable of, and to that effect, He is willing and eager to invest in us. Remember, the enemy of faith is not unbelief; it is memory, because negative memories bind us to the past, whereas faith reveals all the positive things that are yet to happen. To quote Hebrews 11:1, "Now faith is the assurance of *things hoped for,* the conviction of *things not seen*" (emphasis added).

Gideon obviously was not convinced that God was with him, nor that he was a mighty warrior, because he began to argue with the angel that if God was indeed with him, then why hadn't he seen miracles like the ones his forefathers talked of so much.

Why? The ultimate question. It is the one that Satan likes to resort to when we are immersed in a deep personal crisis. When our faith in God begins to wane, he leverages the crisis with that question, knowing that only God can provide the answer, but our weakened faith will not allow us to access it. As a result, we are driven deeper into despair and defeat.

The more we fixate on this question, the more prone we become to doubt the power of God and the reality of miracles, which are precisely what we need in order to get out of our predicament. So it was with Gideon (see Judg. 6:13).

It is very revealing that at this point God Himself replaced the angel in the scenario. We understand that the "angel of the Lord" in the Old Testament is a reference to the pre-incarnate Christ, which is why we know that the next voice heard is God's. I can imagine God saying, "This is a tough case that requires My personal attention." Then, ignoring the "why" question that will lead to nowhere, and because time was of the essence, God proceeded to give a direct command—illogical, improbable and without explanation: "Go in this your strength and deliver Israel" (Judg. 6:14). I say "improbable" because Gideon had hardly any strength left, and whatever strength he had was not adequate to save himself, much less the nation.

But there is a powerful principle at work here. In essence, God was telling Gideon, "Stop thinking about personal survival and trust Me for something that will save you and everything around you."

If we remain fixated on mere survival, struggling to come up with well-meaning (albeit temporary), short-term solutions, then we will never reach our destiny. Saving an industry, a city or a nation requires total dependence on God and access to new ideas, new power, new anointing. We need to believe the report of the Lord instead of a report that is the sum of our fears and doubts.

A Personal Illustration

In 1980, following a week of medical tests, I sat down with my doctor to hear him state that I had a maximum of two years to live. A neurological disease had taken up residence in my body and medical science did not have a cure for it.

I vividly recall how he walked up to a blackboard (this was 1980 and we were meeting in a teaching hospital) and drew first an X to indicate where I was, health-wise, that day, and then drew a line that at first was level but after a short while took an abrupt turn downward. At that point he said, "Sooner or later, this will happen to you." His descending thrust caused the chalk to hit the chalk-holder tray and it broke in two pieces. One fell to the floor and began rolling in my direction, and the shocking, sobering reality of the moment gripped my mind. I thought, "This chalk represents my life today. I am still rolling but it will soon come to a stop."

My doctor's prognosis was confirmed by other specialists and by the body of literature I read on my illness. All this information got stored in my mind and became a bulwark in my memory. Every visit to the doctor was a reminder of what I had been told: "Two years and counting." Two years is a frighteningly short time when you are 35 years old with a wife and four children ranging in age from 2 to 11.

Every piece of information I had stored in my brain pointed toward my early demise and began to control my thoughts and my actions. All I heard were "medical facts" that preempted any miraculous intervention. That was the case until I discovered the power of intercession. As I tell the story in my book *That None Should Perish*, I made a decision to set aside three days to seek God and inquire not into the past, but into the future. My question to God was direct and simple, "Is this an illness unto death or unto life?"

For nearly three solid days I interceded, beseeching God and seeking His face. After 2 days, 23 hours and 45 minutes had gone by with nothing but divine silence, and with only 15 more minutes to go, I said to God, "I have enjoyed your presence and I am grateful for the privilege of being able to bring up this matter. I submit to your will. If your silence is the answer, as much as I dislike it, I accept it. But with all due respect, allow me to say that it would have been very nice for me to hear from you, even if it was to confirm what the doctors have already told me."

I was heading toward our retreat center in San Nicolas, Argentina. With just minutes before the self-imposed deadline and less than a mile to go before I would have to resign myself to what my memory had been saying all along, all of a sudden the presence of God invaded the car. It was so powerful that He became tangible. I could feel and sense Him all around me. The car became a chariot of fire and, as if riding on the wings of angels, I made it to the retreat center. Once there, His Spirit took over mine and for the rest of the night I was praying *with Him* with groans too deep for words, as Romans 8:26 teaches.

When dawn came, my body was still sick, but I had received, *by faith*, a promise that God was going to heal me. I had nothing in the natural to pin it on but just plain, raw faith. I had come to a "Y" in the road. If I looked at the past, I would die. If I dwelt on my present condition, I would whither. But if I gazed into the future, penetrating the ever-present memory-fed fog of doubts with my newfound faith, I knew that I would live.

And I chose *life*!

For the next six months, I went through medical hell. I had to be rushed to the emergency room when my white blood cell count became dangerously low. I was hooked for hours to machines twice a week to cleanse my blood with a procedure called plasmaphoresis. My days were measured from injection to medication to time for another injection. But every day I would choose to look into the future—often from a deep rut in the road—to salute from a distance the promise that I would live and not die. It was a gargantuan battle between memory and faith. And faith won. The 2 years that were to have ended in death have become 27 years to-date, filled with the most exhilarating life, fully focused on bringing transformation to cities and nations.

Heading for Victory

I want to say to you with great confidence in God and full assurance emanating from His Word that as it was with me your true destiny awaits you at the end of a path guarded by menacing giants, and fear is one of them. You must press on knowing that *God has a very positive opinion of you and He is commanding you to shift from survival mode to conquering mode.* Firmly take hold of your Father's hand in fullness of faith! Let Him lift you up and lead you to where He has destined you to go. Look beyond the ominous clouds of today's momentary crises to the lasting transformation that He has called you to bring to your sphere of influence in the marketplace. He is there to enable you. He believes in *you as He believed in fear-ridden Gideon* when He told him to save the nation.

Next, God instructed Gideon to go to his father's house to tear down the altar of Baal and the image of Ashera adjacent to it, and to use the stones from the former and the wood from the latter to build an altar to the Lord upon which to sacrifice Gideon's dad's prized bulls.

Gideon was again struggling with fear because he was the youngest in his father's household and his own family was not a prominent one in Israel. His dad would be more than angry when he discovered that two of his prize bulls had been sacrificed. The economy of his family would be put in further jeopardy. And as soon as the elders of the city found out that the altars had been torn down, they would put the severest demands on his dad for punishment and restitution. Even Gideon's lynching would be a strong possibility. Yet, in spite of his fears, Gideon chose to obey. Not yet bold enough to do it in the daytime, Judges 6:27

tells us that he carried out the assignment under cover of darkness when no one was watching. But he did it.

The next morning when the elders found the altars missing, they wasted no time in finding out that it was the work of Gideon, and reported it to his father. All of Gideon's fears were about to become realities. What's more, he knew that his family's humble ranking would be no match for the angry demands of the prominent city elders.

■ ■ ■

God has a very positive opinion of you and He is commanding you to shift from survival mode to conquering mode.

■ ■ ■

But against all odds, Gideon's father took sides with him and told the elders, mockingly, that if Baal had an issue about what his son had done, then Baal should defend himself. In fact, his dad became so pleased with Gideon's actions that he changed his name to Jerubbaal, which means, "The one that Baal has to contend with." In other words, he was saying, "My son can knock Baal down. Now Baal, if he is who he says he is, needs to get up and defend himself against the God my son is serving" (see Judg. 6:28-32).

Why such a dramatic turn in Gideon's life? We find the answer in the second principle: Not only does God have a better opinion of you than you have of yourself, but also when you agree to shift from survival mode to overcoming mode, *He will cause your family and elders to develop a better opinion of you than you think is possible.*

Today, too many believers are pinned down in their faith by what others think of them *or what they think others might think or do*. Memories of past failures have erected altars of impotence on the hills surrounding the valley of helplessness, where they struggle in spiritual indenture. When they try to lift their eyes to the Lord, their gaze is blocked by those hills, dotted with so many memorials to old setbacks. And what makes those shrines so formidable is that their elders have built them, which means that to tear them down we will have to do what they have not been able to do: in essence, to fear God more than men.

Tear Down the Strongholds

In his book *God Out of the Box,* Chuck Ripka, the banker who is one of the key players in the transformation of Elk River, Minnesota, grew up in a dysfunctional home devastated by the alcohol that both of his parents consumed, and the misery that it brought upon the children.[1] Fights between his dad and mom had to be broken up by Chuck and his brothers. Insults and abuse were common all around. He did not study past high school. His teenage wife was already four months pregnant with their first child when they got married. He did not have a trade or a career.

As a young man, when he looked around, everything was dotted with monuments to family failures, some small, some big. But Chuck and Kathi met Jesus and decided to set their gaze beyond those hills, and they received the strength to tear those altars down, even when doing so involved a direct challenge to family beliefs.

Today, Chuck and Kathi have a loving marriage, precious children, and a home that is a haven of peace to friends and strangers. In addition, Chuck has become the founder and president of an international bank that invests 51 percent of its profits to transform nations. His testimony and his actions have touched and impacted presidents, Generals, CEOs, and myriads of common folks. But none of that would have happened had Chuck and Kathi not dared to tear down ancestral curses.

If you are struggling with similar shrines of ancestral failure, it is time that you choose to obey God. Even if you are afraid and need to do it at night, so to speak, do it. Tear them down, especially the ancestral ones that perpetuate failure in your lineage by imposing a ceiling on what *God can do.* Reject the notion that it cannot happen because it has never happened before. Believe God, not the past!

Imagine the impression that a timid Gideon must have made on his father with this sudden but calculated demonstration of godly courage that dismantled every false spiritual anchor the family had, and with astounding resolve. You must obey the word of the Lord and walk through that challenging threshold that is always framed by fear on one side and faith on the other, and tell everybody in your circle that you have chosen to stand on the side of faith *because God said so, even though in the natural it looks impossible.* You will be surprised by the unexpected results once you tear down those altars because it is impossible to develop faith while living in the shadow of failure.

When Francis Oda was asked suddenly and unexpectedly by the president of Tahiti to find a solution to a problem that had baffled 13 top French engineers for the previous six months, Francis knew that he needed to look beyond those shadows—and quickly, as he only had a few hours before he was expected at the president's residence for dinner.

He did not turn to the French architects—they had already failed. He did not ask any "impossibility" thinkers. Instead, he accepted the assignment and looked to God. That was the turning point. Without speaking a word, he spoke volumes, and his acceptance of the challenge declared, "My God will provide the answer." God loves that childlike faith and He delights Himself in bestowing extraordinary answers to those who dare to pray extraordinary prayers. Francis's wise choice resulted in the salvation of the president and key members of his family and inner circle, because his obedience brought down the pagan altars that until then had blinded them to the light of the gospel.

Once Gideon's self-image and the opinion of his family and peers had been reshaped to reflect God's perspective, God instructed him to go to the enemy's camp in a journey intended to show him how victory over the Midianites would be obtained. As expected, this worrier-now-makeshift-warrior stuttered to a halt, and to counter it, God made another incomprehensible and almost comical proposal to Gideon in Judges 7:10: If Gideon was afraid to go down by himself, he could take his servant Purah with him! This suggestion comes across like a touch of divine humor because Gideon's enemies numbered in the thousands—135,000 soldiers to be exact, plus their entourage. What difference would it make for Gideon to go by himself or with one other person?

All we know is that Gideon decided to exercise the option offered by God and took Purah with him. Upon arriving in the camp in the dead of night, Gideon became privy to a conversation going on inside one of the tents. A Midianite soldier was relating a strange dream in which he saw a loaf of bread blown into the camp and striking the main tent, causing it to collapse. His tent mate immediately provided an interpretation that I am sure surprised Gideon more than anyone else: "This is nothing less than the sword of Gideon . . . God has given Midian and all the camp into his hand" (Judg. 7:13). And that is exactly what happened shortly afterward.

That reveals the third principle: Not only does God have a better opinion of you than you have of yourself, and not only will He cause your elders, family and friends to think better of you than you think is possible, but *God will make your enemies develop a better opinion of you!* But for this to happen, you need to go to the enemy's camp. That is where that type of divine revelation is bestowed. The farther you get from the wine cellar, the bolder God's interaction with you will be; and the greater your interaction with Him, the stronger your faith will become.

It is interesting to note that the very fearful spirit that neutralized Gideon in the beginning was the same spirit of fear that overtook the Midianite armies *once Gideon replaced fear with obedient faith.* One hundred twenty thousand soldiers slaughtered themselves that night under the light of 300 candles and the raucous noise of 300 blaring trumpets. The 15,000 who remained ran for their lives, but the run was a short one and their demise was quick. It was a most unpredictable victory by every human standard, but human standards are never the order of the day with God.

God has already decreed victory for those who agree to carry out His assignments, even if like Gideon they shake in their boots. As long as they obey and move forward, God will deliver the promised victory because He *has already told your enemies that you will overcome them.* Jesus stated unequivocally that the Gates of Hades would not prevail against us. This is a given. But for us to see it happen, we must leave the pseudo-protection of the wine cellar and fight for our destiny, for the transformation of our nation. We must stop looking down and instead lift up our eyes to the One who made the heavens and the earth.

Memory vs. Faith

The crowning point that we must not miss in Gideon's story is this: The enemy of faith is not unbelief; it is memory, because memory is the record of what has already taken place, whereas faith is the revelation of what is yet to happen. Even good memories can be bad if they keep us from believing God for something better by enticing us to settle for the good we know instead of for the best we have not tasted yet.

Gideon's faith was limited by the loudness of negative recollections that echoed through the corridors of time. His memory, by ambushing his faith, made him a slave to his circumstances.

How can we get out of those canyons of despair? It is very simple: Hear God say to you, "Saddle up and go get 'em!" Believe that He has a better opinion of you than you have of yourself, because He knows what you are capable of and *He knows the victories that are in store for you!*

Let His faith *in you* energize what little faith you have *in Him* and you will pivot from the wine cellar toward your destiny. God sees the nations in the grip of the evil one, doing what they are not supposed to do and being led by an evil crafty "bull," and He says to you, "Go get 'em!"

He believes you can do it. You should believe that too. That is why I say to you in the name of Jesus: "Mighty warrior, arise and ride, because the Lord believes in you!"

CHAPTER 20

The Rest of Your Life: Monument or Legacy?

Rick Warren's classic opener to *The Purpose-Driven Life* declares, "It is not about you." Warren is right. Life, in the final analysis, is not about us; ultimately it is about God. At the same time, God is neither an island nor a terminus. God is love and love cannot exist in a void because love needs an object due to its giving nature. In fact, none of His attributes have purpose in a vacuum. God is about relationships. God himself is a Trinity—three persons in one. He relates to angels and to everything in his creation. But only man was made in the likeness and image of God, and all biblical and practical evidence shows that He has a unique relationship with human beings

From the beginning of human history, God made this relational design evident. He instructed Adam and Eve to be fruitful and multiply (see Gen. 1:22), a mandate to populate the earth, to produce *more people*. As their descendants materialized, God connected with them first as families and clans and then eventually chose Abraham to give birth to a nation that would be God's staging ground to touch other nations, plural.

God relates to individuals, but His blessings are meant not just for the recipient but also for his or her descendants. The Old Testament is dotted with references to the *God of Abraham, Isaac and Jacob,* particularly at the moment when those blessing were imparted, to underscore the exponential generational dimension of the process. The blessings initially given to Abraham were augmented by those entrusted to Isaac, and the sum of those two by Jacob's, and so forth. God designed people to be a blessing to those coming after them.

Consequently whatever you do today will have an impact not just on you but also on your children and your children's children. We are keenly aware that God visits the sins of the fathers upon their children up to the fourth generation, but we are not as sure that He will do the same with blessings, *or that He will do it beyond the fourth generation.*

But He will.

This principle is the spiritual equivalent of compound interest. It gets exponentially bigger with age. Every time you choose to do God's will, to embrace righteousness instead of wickedness, to bless when you could easily have chosen to curse, you will be rewarded; but more important yet, you will be making a deposit in your descendants' accounts.[1]

God remembers our godly choices. David's righteous decisions generated deposits of mercy for his descendants to access in times of need. Solomon built the Temple not as a result of personal merits but because of his father's relationship with God. Later, during the awe-inspiring dedication of the Temple, it was right after Solomon's reference to David's walk with the Lord that God's presence invaded the place, majestically overwhelming everyone as a way to underscore that point (see 2 Chron. 6:4–7:2). By choosing righteousness time and again, David made deposit after deposit into his descendants' accounts and Solomon was the first beneficiary.

Those deposits came to the rescue when David's descendants fell into sin. When Solomon, ignoring God's explicit instructions, married foreign women and turned to their gods, God's judgment fell on him and the nation. But when it was meted out, it came with a measure of grace on David's account, for God said to him, "Because you have done this I will surely tear the kingdom from you but I will not do it in your days *for the sake of your father David*" (see 1 Kings 11:1-12).

When David's grandson Rehoboam sinned and was in danger of losing his hold on Judah, God strengthened his position with a mass migration of priests and godly people from the northern kingdom, Israel, "they walked in the way of David and Solomon" (2 Chron. 11:17).

Five generations later, David's great-great-great grandson Jehoshaphat did enough evil things to deserve to have his kingdom obliterated, but God did not destroy it, "because of the covenant which He had made with David" (2 Chron. 21:7).

Hundreds of years later, King Hezekiah found himself surrounded by pagan kings with thousands of soldiers foretasting a sure victory. Hezekiah cried out to God for deliverance (see 2 Kings 19:34). Hezekiah and his army went to bed facing certain annihilation but awoke the next morning to find their enemy slaughtered by the Angel of the Lord. The reason? His great-great-great-great-great grandfather David's walk with God (see 2 Kings 19:34).

After a season of prosperity, Hezekiah fell mortally ill. Again in desperation, he turned to God to plead his case (see 2 Kings 20:3). Hezekiah's argument was strong—he had walked righteously before God. His pain was intense and evident, adding credible urgency to his entreating. God responded favorably, not because of Hezekiah's record, but on the basis of *someone else's actions many years before*: " I will heal you . . . for my sake and *for the sake of my servant David"* (2 Kings 20:5-6, *NIV,* emphasis added). What a rich and empowering heritage David left for his descendants, setting an example that life ultimately is about *leaving a legacy for others.*

All of us can look back on good things that came to us for free because somebody in our ancestry paid the price

Ruth and I constantly thank God for the godly heritage that upstreams to our parents and grandparents. Much of what I teach today to pulpit and marketplace leaders has its genesis in what I saw my father demonstrate as he strove to break a legacy of evil and launch one of righteousness as the first adult in our family to receive Christ.

Even in his pre-Christian days, my dad made choices that became deposits in my account and my sister's account. And he made them in what is perhaps the muddiest arena: politics. He was part of the revolution and the subsequent civil rights movement that Juan Perón and his legendary wife, Evita, launched in the early 1940s. Those were the days when factory bosses "owned" the workers. In the large haciendas, the "Dons" paid the laborers with coupons that could only be redeemed at the company store. There were good labor laws on the books, supposedly to protect the underprivileged, *the shirtless ones,* as Evita came to call them, but those laws were not being enforced because the judge, the chief of police, the mayor—the city elders—were appointed by the oligarchy running the country. The very few who dared challenge the system were soon eliminated—physically, socially, or both.

My father joined the movement on day one and began to mobilize and organize people to vote and to stand for their rights, even if there was no judicial system willing to enforce them. On October 17, 1945, the day that unprecedented masses of people marched onto Plaza de Mayo, the site of the national government, to demand the release of Perón (whom the oligarchs had jailed)—a day that proved how vulnerable the ruling elite was if the people united—my father led a column of marchers, putting himself in harm's and history's way.

Later on, when Perón won the elections, my dad became influential in the Party. I remember the portrait of *El General*, as his followers called him, that Perón had autographed for my father occupying a place of honor in our house. I used to look at it with a deep sense of pride that *El Hombre* (the man), as Perón was also referred to, had inscribed it with his own hand for *my dad*.

I recall the day my dad returned from a trip where he had met with Evita to propose social relief for needy people in our area. He told us how beautiful she was, what dress she wore, how her hair was done, how magnetic her personality was, and how supportive she was of the proposals put before her. I peppered him with questions about *La Señora*, as she was respectfully called by the masses, but the true source of my pride was that *my dad* knew her.

Dad kept rising in the ranks and eventually was elected Secretary General of one of the major labor unions in the country. The backbone of the Peronist movement was the newly formed, or energized, unions, an absolute must to stand for the rights of the underdogs against a system that, not unlike the Old South, saw no value in making social peers of the underclass.

He became powerful, politically speaking. To our house came many influential people. In the typical style of Argentine families, we kids were allowed to sit in and listen, even late into the night as long as we did not interrupt. I got an education in social issues and political strategy at the feet of those illustrious visitors.

But then the movement, so idealistic in the beginning, became corrupt. The principles for which the pioneers fought succumbed to the moral stupor emanating from the accumulation of power. My father stood at a crossroad. One night I overheard him tell my mother that he had resigned his position in the party. That night, he had arrived home later than usual because he had chosen to walk home rather than be chauffeured by the party he now considered irremediably lost to corruption.

He could have had his share, a big one, in the loot available if he chose to stay, but he valiantly walked away from it for the simple reason that he believed it was wrong to access something for which he had not worked.

His decision was not easily understood. Power-grabbers saw it as raw stupidity. The corrupt ones that were milking the system sought to neutralize their exposure by discrediting my dad. To him it did not matter. He held his chin up and kept telling us, "At night I sleep with a clean conscience." He was fully vindicated when the Peronist movement was overthrown and its leaders jailed. My father's name never came up in any investigation. Everybody, Peronist and non-Peronist, knew he was a man of integrity.

My second memory is of when he set up two loudspeakers on the roof to tell our neighborhood about his newfound faith. That was before telephones, faxes or emails were available. Those were the days when neighbors did a lot of "frontporching." With dinner over and the sun beyond the horizon, people would bring their chairs to the front of their houses, from which they had a generous view of the block, and enjoy a moment of unscripted leisure. For the adults it consisted of drinking *mate* (MAH-tay), the Argentine green tea, trading innocuous gossip, catching up on mutual friends, telling jokes. For the children, it meant pick-up soccer on the sidewalk, or a game of marbles, or simply shooting the breeze. Those were the days when school homework did not invade family time. School was something you occupied yourself with during the day, but family and neighborhood you enjoyed in the evenings.

It was in one of those days that my father *went public* with his faith. Our neighbors had known him as an eloquent atheist, not the norm in a country with an "official religion" that held considerable sway over the life of the people. Those foolish enough to debate him were left to regret it because my father was a modern-day Apollo. He devastated them with his unmatched eloquence.

But rumors had been circulating that *Don Omar,* as he was called, had embraced religion, not the official one, but some sort of foreign "cult." To put it in cultural perspective, being a Protestant in Argentina in those days was as welcomed as an al-Qaeda cell member working at the Pentagon.

None of that mattered to my father. He was going public with his faith. He was fearless . . . but not me. Deep inside I am shy and I prefer nuances to dogma when broaching difficult or controversial subjects. On that fateful evening, I watched events unfold with such a balanced mixture of fear and pride that it produced an absolute physical gridlock that prevented me from running in either direction. As an insecure teenager, I stood paralyzed on the sidelines, close enough to be identified with my dad, but distant enough to avoid embarrassment.

After testing that the volume was at the maximum level, he approached the microphone, greeted his neighbors in his best public voice and said, "You have known me as an atheist who looked down on those who believe in the existence of God. But today I stand before you to admit that I was wrong. There is a God and I wish to ask your forgiveness, especially from those that I debated and belittled because of your faith." He quoted John 3:16 and, with the spontaneity and simplicity of a new believer, shared with the people about the real Jesus. He closed with an offer to answer questions if anyone cared come where he stood. One couple that lived across from us did so and that night they received Christ.

I was so proud of my dad! Drowning in the insecurities typical of teen years, I had no expectation of ever becoming like him, but somehow that evening I felt that precious seeds had been deposited in my soul.

In those pioneering days, it took tremendous courage to swim upstream, especially against an institutionalized tide of corruption. To act righteously when the opposite was the norm was something his peers did not conceive as possible, much less as advisable. But he did it, even if people did not understand why he would tell the truth when a lie would serve him better. Why would he return money that he could have kept? Why would he own up to a mistake that he could blame on a subordinate to advance his position? I am sure he often felt like Noah preaching about the flood when rain was non-existent.

I know my father intensely felt the tension of the daily clash between the righteousness of God and the corruption that was such an integral part of the system he operated in. Many of his contemporary fellow-Christians, who also had social visibility, chose to be "secret disciples" to minimize their risks in case they stumbled so that the loss of face would be minimal—but not my father. He was a *totalist*. It was his pattern, even before becoming a Christian, to either go for something or to go against it or to not touch it, and this became even more marked when he became a believer. He never did anything half way.

A few years later I found myself facing a moral dilemma, and the fruit of those seeds came to the rescue. Everybody at work knew that I was a Christian but most, if not all, of my colleagues considered me "strange" because of my convictions and my Protestant religion.

At the time I was on the fast track to run one of the best international hotels in the country. I had been steadily moving up through the ranks and I felt in my soul that I had a very good shot at the coveted position. But there was a challenge: We were under orders to overcharge American customers every time they placed an international call.

Caught between my convictions and my boss's orders, I had smartly dodged placing international calls for our guests, but the unavoidable day finally came. As soon as I placed the call, everybody's eyes turned in my direction, as if to shout, *"What are you going to do now, Mr. Honesty?"* I was lectured sternly on how unforgiving our boss was when his directives were ignored, followed by a torrent of condescending lectures about our unforgiving boss. It was just me against everybody else, a throwback to that evening in my neighborhood, except that the player was not my father but me, and what was at risk was not a public perception but my chances at the top position, perhaps even my job.

I have no distinct memory of recalling my father's example at that moment, but I do remember instinctively tucking my chin and in my father's style answering in a firm voice, "I intend to charge the right amount. I am a Christian."

Dropping a bomb would not have caused the blast of emotions my statement unleashed among my coworkers. Some told me they were sure that I did not mean it. Others bet that at the last moment I would chicken out. Still others reminded me that my promotion and my job were on the line. The boss's secretary, who also happened to be his mistress, walked up to me and, rolling her eyes, purred, "You better do as the boss said or I will tell him. And you know that he likes me better than you." Notwithstanding the pressure, I decided to do the right thing. And my colleagues did what they promised: They told the boss.

A couple hours later, *El Jefe* (the boss) stormed into my office, his eyes on fire, rage written all over him, anger exuding from every pore. Pointing his finger, he vociferously hurled non-stop verbal abuse at me for what seemed an eternity. He insulted me in every imaginable way with every cuss word known plus some new ones I learned on the spot. And worst of all, everybody was privy to this tirade since the door to my office had been left open.

Finally my boss ran out of steam but with a still-angry voice and bulging eyes he demanded, "Why did you disobey my orders?" I had been so pummeled by his outburst that my brain felt frozen, but to my surprise, I heard myself saying, "Sir, if I refuse to steal from a Gringo who will never know what I did to him, can you imagine how sure you can be that I will *never* steal from *you*?"

The logic was so fulminating, the argument so disarming and my response so unexpected that it had the effect of an emotional knockout punch. I can still see the shock that swept across his face. He gave a loud snort, turned around, rushed out of the room, and slammed the door with such violence that it all but tore the hinges off.

Who put those words in my mouth? The Holy Spirit did. And because greater is He who was in me than the one who is in the world, victory was snatched from the jaws of defeat. A few hours later, in typical Latino macho fashion, instead of apologizing, my boss had dinner served for both of us in my office, in plain view of everybody else. I am sure Mordecai must have felt a similar sense of satisfaction when the king chose to honor him in front of his nemesis, Haman. And I did get the promotion and became the boss of those who had bet I would lose my job.

My reflex actions that day were the result of the deposits my father had made many years earlier when he turned his back on a corrupt system and also later on when he faced his neighbors to openly proclaim his newfound faith.

Yes, life is not about us but about God, and God is about others, and the first circle of "others" consists of our children. We parents must provide our young with three things: feet to stand on, wings to fly with, and a moral compass to know where to go. Sequentially speaking, feet come first since they constitute the foundation from where to alight. If we do a good job, our children will eventually undertake their first solo flight, establishing a constructive independence. From time to time they will come back to the place from where they took off for rest, fellowship and guidance when needed; but like a healthy adult bird, they will know they have wings to go places and the will to use them. And that is when the moral compass becomes crucial, to show them not just where to go but also *when* to do it and *how* to get there.

My dad modeled this for me. He gave me convictions to stand on. He showed me how to spread my wings and not to fear the wind on my face but to use it for uplift; and by modeling morality, he made sure I knew which way to turn. He gave me a compass that always pointed to the true north.

This equipment trilogy was put to the test when puberty hit me, not just with hormones that made me aware that my days of innocence as a child were passing away, but also with ideals, some of them potentially dangerous. Those were the days when the message I heard in church was artfully challenged and redefined by eloquent revolutionary voices sweeping Latin America on the heels of Fidel Castro and Ché Guevara's infamous takeover of Cuba.

Idealism comes naturally to youth; it is air in their lungs, blood in their arteries. Such idealism is the springtime of society. It causes that which has lain buried in the recesses of the soul to sprout and to bloom. It brings the promise of renewal to that which has grown old or become dilapidated. The strident calls issued in Cuba for the youth of Latin America to embark on revolution and wrestle to the ground the evils of society were impossible to ignore. Today, with the perspective of half a century, it is easy to differentiate between rhetoric and reality, demagoguery and substance, but in the decade of the '60s the call to change the world was deafening. While the USA was upset by youth who left their homes to smoke marijuana, lose their virginity and turn into hippies, in our part of the world masses of young people left their cities and took to the hills to join the guerrilla movement.

To our youthful idealism, it seemed *so right*! The appalling social conditions of so many around us made the call compelling and urgent in extreme. I was no exception. I wanted to change the world too. I flexed my wings and noticed them getting stronger by the day, and I was tempted to take off in that direction, but my compass kept saying *no*.

I don't know of any other two forces that can clash so loudly and with so much brutal force in the minds of young people than idealism and realism. One feels torn apart, and more so when peer pressure comes into play. Many of my schoolmates joined the movement and became part of a struggle that at first was romantic, but eventually threw Argentina into chaos, with thousands slaughtered in an all-out urban war between guerrillas and the army.

As I stood on that threshold, feeling the relentless pressure of my peers, clashing with the force of deeper convictions, like my dad before me, I decided to "walk home"—*alone*.

I knew social change was necessary, but somehow I felt that what I saw emerging was not the right course, and I decided, reluctantly, to sit it out. I wish I could adequately describe the overwhelming frustration, even desperation, that envelops a revolutionary when he lives in a land rocked by a revolution that he has chosen not to be a part of.

But having wings does not mean we *have to* fly.

In the ensuing years, many of my classmates were killed. I sat down to comfort parents who would no longer prepare a meal for children who had "disappeared." That was the euphemism used since, once detained or captured by the security forces, people simply evaporated. Thousands upon thousands of young people were drugged, bound and dropped from military airplanes into the unforgiving waters of the Atlantic Ocean. Others were buried in unmarked graves.

Eventually Ruth and I came to the States to study, and in 1974 we returned to Argentina as part of the Luis Palau Evangelistic team to establish its ministry in Argentina. But the civil war was at full blast and we found ourselves caught between the warring factions, both of which threatened us with death. The leftist guerrillas considered us "traitors and agents of the CIA," and the right-wingers classified us as enemies of the state. It was not comfortable, but this time we knew that this was the time to spread our wings and fly. We knew that Argentina needed the message we brought and, risking our physical safety, we decided to soar. A fierce wind was on our face, but that was good; we used it for uplift. And that lift became more than necessary; in fact, it became vital to give us a higher perspective as we faced a kidnap attempt on one of our children, armed robbery, shootouts, clashes between the army and the guerillas on our sidewalk, and bombs exploding in our neighborhood.

My father died four years after our return, but his final words energized me immensely, even though they were not spoken to me directly but relayed through my mother. The morning I received the news that he had died unexpectedly, I drove through pouring rain the 40 miles that separated our homes. As I watched the rain relentlessly hit the windshield, I became aware of a bigger storm of grief and doubts buffeting my own soul.

I was sure that my dad had loved me and I was deeply grateful for what he had done for me, but I was also uncertain if I had measured up to his expectations. The fact that he died suddenly robbed me of the opportunity to ask him that important question. My grief at losing him was exponentially increased by that question, which now I felt I would never get answered.

However when I got to the ancestral home, after embracing and comforting my mother, she told me she had a message from my dad. Before dying—as he was saying goodbye to his wife of 34 years—he asked her to tell me, "What a great *pibe* Ed is." The word *pibe* is an endearing Argentine term used to describe a winsome, pleasant young person. For the older generation, it is the equivalent of "cool" to high-schoolers today.

The moment the message registered, the weight I had been accumulating was lifted from my heart. Even as he was departing this earth to take his place in the cloud of witnesses described in Hebrews 11, he had made a last deposit, and one that I needed very badly, in my account. He turned his "taps" into a "reveille" for me and in so doing inspired me to go farther and higher.[2]

With renewed energy, Ruth and I, along with our children and our new ministry team, embarked on a spiritual revolution. Out of that came Resistencia, the first city in modern times reached for Christ. This led to the launch of our International Institute and the writing of several books that took to the four corners of the world the principles of prayer evangelism and city transformation. As our circle of influence grew and our platform expanded, we began to see regions and states transformed. Today we stand on the threshold that leads to nation transformation.

■ ■ ■

We are part of a revolution, but our leader is not someone from the left or from the right but from above: Jesus Christ.

■ ■ ■

We know *that we know that we know* that soon the first of many nations will be transformed. We are part of a revolution, but our leader is not someone from the left or from the right but from above: Jesus Christ, the Lord of lords and the King of nations.

Our weapons and bullets are not made of steel to kill, destroy or maim, but they are powerful in God to tear down spiritual strongholds in people's minds and to reclaim the marketplace for His kingdom. Instead of bayonets and machetes, we have been outfitted with scalpels to remove malignant ideological tumors in the minds of people made sick by the Babylonian system and to do heart transplants, the kind that turns rebels into revolutionaries to make the world a better place by causing the will of God to be done on Earth as it is already done in heaven.

The task is so huge and our resources so few! What can we do with the few things at our disposal? This is where David's example becomes a guiding beacon. His life and his epic fight with Goliath are well known, but as I bring this book to a close I wish to bring to light often-overlooked insights that are capable of turning you into a far mightier person that what you think is possible. Please read carefully.

David faced a giant that was stronger, better armed and more skilled at war than he was, but he overcame him. David loved God. He was righteous. He was courageous and endowed with many other positive characteristics. But the victory over Goliath came primarily as the result of David's having *a bigger vision than the giant*. He who has the greater vision wins at higher levels. And he who offers the greatest hope will lead. And David had both vision and hope.

Goliath had a very narrow and shallow vision. He told David, "I will give your flesh to the birds of the sky and the beasts of the field" (1 Sam. 17:44). That was the extent of his mission statement. He was the source, the means and the end of his own vision, whereas David drew from the unlimited well of God's character and purposes. This became evident when he declared, "I come to you in the name of the LORD of hosts [angels], the God of the armies of Israel, whom you have taunted" (1 Sam. 17:45).

Furthermore, David's vision was all-encompassing and transcendental—encompassing because it drew in God, His hosts of angels and the armies of Israel; transcendental because, unlike Goliath's, his went beyond the immediate. He told the Philistine, "I will strike you down and remove your head from you. And I will give the dead bodies of the army of the Philistines this day to the birds of the sky and the wild beasts of the earth, *that all the earth may know that there is a God* in Israel, and that all this assembly may know that the LORD does not deliver by sword or by spear; for the battle is the LORD's" (1 Sam. 17:46-47).

David's vision was not centered on himself or on his needs, as Goliath's was. To David, his fight with Goliath was a means to a much greater end, one that would bring glory and honor to God and also make God's people, God's enemies, and all the earth aware that God is God. As he rushed to the battle line, he saw himself in an epic struggle to show the world that God saves.

He who has the greater vision wins because vision always opens the door to *pro*vision. He told the giant, "I will cut off your head," when he had nothing to cut it with. All he held in his hands were sticks, as Goliath derisively pointed out. But such lack did not prevent him from announcing what he had chosen to believe: "I will cut off your head. How, I don't know, but I will do it. I don't have a sword but that is a *minor* detail. My vision is not determined by what I have now but by what God will make available as I pursue it into the future."

And that is exactly what happened. We read that David knocked Goliath down, but no sword was found in David's hand with which to decapitate the giant as he had promised. Such lack did not pose a problem to the young shepherd since the deciding factor was not the tools or the weapons in his hands, but the vision in his heart. David "borrowed" Goliath's sword and proceeded to cut off Goliath's head (see 1 Sam. 17:50-51).

This is the beauty, the majesty and the power of a vision fueled by uncompromising faith, faith in a God who is omnipotent, and not by the resources at hand. Faith always gazes into the future and assures us that provision is there to undertake with confidence that for which our current resources are insufficient.

Vision creates provision, but for provision to materialize it must be preceded by obedience. In the alphabet, the letter *O* comes before the letter *P* and this is a good reminder that in "God's alphabet" obedience always comes before provision. If we obey the divine command to rush to the battle line to slay the giants—such as the Babylonian system—God will cause provision to materialize, sometimes through the giants themselves. *Vision* is the key.

When David's father, thinking that David was too insignificant, "forgot" to include him the day Samuel came to identify and anoint the future king, David did not seem disturbed. When he was finally summoned, he acted as someone who had seen it first in his heart before it became evident to those around him (see 1 Sam. 16:13).

When King Saul drafted him as a musician and used him also as an armor bearer, he did not mind (see 1 Sam. 16:21). Either way, David was in the palace, the place he knew was his eventual destiny. Saul saw him as another servant, but David, in his heart, knew that he was destined to be a king.

When on numerous occasions Saul tried to kill him while David ministered to the demonized king, David did not hold a grudge or take revenge. He recognized that he was destined for the throne and there was no need to rush things. His vision sustained him (see 1 Sam. 18:10-11; 19:9-10).

Later on, during a leave of absence as Saul's therapist, his father sent him to the battleground as a caterer; such a menial assignment did not prevent him from volunteering to fight the giant that no one else dared to confront. His vision of himself was bigger than the assessment his father had of him (see 1 Sam. 17:10-20).

When everyone believed that *God* could slay Goliath, only David believed that *he* could do it unto the glory of God (see 1 Sam. 17:26).

When the king tried to dissuade him because of his youthfulness and inexperience, he replied that he was willing and able to overcome Goliath because of who God made him to be. The king did not have faith in him, but David had faith in himself because of who God made him to be (see 1 Sam. 17:32-37).

When Goliath insulted him, rating him no higher than "a dog catcher" on account of the "weapons"—sticks—that David brought to the fight, he did not flinch. He replied, "I come against you with something stronger and far more powerful than weapons. I come to you in the Name of the maker of heaven and Earth. I am a man of vision. Prepare to die!" (see 1 Sam. 17:43-47).

Goliath did not believe in David, but David believed in himself. The giant rated David by what he saw—sticks in his hands—but David had stones concealed in his pouch, which, like the vision treasured in the recesses of his heart, delivered the devastating hit. David defeated Goliath not because he had better weapons but because he possessed—and was possessed by—a bigger vision, *in spite* of everyone around him.

Vision is crucial for the task before us, the task of bringing transformation to the entire world. But vision is not enough to change the world *unless it is a generational vision,* a vision that transcends its bearer—because its ultimate objective is to bless others, including those yet to come. And this is an area where David was superior not only to Goliath, who saw his mission as simply killing the young shepherd, but also to Saul.

The fundamental difference between Saul and David was that for Saul life began and ended with himself. He was the center of a constellation of humans whom he saw as orbiting satellites around the sun he believed himself to be.

This became evident by the question he asked his commander, Abner, while David was rushing to the battle line: "Whose son is this young man?"(1 Sam. 17:55). Saul knew David but evidently had forgotten who his father was. This is strange since in chapter 16 he had sent Jesse, David's dad, a formal request for the services of his son. Later on, he had granted David a leave of absence from palace duties for the young lad *to help his aging father* now that his older brothers had to serve in Saul's army on account of the war against the Philistines.

In a culture in which genealogy and ancestry were central to daily interactions and where everybody was known as So-and-so's child, it is incomprehensible that Saul would not remember who David's father was. But he did not. He had forgotten. Why? Because from the moment he got David the first time and saw how profitable it was to have him in his service, Saul no longer cared about David's family. He saw David as property, as *his* servant, but never again as Jesse's son. And this sinister trait became evident after David's victory when Saul learned (or remembered) the identity of David's dad: "Saul . . . took him that day *and did not let him return to his father's house*" (1 Sam. 18:2). Saul's world began and ended with him and so did his vision.

David was the opposite. Instead of holding back, he served Saul with distinction and became Saul's son's best friend (see 1 Sam. 18:1); and after Jonathan died, David searched for any surviving descendants of Saul, and when he found Jonathan's son, Mephibosheth, he awarded him unmerited royal treatment (see 2 Sam. 9:1-13).

David had a generational vision—a type of vision that transcended his circumstances by drawing from those who preceded him with the intent to channel those blessings into future generations. This was David's most outstanding quality. He knew better than anyone else that life was not about him but about God and about others.

What about you? Will you be another Abraham? Purah? David? Paul? Will you be another Chuck Ripka, Barbara Chan, Francis Oda, Graham Power, or Father Saaman?

When you depart this earth, will you leave behind a monument to yourself or an inspiring and empowering legacy to your children and your children's children? There is a drastic difference between a monument and a legacy. A monument is tangible and inert and, as such, is frozen in time and pointing to the past. It tells us that someone who is dead did something that we would not be aware of if it were not for the monument itself. Were it not for the monument, we would never have learned about the person.

A legacy is quite different. It is transcendent, and as such it is not confined by time, because it lives through the ages, propelling us in our journey into the future. A legacy is such because it has been bestowed upon us very much like an inheritance, because someone who cared bequeathed it to us, allowing us to turn capital we did not work for into a source of enrichment.

We have only one life to live. We must provide our young ones with feet to stand on, wings to fly with and a compass to guide them. Of these three, *the compass is the most important one*—and it is always set to its "true north" by the decisions *you* make.

The best decision you can make today is to invest the rest of your life and the sum of all your resources into discipling nations. Doing so will show your children that life is about God. By charging against formidable and well-armed giants with a compelling vision and absolute faith that God will make possible the impossible, you will give your children a solid foundation to stand on, you will show them how to spread their wings and not be intimidated by adverse winds but to use them for uplift. And above everything else, you will teach them to align their compass with God's true north.

I am not ignorant that the fight will be fierce and that martyrdom is a possibility, even more so as the end times descend upon us. I believe that and much more is in the mix before the Babylonian system is finally debunked. But I have deliberately dwelt on the ultimate victorious outcome—the one predicted by Jesus when He stated unequivocally that the Gates of Hades *shall not* prevail against His Church—to counter the defeatism that has permeated us for too long because we have been focusing too much on the end-time tribulations and not enough on the victory that will follow them. There is no victory without war. There is no champion without a fight. The kingdom of God will suffer violence, but those who do not run away will inherit it.

This is the most important lesson we can teach our children. Rush to the battle line. Slay the giant that others consider invincible for the earth to know that God is the God of all its nations. When the majestic parade described in Revelation 21:24-27 finally happens, you will march along with millions of others, including heads of state, whose inclusion will have been made possible because you chose to reach the destiny that God set for you.

Go for it, there are nations waiting to be discipled *by you*!

Endnotes

Chapter 5: What on Earth Did Jesus Come to Do?
1. For an in-depth discussion of this definition of the marketplace, see Ed Silvoso, *Anointed for Business* (Ventura, CA: Regal Books, 2006), chapters 1 and 2.
2. For a visual report on this extraordinary story, go to www.harvestevan.org/bookstore, where you can order and/or download a documentary DVD.
3. "Atonement" is a theological term to refer to the death of an innocent on behalf of someone guilty. When used in the context of Jesus' death on the cross, it refers to Him paying with His life for the sins of the world (see John 3:16)
4. Chuck Ripka is the author of *Out of the Box* (Lake Mary, FL: Charisma House, 2007).
5. This and other Transformation DVDs are available at www.harvestevan.org/bookstore.

Chapter 6: Bridging the Pulpit and the Marketplace
1. For a detailed treatment of these four misbeliefs, see my book *Anointed for Business* (Ventura, CA: Regal Books, 2006), pp. 20-21.
2. For additional details on this, see Rick Heeren, *The Elk River Story* (Minneapolis, MN: Transformational Publications, 2004). You can acquire it at www.harverstevan.org/bookstore.

Chapter 8: Doing Church 24/7 in the Right Place
1. For additional details on this story, order or download the DVD *Transformation in the Marketplace with Ed Silvoso*, "Government and Elected Officials," at www.harvestevan.org/bookstore.

Chapter 10: Giving the Devil a Heaven of a Time
1. For additional details on this story, order or download the DVD *Transformation in the Marketplace with Ed Silvoso*—Transformation Churches (USA), at www.harvestevan.org/bookstore.
2. See Ed Silvoso, *Prayer Evangelism* (Ventura, CA: Regal Books, 2000), chapters 2 and 3.

Chapter 11: Systemic Poverty
1. Ed Silvoso, *Prayer Evangelism* (Ventura, CA: Regal Books, 2000), p. 207.

Chapter 12: The Early Church and Poverty
1. For an in-depth treatment of this subject, see Ed Silvoso, *That None Should Perish* (Ventura, CA: Regal Books, 1994), chapters 3 and 5.
2. Because the conversion of men also meant the salvation of their household, estimating 10 people per household, just the 8,000 men reported as saved in Acts 2 and 4 would comprise a community of 80,000 individuals.

Chapter 13: Really Good News to the Poor
1. According to the online encyclopedia Wikipedia, "Cold fusion is the name for effects which could be nuclear fusion reactions occurring near room temperature and pressure using relatively simple and low-input energy devices." It has not been proven as feasible yet. If and when it does, it will represent the most extraordinary energy bonanza of all times.
2. Ken Eldred, *God Is at Work* (Ventura, CA: Regal Books, 2005), p. 76.
3. Ibid.
4. Ibid., p. 80.
5. Ibid.
6. Canada and Australia are exceptions, but in both cases, natives were overtaken by whites by extermination of the former and by massive immigration of the latter. As a result, those in government at the time of independence were whites, something that may have made it easier and appealing for entrepreneurial and wealthy Brits to migrate and be assimilated into.
7. For a visual report on the transformation of Garbage City, go to www.harvestevan.org/bookstore or to Mediavillage.com to order or download the El Zabaleen DVD documentary.

Chapter 14: Integration

1. Tod Bell is South East Director of Harvest Evangelism. He is based in Nashville, Tennessee, and is the author of *It Can Be Done!* (San Jose, CA: Transformation Publications, 2004). For an in-depth treatment of this subject, see Ed Silvoso, *Anointed for Business* (Ventura, CA: Regal Books, 2006), chapter 7.

2. A. T. Robertson writes, "*I will build my church* (oikodomhsw mou thn ekklhsian). It is the figure of a building and he [Jesus] uses the word ekklhsian which occurs in the New Testament usually of a local organization, but sometimes in a more general sense. What is the sense here in which Jesus uses it? The word originally meant 'assembly' (Acts 19:39), but it came to be applied to an 'unassembled assembly' as in Acts 8:3)." A.T. Robertson, "Commentary on Mt. 16:18," *The Robertson's Word Pictures of the New Testament*, copyright © Broadman Press 1932,33, renewal 1960. All rights reserved. Used by permission of Broadman Press (Southern Baptist Sunday School Board).

3. Ed Silvoso, *Anointed for Business* (Ventura, CA: Regal Books, 2006), p. 37.

4. In my book *Prayer Evangelism,* I describe prayer evangelism as "talking to God about the lost before talking to the lost about God" and I explain the four-step strategy based on Luke 10:5-7: *bless* the lost, *fellowship* with them, *minister* to them, and only then *proclaim* that the kingdom of God has come near them.

5. For additional details on this story, order or download the DVD *Transformation in the Marketplace with Ed Silvoso,* "Indonesia," at www.harvestevan.org.

Chapter 15: The Healing of Nations

1. Whereas "saving grace" is entirely dependent on the person believing in Jesus as his or her savior, "general grace" is the favor of God bestowed on every person on Earth, whether or not they believe in Jesus.

2. Meaning "according to the number of the angels" following, as most Old Testament scholars do, the third-century B.C. Greek version of the Old Testament, called the Septuagint, and following the Qumran versions of the text of Deuteronomy 32:8.

3. The administrative role of fallen angels over affairs on Earth is also present in Ephesians 3:10.

Chapter 16: The Babylonian System

1. According to Wikipedia, the ancient name for the Babylonian's tower-type construction is "ziggurat." It is generally known that the ziggurat temple in ancient Mesopotamian architecture was used for worship and interaction with demonic powers of high caliber. The Great Ziggurat was built as a place of worship, dedicated to the moon god Nanna (or "Sin"), in the Sumerian city of Ur in ancient Mesopotamia (30° 57? 46? N, 46° 06? 10? E). The temple, a huge stepped platform, was constructed approximately in the twenty-first century B.C. by King Ur-Nammu. In Sumerian times it was called Etemennigur.

2. In Matthew, Jesus used the word *ergazomai*, meaning "to work" or "to trade." In Luke, He used a stronger Greek word, *diapragmateutomai*, a technical word from the financial world meaning "to gain by trading." Taken from C. Peter Wager, "The Parables of the Money Managers," unpublished article, p. 4.

3. (A) Pieter Bos, "Europe—Africa; Berlin Congo I: Hist. Overview," November 2, 2002, http://www.servingthenations.org/article.asp?ArticleID=15; (B) "The Berlin Conference," *The African Independent,* http://www.africanindependent.com/BerlinConf.html; (C) "Berlin West Africa Conference," *Encyclopedia Britannica,* http://www.britannica.com/eb/article-9078808/Berlin-West-Africa-Conference#34221.hook; (D) "Berlin Conference," Wikipedia.org, wikipedia.org/wiki/Berlin_Conference. To view the conference text document, go to http://www.homestead.com/wysinger/berlin-conference-doc.html.

4. King Leopold II turned his "Congo Free State" into a massive labor camp, made a fortune for himself from the harvest of its wild rubber, and contributed in a large way to the death of perhaps 10 million innocent people. See Mark Dummett, "King Leopold's Legacy of DR Congo Violence," http://news.bbc.co.uk/2/hi/africa/3516965.stm.

5. (A) "Colonialism, Western: The Race for Colonies in Sub-Saharan Africa," *Encyclopedia Britannica,* http://www.britannica.com/eb/article-25932/colonialism-Western#311557.hook; (B) Dummett, King Leopold's Legacy of DR Congo Violence."

6. Andrew Rugasira, "The Case for a New Paradigm," paper presented on February 1, 2007, at The Royal Society, the United Kingdom's National Academy of Sciences.

7. Ibid.

8. (A) Timothy A. Wise, "The Paradox of Agricultural Subsidies: Issues, Agricultural Dumping and Policy Reform," May 2004. http://www.globalpolicy.org/socecon/trade/subsidies/ 2004/05wise.pdf. (B) "Common Agricultural Policy," Wikipedia, June 2, 2007. http:// www.wikipedia.org/wiki/Common_Agricultural_Policy. (C) Mr. James D. Wolfensohn, World Bank president until 2005: "OECD member states spend US$350 billion every year in agricultural subsidies, which is seven times their development aid budgets." Merrell J. Tuck-Primdahl, "Commonwealth Secretary-General and World Bank President Call for Reduction in Agricultural Subsidies," speech delivered at the World Bank in London, on November 13, 2001. http://web.worldbank.org/WBSITE/EXTERNAL/NEWS/0,,contentMDK:20015945˜ menuPK:34463˜pagePK:34370˜piPK:34424˜theSitePK:4607,00.html. (D) "Statement from Mr. James D. Wolfensohn, President of the World Bank, Delivered on His Behalf by Mr Ujri Dadush, Director, Economic Policy Group," World Trade Organization, Ministerial Conference, fourth Session, Doha, November 9-13, 2001. http://www.wto.int/english/thewto_e/ minist_e/min01_e/statements_e/st25.doc.

9. Spanish Source: Tercer Mundo Economico: No. 176/177 - Enero/Febrero 2004. Ex Alta Comisionada de Derechos Humanos de la ONU .Subsidios a la agricultura impiden que el Sur salga de la pobreza. por Kanaga Raja. http://www.redtercermundo.org.uy/tm_economi co/texto_completo.php?id=2380.

10. (A) Geraldine Bedell, *Make Poverty History* (New York: Penguin Books, 2005), p. 43. (B) According to the United Nations' Word Food Program, 10,000 die of hunger alone. See http://www.wfp.org/aboutwfp/introduction/hunger_who.asp?section=1&sub_section=1. (C) For the United Nations/Millennium Campaign, see http://www.millenniumcampaign.org/ site/pp.asp?c=grKVL2NLE&b=185518. (D) "Make Poverty History: Live 8 Canada Facts and Stats." http://www.abolissonslapauvrete.ca/e/resources/live8-factsheet.pdf.

11. Oxfam International is an international confederation of 13 independent non-governmen-tal organizations. It was founded in 1995. Oxfam Great Britain is based in Oxford, UK. It was founded in England in 1942 as the Oxford Committee for Famine Relief. Oxfam works with over 3,000 partners in more than 100 countries to achieve greater impact by their col-lective efforts to find lasting solutions to poverty and injustice. See "Oxfam," Wikipedia, http://en.wikipedia.org/wiki/Oxfam_International.

12. "Oxfam Dismisses US Cotton Market Access Offer as 'Empty Promise,'" Oxfam International Press Release, 15 December 2005. http://www.oxfam.org/en/news/pressreleases2005/ pr051215_wto.

13. (A) "U.S. Must Reform Agricultural Subsidy Program," Oxfam International: http://www. oxfam.org/en/news/pressreleases2006/pr060901_wto_cotton_subsidies. (B) Andrew Rugasira, "Africa Needs Trade Not Aid: The Case for a New Paradigm," speech given at The Royal Society for the encouragement of Arts, Manufactures and Commerce (commonly known as the RSA, which is the forum where he did the speech), February 1, 2007. http://www.rsa.org.uk/acro bat/rugasira_010207.pdf.

14. The European budget for sugar subsidies amounts to ?1.5 billion per year and is funded by tax-payers, but the vast majority of benefits go to a small number of sugar growers and processors in Europe. Consumers pay about ?7.5 billion per year in higher prices due to the EU sugar regime. See "European Sugar Leaves Environment with Bitter Taste," WWF, November 22, 2004. http://www.panda.org/about_wwf/what_we_do/freshwater/news/index.cfm?uNewsID=16618.

15. Interview of Winston Bosch, CRWRC Mali staff, in Korin, 2003.

16. Susan Crickmore, "Cotton Subsidies Hurt African Farmers," CRWRC West Africa, August 2004.

17. "The Bretton Woods system of international monetary management established the rules for commercial and financial relations among the world's major industrial states. The Bretton Woods system was the first example of a fully negotiated monetary order intended to govern monetary relations among independent nation-states. Preparing to rebuild the international economic system as World War II was still raging, 730 delegates from all 44 Allied nations gathered at the Mount Washington Hotel in Bretton Woods, New Hampshire, for the United Nations Monetary and Financial Conference. The delegates deliberated upon and signed the Bretton Woods Agreements during the first three weeks of July 1944." "Bretton Woods System," Wikipedia. http://en.wikipedia.org/wiki/Bretton_Woods_system.

18. Bedell, *Make Poverty History*.

19. "Let him who steals [-1] steal no longer [0] but rather let him labor [+1], performing with his own hands [+2] what is good [+3], in order that he may have [+4] something to share [+5] with him who has need [+6]."

Chapter 17: The Demise of Babylon

1. The struggle that opens with the Lord's crowning in 11:15 moves on to the angelic triumph over Satan (see Rev. 12:9) and ends with the saints' victory over him in 12:11, which has as its prize the kingdoms of the earth (see Rev. 11:15-18; 12:9). I suggest that this segment renders in summary what later on is portrayed in minute detail in Revelation 12-22. It is a synopsis of the rest of the book of Revelation and ends on a very high note: "For this reason (the saints having defeated the devil on earth), rejoice, O heavens and you who dwell in them" (Rev. 12:12a), because it describes the final victory depicted in Revelation 21:24-27, with the nations of the earth walking in God's light. This summary is followed by a detailed description in chapters 13 through 18 of the devil trashing the earth, hence the lament, "Woe to the earth and the sea, because the devil has come down to you, having great wrath, knowing that he has only a short time" (Rev. 12:12b). Undoubtedly, Satan will soon be engrossing his ranks with the Beast and the False Prophet in a futile attempt to preserve Babylon (his command and control center), which eventually falls (see Rev. 17-18). The Unholy Trinity (the Devil, the Beast and the False Prophet), along with their followers, are also defeated and vanquished forever into the lake of fire.

2. On May 6, 1954, the Englishman Roger Bannister ran the first sub-four-minute mile in recorded history at 3 minutes 59.4 seconds at the Iffley Road Track in Oxford, England.

Chapter 18: It's Beginning to Happen

1. Geraldine Bedell, *Make Poverty History* (New York: Penguin Books, 2005).

Chapter 19: God's Faith in You

1. Chuck Ripka with James Lund, *Out of the Box* (Lake Mary, FL: Charisma House, 2007).

Chapter 20: The Rest of Your Life: Monument or Legacy?

1. I received inspiration for this teaching while listening to Joel Osteen, pastor of Lakeland Church in Houston, Texas, deliver a message on the value of right choices.

2. "Taps" is a bugle call to signal the end of a day in a military camp. "Reveille" is the sounding of a bugle to awaken and summon military personnel at the beginning of the day.

Acknowledgments

I wish to thank the many friends and associates who helped me produce this book, especially those who allowed me to share their stories and those who gave helpful suggestions. And especially Steven Lawson, Gary Greig, Brenda Usery and Mark Weising at Regal Books, and Dave Thompson and Cindy Oliveira at Harvest Evangelism, without whose help this book would have never seen the light.

Additional Works by Ed Silvoso

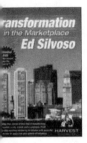

TRANSFORMATION IN THE MARKETPLACE *DVD Series*

This DVD series presents riveting true stories of how God is transforming businesses, schools, churches, government, legal and prison systems, cities, states, and a continent, PLUS each DVD includes a step-by-step "how-to" teaching section by Ed Silvoso with powerful insights on how to apply it in your sphere of influence. Titles currently available:

- Olmos Prison, Elk River Story, Transformation Hawaii, The Power of One (four stories on one DVD)
- Transformational Churches
- Transformation in Government and Elected Officials
- Transformation in Youth
- Transformation in Sentul City and Jakarta

THAT NONE SHOULD PERISH *Video Seminar*

Based on the best-selling book *That None Should Perish*, this video seminar shows how prayer for the lost can be an effective tool for reaching cities and communities for Christ. Eight hours of teaching (in 30-minute sessions) instructs viewers in the fundamentals of prayer evangelism. Ideal for small groups and Bible studies (includes workbook). *Now available on DVD!*

VICTORY AT HOME *Audio Series*

A dynamic, insightful series by Ed Silvoso designed to help couples rediscover intimacy and learn how to prepare children for adolescence with Kingdom values. Rich in biblical and practical insights, this is an ideal tool to restore families to God's intended fullness. *Now availabile on CD!*

BECOMING AN OVERCOMER *Audio Series*

In this powerful series, Ed Silvoso shows how to identify and dismantle spiritual strongholds. Ed defines a stronghold as *a mindset impregnated with hopelessness that forces us to accept as unchangeable situations that we know are contrary to the will of God*. A session on how to forgive the unforgivable is also included. *Now available on CD!*

Visit the Harvest Evangelism website to acquire these and other titles, to learn about upcoming seminars in your area and Argentina training trips, and to access a variety of practical "how-to" tools by Ed Silvoso and the Harvest Evangelism team.

www.harvestevan.org
1.800.835.7979

HARVEST
EVANGELISM

P.O. Box 20310 • San Jose, CA 95160-0310
Tel 408.927.9052 • Fax 408.927.9830 • info@harvestevan.org

Also Available from Ed Silvoso

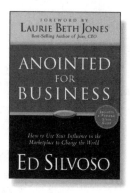

Anointed for Business
How to Use Your Influence in the
Marketplace to Change the World
ISBN 978.08307.41960

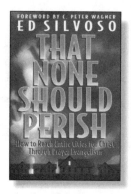

That None Should Perish
How To Reach Entire Cities For
Christ Through Prayer Evangelism
ISBN 978.08307.16906

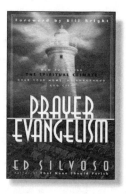

Prayer Evangelism
How to Change the Spiritual Climate
Over Your Home, Neighborhood and City
ISBN 978.08307.23973

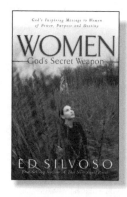

Women: God's Secret Weapon
God's Inspiring Message to Women
of Power, Purpose and Destiny
ISBN 978.08307.28879